PAUL E. BIERLEY, a graduate of Ohio State University, is an aeronautical engineer, musician, and musicologist. As a tuba player with the Columbus Symphony Orchestra, he recently performed with the World Symphony Orchestra. Since 1961, he has been assistant conductor of the North American Rockwell Concert Band, an industrial band which he helped organize.

Bierley, considered by many to be the leading authority on the life and music of John Philip Sousa, has contributed to books, magazines, newspapers, radio and television programs, and record jackets on this subject.

JOHN PHILIP SOUSA

BIERLEY, Paul E. John Philip Sousa; American phenomenon. Appleton-Century-Crofts, 1973. 261p il bibl 73-1712. 8.95. ISBN 390-X-09111-1

This investigation into the life of John Philip Sousa represents the author's total scholarly dedication for the last seven years; Bierley has amassed a wealth of accurate and significant information on Sousa as a man, composer, and patriot, from his boyhood to the final years of the Sousa Band. Certainly Bierley's zeal was motivated by the enthusiastic response evoked from the professional performance of Sousa's music, which is mentioned in the foreword by Arthur Fiedler, who speaks in support of Sousa's taste and breeding, both as composer and conductor. Bierley states in his preface: "I deemed it more important to tell the true story of his life and to bring to light the forgotten and heretofore unknown Sousa works. It is my hope that this book will assist the reader to refine his perspective of Sousa as a prominent American composer and to better appreciate his role in the entertainment world." The contributions of many persons — from Leopold Stokowski to Arthur Fiedler and Edwin Franko Goldman, musicians of note, librarians, and government institutions — are acknowledged. The body of the book discusses Sousa's creativity, his humanism, and his band. Bierley shows Sousa as director of the U.S. Marine Corps Band, violinist, operetta composer and director, gentle employer and champion of the performers in his famous Sousa Band, equestrian, sportsman-hunter, educator, and patriot. Sousa's creative process and compositional techniques, as well as his rehearsal procedures, are discussed at length. The book's more than 100 excellent photographs are representative of the author's scholarly and intrepid sleuthing. Comprehensive bibliography and index conclude one of the best-researched biographies read by this reviewer. Recommended for libraries and students of all ages, undergraduate and graduate.

John Philip Sousa (1854-1932)

JOHN PHILIP SOUSA

American Phenomenon

PAUL E. BIERLEY

New York

APPLETON - CENTURY - CROFTS
Educational Division
MEREDITH CORPORATION

73 74 75 76 77/10 9 8 7 6 5 4 3 2 1
Library of Congress Card Number: 73-1712

PRINTED IN THE UNITED STATES OF AMERICA
390-X-09111-1

This book is respectfully dedicated to the memory of the man who inspired it.

Contents

Illustrations

Foreword

As Musical Director of the World Symphony Orchestra when it was organized in the fall of 1971, I was faced with the perplexing problem of selecting appropriate program material. I had before me musicians from sixty-six nations. To recognize the sponsoring country, the United States, I decided to begin the concerts with Copland's *Fanfare for the Common Man* and end them with Sousa's "The Stars and Stripes Forever," the latter being used as an encore.

Spokesmen of the sponsoring organizations were somewhat critical of me for performing the Sousa piece—they feared it might be considered flag-waving. But I put my foot down, explaining that "The Stars and Stripes Forever" was great music and that it would stand on its own merits. As things turned out, it was a grand concluding number, bringing standing ovations at every concert. The foreign members of the orchestra played it with much enthusiasm and actually seemed gratified to be playing it.

When the brass players stood up for the march's brilliant finale, as is now customary, the man most sympathetic to my choice was undoubtedly our tuba player, Paul Bierley—the author of this book.

This particular Sousa march and many of his other marches are known throughout the world. If you ask why they have such universal appeal, it is simply because they are the best of their kind. I have dared to say that a Sousa march is as good as a Beethoven symphony—of course, in its own category.

I've always been an admirer of Sousa's, perhaps because his philosophy of music was similar to mine. This philosophy, simply stated, is to perform the things people appreciate and to perform them as well as possible.

It is absurd how much stuffy, uninteresting music is pawned off on the public under the guise of culture. Do people actually benefit from this? Do they understand it? These thoughts occurred to Sousa early in his career, and thereafter he went to great lengths to find out what people really wanted to hear. He then proceeded to give it to them. His programs ranged widely from classics to common street melodies—anything he thought his audiences would appreciate. But he was uncompromising in the matter of execution; even the most insignificant tune was played to perfection. Sousa probably did more to diminish musical snobbery than any other conductor of his time.

Sousa chose the concert band as his vehicle of expression, but his principles apply to all musical organizations. Having a consuming interest in *all* musical forms, I am a believer in these same principles. I've learned that one catches more flies with honey, as did Mr. Sousa. Sousa became a wealthy man by applying these principles, so he must have been doing something right. The chapter entitled "Sousa's Philosophy of Music" should be of interest to everyone.

It is high time that an authentic biography of John Philip Sousa has finally been written, and the thoroughness of the author's research will be obvious to the reader. This book fills a long-standing void in the musical history of America. Hopefully it will come to the attention of all who believe in the ideal of a wide gamut of wholesome, entertaining music and to those who wish to learn more about one man who dedicated his life to the preservation of that ideal.

Arthur Fiedler

Preface

John Philip Sousa was an American phenomenon, a product of the era in which his country emerged as an international power. Because of his profound influence on America's musical tastes and his impact abroad, he ranks as one of America's most important composers. A major biography of Sousa had never been written because it would have been impossible without intimate knowledge of his entire music—and literary—output. Then too, Sousa traveled so widely that biographers shuddered at the thought of retracing his steps.

This book came about through my lifelong interest in Sousa's marches and my curiosity about his colorful titles, which have puzzled several generations of musicians. In investigating the origins of these titles I learned why the comprehensive biography has never been written and why a complete catalog of his music has never been compiled. There are several reasons. First, Sousa was so absorbed in his creative processes that he never bothered to keep a diary or make a list of his own compositions. Also, as mentioned above, he was constantly on the move during the second half of his life. In addition, his music was printed by many different publishers. Most importantly, however, the manuscripts at his Long Island estate were not available to scholars until thirty-eight years after his death.

I was fortunate in gaining the confidence of Sousa's daughter, Mrs. Helen Sousa Abert, the only surviving member of his immediate family. She permitted me to study manuscripts, press books, and other documents in the family archives. With these materials as a foundation, I proceeded to piece together Sousa's life and works through the study of all other available sources.

Over nine years were devoted to basic research. Among the most important materials studied in detail, in addition to the manuscripts and press books, were Sousa's published music; his tour schedules; scattered sections of his band's music library; U.S. Marine Corps and U.S. Navy records; Masonic records; phonograph recordings with which he was associated; early Washington and Philadelphia newspapers; vital statistics and church and cemetery records of Sousa's relatives, particularly his brothers and sisters; other writings about Sousa; and issues of the Sousa

Band Fraternal Society newspapers. Interviews with Sousa family members and domestic help of the Sousa household were especially fruitful. Of considerable significance was the compilation of all copyright registrations, including renewals, of the original editions of Sousa's music.

If I could single out the most rewarding facet of my research, it would be the personal interviews with some fifty persons formerly associated with the Sousa Band. These interviews took me to all four corners of the continental United States. Though all of these men and women led eventful professional lives, their Sousa Band careers invariably were the most vivid of their recollections. It is a matter of deep personal regret that many of those whom I interviewed did not live to see the book they made possible.

In this volume no attempt has been made to analyze musically Sousa's compositions. I deemed it more important to tell the true story of his life and to bring to light the forgotten or heretofore unknown Sousa works. It is my sincere hope that this book will assist the reader to refine his perspective of Sousa as a prominent American composer and to better appreciate his role in the entertainment world.

Acknowledgments

I wish to express my appreciation to many persons whose help and encouragement transformed what seemed an endless research project into a labor of love.

First, the members of Sousa's family. I am most grateful to Helen Sousa Abert, his daughter, for permitting me to study music manuscripts and other documents which had previously been unavailable to scholars. Without her assistance this book would be less complete.

My special thanks go to Jane Priscilla Abert and John Philip Sousa III, for making their grandfather's personal possessions available for study, and to Col. Osmund Varela, the composer's nephew, for his research of family history and for locating and personally processing many rare photographs. For other aspects of Sousa family history I am indebted to three nieces of the composer, Katheryn Pugh, Vida Geiger, and Katherine Clark, and to two nephews, Harry Sousa and William Bellis.

The kindness of Dr. Frank Simon, former Sousa Band cornet soloist and assistant conductor, is also gratefully acknowledged. Dr. Simon greatly increased my understanding of the meaning of Sousa's marches. Our meetings were an inspiration to me, and I hasten to add that recommendations he made in my behalf were of extreme importance.

I also wish to acknowledge the efforts of two men whose flexibility and willingness to help in a multitude of ways were of great benefit. My sincere thanks go to Richard Harris for much library research, critical comment on my manuscript, and guidance in the study of the Sousa Band music library at the University of Illinois. My sincere thanks also go to T. H. Corrie of England, whose tireless efforts in collecting data on Sousa's European activities and in reconstructing some of Sousa's compositions were of considerable help.

I am also very grateful to Dr. Leonard Smith of Detroit. By virtue of his consuming interest in the history of American band music, he proved to be a veritable storehouse of information. I was extremely fortunate to receive his advice on musical matters. Over the years I have discovered that his career as a march composer and conductor has been in many respects like Sousa's. It is therefore a privilege to know him personally, and in following his career I feel that I have a greater insight into the life of Sousa himself.

I am also very grateful to Professor Raymond Dvorak of the University of Wisconsin for sharing his knowledge of Sousa Band history and for the stories of his personal association with Sousa. His encouragement often manifested itself in the form of support from his associates. To say that I was inspired by this magnanimous gentleman would be an understatement; I am a better scholar for having known him.

Thanks to MGySgt. Joan Ambrose of the U.S. Marine Corps Museum, much data on Sousa's Marine Corps career was made available. Her advice, referrals, and encouragement were of inestimable help on many occasions. The assistance of several others in gathering data on Sousa's military career is also acknowledged. They include Col. Dale Harpham of the U.S. Marine Band; Capt. John Dineen, Lts. L. D. Hamilton and L. A. Williamson, and Ens. J. J. McBride, Jr., of the U.S. Naval Training Center at Great Lakes; and Lt. Col. David Schwulst and Doris Davis of the U.S. Marine Corps Museum.

I also acknowledge the help of several distinguished scholars whom I consulted. They are William Lichtenwanger and Dr. Harold Spivacke of the Library of Congress; Professor Wilbur Crist of Capital University; Professors Donald McGinnis, Charles Spohn, and Jack Evans of Ohio State University; Dr. Evan Whallon, conductor of the Columbus Symphony Orchestra; Dr. Boris Goldovsky, the eminent opera authority; and Dr. Richard Franko Goldman, conductor of the famed Goldman Band. I am especially grateful to Dr. Kenneth Berger, author of *The March King and His Band* and numerous other scholarly works, for his generosity in passing on much Sousa music and other information. His advice on avenues of research was both valuable and timely.

With much gratitude I recognize the help of many former members of the Sousa Band it was my pleasure to interview. They were always eager to share their memories of Sousa, and many of them shared their mementos as well. Such was the case with Eugene Slick, former president of the Sousa Band Fraternal Society and for many years editor of the society's newspaper. His knowledge of the activities of former Sousa Band members was most helpful. And much credit must go to Marjorie Moody Glines. As the Sousa Band soprano with the greatest longevity, she knew Sousa better than anyone outside his immediate family. I am grateful for her insights and for her careful examination of sections of my manuscript.

From Louis Morris, Sousa's copyist for several years prior to 1921, I learned much of Sousa's composing process and business dealings, and I am also indebted to him for much historical data. His adoration for Sousa was contagious. Two others whose adoration for Sousa was obvious are Nora Fauchald Morgan and Harold Stephens, whose careers as soloists with the Sousa Band coincided. Accounts of their artistic associations with Sousa fell on receptive ears. Both kindly consented to lend me valuable Sousa Band memorabilia for study.

I am grateful to Vane Kensinger, former clarinetist with the Sousa Band, for his gift of nearly every issue of the *Sousa Band Fraternal Society News*. (This collection has since been completed and donated to the Library of Congress in his name.) Another of Sousa's clarinetists, Edmund Wall, was also generous with the use of his career scrapbooks, and as the most recent editor of the *Sousa Band Fraternal Society News* he shared many interesting stories with me.

To John Heney, the last of Sousa's percussionists, I am indebted for demonstrating the techniques used by Sousa Band drummers and for the loan of his memorabilia. Many thanks also go to Elbert Severance, one of Sousa's press agents, for making available his collection of press releases. And I am grateful to many other former Sousa Band alumni who consented not only to spend time with me but also to lend clippings, scrapbooks, photographs, programs, band schedules, and other materials. They include Roy Miller, Owen Kincaid, William Schueler, Don Gardner, Loren Kent, and Carl Rundquist.

I shall always remember one particular chat with the celebrated European artist Mme. Jellinek (the former Marcella Lindh), just before her death at the age of ninety-nine. Mme. Jellinek was the first soprano ever to sing with the Sousa Band, and her recollections of that era were fascinating. And I shall never forget the touching interview with William Schneider, who met with me under very trying circumstances. For many years Mr. Schneider had been the band's traveling manager, and he revealed many things concerning the business aspects of commercial bands. Through him I caught a glimpse of another side of Sousa's personal life. Still another side was seen in an interview with Jay Sims, the Sousa Band personnel manager. He was incapacitated and unable to converse with me except through his nurse, Margaret Whitaker, but my visit with him was most memorable.

Former Sousa bandsman Don Bassett also provided much insight into the realities of the early touring concert bands. Coincidentally, William Bell, under whom I studied tuba, was one of his close friends and also a Sousa Band alumnus. I shall cherish my few lessons with Mr. Bell because they were interspersed with engaging stories of his experiences with the Sousa Band.

On a trip to St. Petersburg, Florida, I encountered the thoughtfulness which is characteristic of former Sousa Band men. I am grateful to the following eight gentlemen who convened for a highly informative dinner meeting: Joseph Lefter, Edward Heney, George Lucas, Fred Campbell, Noble Howard, John Henry Spencer, John Evans, and Howard Ham. (Mr. Ham played in Sousa's navy band at Great Lakes.)

In my travels I was able to visit several other people associated with the Sousa Band, and I would like to thank them for sharing their wealth of stories. Three of them were charming: Mme. Estelle Liebling, the celebrated soprano and music educator; harpist Senta Hofmann; and Lillian Finegan, Sousa's personal secretary for the last sixteen years of his life.

It was gratifying to spend an afternoon with one of the most famous of all Sousa Band alumni, Meredith Willson. In various parts of the country I also had informative and pleasant visits with Birley Gardner, Earl Foote, Harold Stambaugh, Robin Davis, Herman Johnson, Arthur Franz, Dr. G. R. McRitchie, Fred Pfaff, and Robert Willaman. Invitations to the New York meetings of the Sousa Band Fraternal Society enabled me to meet Albertus Meyers, Joe Lomas, John Bell, Lester Gray, George Ford, Arthur Rosander, Jr., Richard Kent, Herman Schmidt, Fred Bayers, Albert Weber, Paul Howland, and Walter Bender. My sincere thanks go to all these gentlemen

It was not practical to personally interview all the Sousa Band alumni, so many exchanges were made by mail. Several not only corresponded but kindly consented to lend materials relating to their Sousa Band careers. These were James Borreli, Oscar Nutter, Harold Woolridge, and Sherley Thompson. I am grateful to the widow of Mr. Thompson for the gift of several of his keepsakes. Others to whom I am indebted for much informative correspondence were Earl Duncan, E. E. Newcomb, Jaroslav Cimera, Clarence Booth, and Henry Stern.

Descendants of Sousa Band personnel also were very helpful. I greatly appreciate the gifts of mementos from Ralph Corey, Jr., and Robert Rose, whose fathers were soloists with the Sousa Band. I also appreciate the help of A. R. Merchant, Garry Pechin, Clarence Russell, Jr., and George Buys.

Sousa's sphere of influence extended to those who played under him at the Great Lakes Naval Training Station during World War I. I am indebted to James Friberg, for example, who was Sousa's copyist, for much exacting data regarding Sousa's naval career and for his comments on parts of my manuscript. I extend my thanks also to Dr. M. E. Wilson for several enlightening interviews and for the gifts of memorabilia, and also to Victor Grabel and Claud McCarthy for informative correspondence.

For support in the quest for information about various facets of Sousa's career, much credit is due Sue Shivers and Francine Inman of the District of Columbia Public Library and Elizabeth Hartman of the Free Library of Philadelphia. These dedicated women took a personal interest in my project, and I am deeply appreciative. Many others were of considerable assistance in this area of research, including Karl King, the famed American march composer; Margaret Stace and Byron Hanson of the National Music Camp; Nadine Simmons of the American Telephone and Telegraph Company; Mae Tillman of the Forsyth County Public Library, Winston-Salem, North Carolina; Dorothy Shue of the Cumberland County, North Carolina, Public Library; Herschel Anderson of the Sandhill Regional Library, Carthage, North Carolina; Elmer Parker of the National Archives; Jane Stevens and William Orndorff of the Ponca City, Oklahoma, City Library; Fran White of the Tulsa City-County Library; David Mearns of the Library of Congress; Stan Hanson of the Saskatchewan Archives Board; Fred Bard of the Saskatchewan Museum of Natural History; Hugh McKinley of the Amateur Trapshooting Association; Charles Bisbing of the Abraham Lincoln Hotel, Reading, Pennsylvania; David Henkin of the Conn Corporation; Eleanor Devlin of the Ohio State University Library; and Robert Spangler of the Lorillard Corporation.

For research on Sousa's early life I am indebted to Margaret Billings of the Columbia Historical Society, Washington, D.C.; Ethel Maurer of the Lincoln (Nebraska) City Library; Helen McPhail of the Council Bluffs (Iowa) Public Library; Mary Burns of the New Orleans Public Library; and William McMahon of the *Atlantic City Press*.

In exploring historical matters relating to the Sousa Band, the help of the following persons is acknowledged: George C. Galliti of the Kohler Company; Alice Johnson of the Missouri Historical Society; Patricia Harpole of the Minnesota Historical Society; Janice Lang of the State Library of Wisconsin; Susan Lang of the Columbus (Ohio) Public Library; Irene Miller of the Carnegie Library of Pittsburgh; Alan Eckhart of the Harrison Public Library, Raleigh, North Carolina; Eugene Eisenlohr of the Plainfield (New Jersey) Public Library; Erma Patrick of the St. Joseph (Missouri) Public Library; E. M. MacKinnon of the American Broadcasting Company; and Brooks Marshall of the General Motors Corporation.

For cooperation and assistance in the study of the various segments of the Sousa Band music library I am very much indebted to Professors Guy Duker and Mark Hindsley of the University of Illinois; Professor Richard Feasel of Stetson University; Joseph Frantik of Morton High School, Cicero, Illinois; Dr. Mark Foutch of Champaign, Illinois; and Charles Hyde Walker of Port Washington, New York.

There are many persons whose help in documenting the Sousa compositions is gratefully acknowledged. For copyright information I am indebted to Margaret Harman, James Boxley, and John Boyle of the Copyright Division of the Library of Congress and to Nancy Aitel of Ohio State University. For helping locate Sousa manuscripts heretofore unaccounted for I am indebted to Professor Leonard Meretta of Western Michigan University, Marietta Ward of the University of Washington Library, Richard Leonard of the *Milwaukee Journal*, and Maj. E. L. Kirby of the Royal Welch Fusiliers Regimental Museum, Caernarvon,

Wales. For assistance in locating rare Sousa music for study I am indebted to Professor Wesley Shepard of Evansville College and researchers Lloyd Keepers, Sam DeVincent, Mickey Woodman, Wesley Haines, and Edward Martin.

Many people were of considerable help in investigating the background of Sousa's compositions. Those to whom I am most grateful are: John Smucker, Jr., William O'Brien, Edward Kasten, and Gerald Whitaker of the U.S. Army Ambulance Service Association; Walter Ross of the National Music Camp; Ann McCormick and Katherine Spencer of the National Society of the Colonial Dames of America; Professor Howard Shanet of Columbia University; Stanley Adams, President of ASCAP; Philip Lundeberg of the Smithsonian Institution; Micki McDonald, Minneapolis researcher; Wyman Spano and Milton Hallman of the Apache Corporation; Robert Lopez of the *Minneapolis Star*; Virginia Hawley of the Western Reserve Historical Society; John Kilbourne of the Historical Society of Pennsylvania; Allan Ottley of the California State Library; Martina Brown of the Minneapolis Public Library; Dorothy Ginn of the Atlantic City Public Library; Charles Andrews of the Cleveland Public Library; K. C. Harrison of the Westminster (England) Central Music Library; Gordon Mapes and Howard Ferguson of the Curtis Institute of Music; Robert McCarthy and R. N. Hamilton of Marquette University; J. J. Domenech of the Pennsylvania Military College; Col. Lewis Hittemore of the Ancient and Honorable Artillery Company of Boston; Maj. Leslie Pletcher of the 107th Armored Cavalry, Ohio National Guard; Lt. Glendon Wier of the U.S. Naval Academy Band; H. Durston II of the Military Order of the Loyal Legion of the United States; Julius Frandsen of the Gridiron Club, Washington, D.C.; Alfred Lief of Alfred Lief Publishing Projects; Mark Fisher of Strawbridge and Clothier, Philadelphia; J. F. McGlinchy of the Warner-Lambert Pharmaceutical Company; Walter Buechele of the Congress Hall Inn, Cape May, New Jersey; Harry Schwartz of Hillsborough, California; Patrick Foley, Assistant U.S. Attorney, District of Minnesota; Calvin Hawkinson and W. B. Schroeder of Minneapolis; and J. T. Willingham of Leavenworth, Kansas.

In gathering data on members of Sousa's immediate family, I gratefully acknowledge the assistance of Helen Rietheimer, genealogist of Hatboro, Pennsylvania; Kathryn Hutchings, cook and housekeeper at Sousa's Sands Point estate; Ward Hodge of Newport News, Virginia; Al Johnson of Congressional Cemetery; the Reverend Donald Seaton, Jr., the Reverend Carl Schroer, John Scherger, Ruth Blackburn, Marjorie Wilson, and Col. and Mrs. John Goodley, all of Washington, D.C.; Bernard Anderson of the District of Columbia Department of Public Health; Helen Wasson of the District of Columbia Department of Public Welfare; Elda

Galli, Priscilla Sousa's personal nurse; and John Daly of the Philadelphia Department of Records.

For information on the various Sousa memorials the help of the following persons is acknowledged: Lt. Col. George Howard and James Dixon, co-chairmen of the John Philip Sousa Memorial in Washington, D.C.; Lt. Col. William Santelmann, former leader of the U.S. Marine Band; the Honorable Samuel Devine, member of Congress from Ohio, and his staff; June and Floyd Mackey and Gay Pearsall of Port Washington, New York; Susan Emery of the John F. Kennedy Center for the Performing Arts; Lt. Col. Gilbert Mitchell, associate bandmaster of the U.S. Army Band; C. W. Geile and Irene Phillips of the American Legion; and Nick Rossi of Rossana Productions.

A study of recordings of Sousa's music was essential to my research, and there are two gentlemen in particular whose assistance in locating many rare recordings was of considerable importance. They are Robert Hoe of Poughkeepsie, New York, and Oliver Graham of Westerly, Rhode Island. Mr. Hoe shared his unique collection of both recordings and music and was of tremendous help in many ways. And, thanks to Mr. Graham, my understanding of American professional bands of bygone years was greatly increased. Others whose help in locating many recordings of Sousa's music I would like to acknowledge are Captain Frank McGuire of Ottawa, Sgt. James Hedges of the U.S. Marine Band, Sid Rosen and Loyd Bulmur of Toronto, and the following record collectors: Darwin Maurer, Harold Hudson, Steve Gilman, Maurice Belanger, S. A. Langkammerer, John Frankevich, Thomas Gemmill, Jr., Ralph Sim, and Karl Kasky.

The help of several other record collectors in locating recordings of other march composers for study is also acknowledged. They are Thomas Bardwell of the R. B. Hall Memorial Band Tape Anthology, Maj. Ted Connin of the U.S. Air Force, Uno Andersson of Sweden, and Clare Krueger, recordist, of Cincinnati.

In compiling a catalog of Sousa Band recordings for study, I am grateful to the foremost scholar in this area, James Smart of the Library of Congress. Mr. Smart's comprehensive study was in progress as this book was being written and has since been published *(The Sousa Band: A Discography)*. The information he so graciously provided is reflected in several areas of this book.

I am also most appreciative of the assistance of Glenn Bridges, author of *Pioneers in Brass*, who provided much insight into the early recording practices of American professional bands. Copies of his recordings of Sousa's contemporaries proved to be of much historical interest.

Inasmuch as Sousa was associated with several Masonic organizations, it was essential to learn the details of these associations. For much of the data I am indebted to Brothers Arthur Glenum and Frederick Hardin of Columbia Commandery No. 2, Knights Templar and Almas Temple A.A.O.N.M.S. of Washington, D.C. My visit with Brother Glenum was especially informative because he was a former member of Sousa's Band.

Of the scores of persons who helped in various phases of my research, the names of a few stand out. The work of my daughter Lois and my son John, in tasks too numerous to mention, was of considerable help. Several others, such as Professor Harold Bachman, the eminent band historian, music educator, and conductor, provided encouragement at critical times. My sincere thanks also go to Tony Thomas, free-lance producer of the Canadian Broadcasting Corporation; Forrest McAllister, editor of the *School Musician*; Kathleen Motz, editor of the *Wilson Library Bulletin*; MGySgts. Charles Walls and John Burroughs of the U.S. Marine Band; Carol Wade of the Library of Congress; Ruth Bleeker of the Boston Public Library; Olga Buth of the Ohio State University Music Library; Katheryn Sandy of the Port Washington (New York) Public Library; Harold Merklen, John Miller, Philip Miller, Richard Jackson, and George Hill of the New York Public Library; James Heslin of the New York Historical Society; Dr. Theodore Trost, Sr., of the Colgate-Rochester Divinity School; Dr. William Revelli of the University of Michigan; Professor Donald Steele of the University of New Hampshire; Professor Al Wright of Purdue University; David Stackhouse, biographer of the march composer D. W. Reeves; Karl Anton Doll of Germany, biographer of the march composer Carl Teike; John Hottensen of the Theodore Presser Company; Eric von der Goltz of Carl Fisher, Inc.; Leonard Greene of the Sam Fox Publishing Company; F. E. Rogers of Chappell and Company, Ltd.; Herbert Johnston of the American Bandmasters Association; Sir Vivian Dunn, former director of the Royal Marines School of Music, England; Major James Howe, director of music of Her Majesty's Scots Guards Band of England; Leonard Kitcher of the British Mouthpiece; Dr. Charles Payne, conductor of the Long Beach (California) Municipal Band; Verla Allison of Otterbein College; Margaret Firth of the United Shoe Machinery Corporation; W. E. McFee of the Armco Steel Corporation; Francis O'Connor of the Social Security Administration; John Kileen, Chief of Police, Pittsfield, Massachusetts; Thomas Slatter of the Public Archives of Philadelphia; and a gentleman who prefers to be known only as Gidaon.

Others whom I would like to thank for their help in various areas of my research are Dr. Charles Church, Jr., Dorothy and Stanley Clayton, Margaret Whitaker, Delores Smallwood, Pamela Peterson, Judy Condron, Dean Phillips, M. P. Myers, Warren Walker, Edward Petrushka, Norman Hinkel, Lynn Sams, Judd McLevey, John Stanton, Penn Virgin, Harrison Elliot, E. J. Fitchhorn, Robert Fisher, Gordon Fisher, Howard

Roley, John Hull, Dan Wycoff, Edna Jellinek, Ronald Moehlman, Harold Parks, Kurt Linden, and Leslie Zeiger.

To my friends and associates who critically examined parts of my manuscript I give my heartfelt thanks. Foremost were Jane Koerner and Ainsley Smithyman, who generously gave many hours to editing and reediting. The same is true of Dr. Paul Droste of Ohio State University and Professor Nicholas Perrini of Capital University. Others who also gave generously of their time to scrutinize various parts of the manuscript were Professor Robert Hightshoe, Daniel Stevens, David Cloyd, James Porter, James Asmus, Milton Schwartzberg, Richard Fisher, Elmer Stasney, John Callender, Frank Koerner, Enoch Balcer, Kenneth Mackay, Samuel Jackson, Paul Matthews, Charles Pearce, Gilbert Lester, Samuel Ghianni, Charles Bailey, Frederick McQuilken, Harry Fuller, Pierce Robinson, Clyde Greer, Thomas Banks, and Walter Crusoe.

In acknowledging the help of my wife, Pauline, I have saved the most important until last. Her patience and unfailing support were far more than I deserved. She sacrificed much vacation time over a period of seven years to be of assistance in my research. I have no doubt that without her help in interviewing, recording information, typing, proofreading, and in many other ways, this book would have been another year in the making.

JOHN PHILIP SOUSA

1
Minor Composer in a Major Role

Sousa is a genius whose music stands supreme as a symbol of the red-bloodedness of humanity in general.

—Leopold Stokowski[1]

To better understand the man about whom this book is written, let us take ourselves back fifty years or more to a typical Sousa Band concert in Philadelphia. There he was admired and loved by the entire population, sophisticated and unsophisticated alike. Let us board a trolley and ride for half an hour through the scenic countryside, past well-kept estates with stone fences, to beautiful Willow Grove Park. It is a Sunday evening in early September, and Sousa's Band is playing the last concert of the season. Thousands are converging on the park from all directions.

We arrive early enough to enjoy some of the amusements, but too late to find a vacant seat in the pavilion where the band is to play. So we join others outside the pavilion on the grass. People are in their finest attire, for the park has always been a fashionable place. It is immaculately clean. A few couples are holding hands, but there is no petting—the patrolmen see to that. No one seems in a hurry; this is a different age.

The stage is lighted now, and one by one the black-uniformed band members take their places. They study the music just put on their stands by the librarian. By the time they are all in their seats it is past 9:30, and the concert is soon to begin. Looking around, we see that thousands more have left the amusement areas and concession stands and have gathered around the bandstand, some seated and some standing.

[1] From an address given on May 15, 1924, at the Wanamaker Store in Philadelphia. Used by permission.

It is 9:45 exactly, and there he is—the "March King"! He is greeted with enthusiasm. He is the picture of grace and dignity, looking every bit a king in his resplendent, closely tailored white uniform. An appreciative smile is almost hidden by his graying beard. He looks us over and bows once, twice, and then quickly springs onto the podium. The band is ready, and immediately we hear the opening strains of the *William Tell* Overture. It is superbly played. The softer passages are as smooth and delicate as if played by a great symphony orchestra, but the finale is an exhibition of precision and beautiful power. On the final chord Sousa and his band are rewarded with brisk applause. He turns and bows. Five seconds . . . six seconds . . . seven . . . eight. He has swung around and lifted his baton. It comes down, and the band interrupts the applause with a familiar march. A placard is held high and turned about for all to see, and we know the piece is Sousa's "El Capitan." We express our approval. As it ends the applause is even louder—we want more. Sousa knows. He turns to the band, and here is another familiar Sousa march, "The High School Cadets." It too is received with resounding applause, but two encores are sufficient; the show must go on.

In half a minute the applause has died away and the handsome, moustached, middle-aged man at Sousa's right rises and comes to the front of the stage. He is Herbert L. Clarke, hero of every budding cornetist in America. The program says he is to play one of his own compositions, "Bride of the Waves," and he is given a rousing cheer. Sweet, crystal-like tones issue from his silver cornet. The band responds perfectly to his expressions, as though they have but one common soul. As the pace quickens we hear a dazzling display of technical skill. He is ending on a high note . . . still another, even higher . . . then finally a high F, climaxed by a solid chord from the band.

Our response is spirited. Clarke smiles, bows politely, and takes his seat, but we are calling for more. He is on his feet quickly, and the band launches into an encore. From the placard we know he is playing one of Sousa's songs, "Lily Bells," which contrasts with the finale of the preceding number. As the closing chord fades away he is once again met by heavy applause. Sousa makes a gesture toward the brass section, and five other players join Clarke at the front of the stage. The baton comes down, and the placard informs us that we are hearing the "Sextet" from *Lucia*. We all know that one—we've heard it so many times on the old phonograph. As it ends Clarke ascends to a high F again, displaying the stamina for which he is famous. Imagine—he is carrying the top cornet part in his fourth concert of the day, having also played solos in the afternoon and now three more in the evening.

The concert moves on, with "Scenes" from *La Traviata*. The band certainly exhibits its virtuosity this time. As an encore we hear the "Polka" from *The Bartered Bride*.

Presently we see Miss Marjorie Moody make her entrance. She is gorgeous in her light blue evening gown, and we welcome her warmly. Above a light accompaniment she sings "Caro Nome" from *Rigoletto*. Her voice is strong but pleasingly supple. She sings with great warmth. This Sousa surely knows what the public loves, and he obviously has an eye for beauty. Miss Moody is compelled to sing two encores, "If No One Ever Marries Me" and "Carry Me Back to Old Virginny," and she is brought back for another curtain call.

And now the last number on the scheduled program—one we expect at every Sousa concert. It is "The Stars and Stripes Forever." We've heard it many, many times, but when played by Sousa himself, it is a thrill almost beyond comparison. On the opening bar the electric light flag above the band, with its brilliant red, white, and blue bulbs, is turned on. The audience rises. Our spines tingle and we see misty eyes all around us. We are proud to be Americans. The man who is bringing us this stirring march has expressed his patriotic feelings—and ours—as no other ever has.

Four piccolo players come to the front of the stage and add their own sprightly variation to the main melody; then the cornets, trumpets, and trombones line up on either side of the piccolos for a brilliant finale. The bandsmen return to their seats and leave Sousa bowing alone, time and time again. Before the applause is diminished he makes a gesture to the band and hurriedly jumps atop the podium. In three more seconds we hear another lively Sousa march, this time "The Liberty Bell." Toes are tapping everywhere, and some listeners hum the familiar melody. At the conclusion there is a burst of applause and shouting, and Sousa responds with "The Washington Post." Then we are given "King Cotton," and only now have a few people made their way toward the trolley line.

Sousa signals for a drum roll, and "The Star Spangled Banner" is played. Everyone stands and sings with the band. When it is over we simply cannot let Sousa go. He bows and leaves the stage, but only momentarily. He returns, makes another gesture to the band, and we hear the strains of "Auld Lang Syne." He invites us to join in. We are part of a sea of at least 40,000 people crowded around a pavilion which seats only 2,500, all singing our farewell song to a public idol. When the final note dies away, we are still reluctant to bid him good-bye. He bows several times more, then strides offstage. We call him back. He bows and disappears again. He returns and raises his hand toward the audience. What can this be? He has seldom ever been known to address his audiences at concerts. Is he going to speak? A hush falls over the crowd, even in the back rows.

"Can you all hear me?"

Of course, those in the back rows cannot, but those of us who are closer respond in the affirmative. Then we wait in hushed expectancy for his speech. Here it comes. He cups his hands to his mouth.

"See you next year!"

The above reconstructed account of a Sousa Band concert should give the reader some indication of how John Philip Sousa, in his prime, was regarded by the public. He is not held in such high esteem today; his rank as a popular entertainer faded with the decline of the professional touring band. But Sousa the composer cannot be forgotten, because he left a treasury of spirited melodies. He is universally acclaimed as the champion of the march form and as such is known as the "March King."

What is Sousa's place in music, and what, precisely, was his role as an entertainer? This book attempts to answer these questions. While his music is not ranked with higher musical efforts, its enduring quality and worldwide acceptance have earned him a position among the top 100 composers of all time. We shall see why he had such a profound influence on American musical taste, both as a composer and as an entertainer.

THE GREATNESS OF A COMPOSER

If a dozen knowledgeable people, representing all strata of musical endeavor, were asked to name America's greatest composer, a dozen different answers might be forthcoming. There could be no agreement both because of the large number of famous composers from which to choose and because there is no composer of the Western Hemisphere whose fame towers above all others. Few would question the greatness of a Beethoven or a Bach, but the plain fact is that the Americas have produced no composer whose stature approaches that of the accepted master composers.

Greatness has varied meanings, depending upon one's viewpoint. To a lover of serious music, the greatest American composer might be Edward MacDowell, Charles Ives, or Aaron Copland. From the perspective of a jazz buff, however, W. C. Handy or Duke Ellington might be the greatest. Composers such as George Gershwin or Leonard Bernstein, who have successfully bridged these two extremes of style, must also be considered. In between also lie the many-faceted Victor Herbert, Jerome Kern, and Richard Rodgers. Special consideration must then be given to Cole Porter, George M. Cohan, and Irving Berlin, whose popular tunes have had a compelling influence on American musical preferences.

Still another area of importance is that of folk music. Stephen Foster's touching period pieces have become permanent folk tunes of the United States. If Foster is included, the contributions of popular composers of many other American countries must also be considered. There is a tendency to overlook the grass-roots composers of the remaining American countries. While it is true that the cultural growth of the Western Hemisphere has centered around the United States, the composers of other North, South, and Central American countries should be taken into account.

Most authors who have written about American music in general will grant that John Philip Sousa was a significant American composer. They vary widely, however, in their estimates of his rank. Some have assigned him a lower station by comparing his music, which is of a lighter nature, with that of more serious composers. This is unfortunate, because no such comparison is valid.

Sousa's music has endured. This is easily illustrated by asking the man on the street to whistle a melody by Ives or MacDowell. He will probably be unable to recognize most of the works of either of these composers, even if played for him. Yet there are those who insist that one of the two is the greatest American composer. On the other hand, this man on the street will instantly recognize many Sousa melodies, and for that matter, scores of tunes by a number of our popular tunesmiths whose works live on and on. Should writers of lighter works be excluded from the ranks of great American composers simply because their music does not meet the standards of exalted large-scale works? Which music enjoys the greatest endurance?

By consensus, Sousa is ranked as one of the most prominent American composers. The remaining pages of this chapter are devoted to a discussion of why he is so regarded.

THE "MARCH KING"

John Philip Sousa was the symbol of an era and was known as the man who did one particular thing better than any other. He was to the march what Johann Strauss was to the waltz, and he has been described as the "Dickens of Music," the "Kipling of Music," the "Berlioz of the Military Band," the "Knight of the Baton," and so forth. He was one of the Horatio Alger types of premodern music, leading a fabulously triumphant double career for over half a century. He stood alone among composers who toured with their own musical organizations and was the most successful bandmaster in musical history. His band, which many say has never been surpassed, was a living legend, and his art appealed both to a person's emotions and to his intellect.

He came along at precisely the right moment in history, and his marches are an imperishable reflection of his country's spirit. Their bright optimism and driving pulsation said, in effect, "We'll stand up to anything," just as the burgeoning, dynamic United States of America was saying.

Sousa's marches have stood the test of time and have become classics

Before being appointed leader of the United States Marine Band, the youthful Sousa had been a violinist and an orchestral conductor with a promising future in theater music.

of a sort. Amazingly, they were not only marched to but they were also widely used for dancing for a period of about twenty years. His "Washington Post" became the standard of the ballroom as the two-step replaced the waltz for dancing. Evidence of his popularity is preserved in such contemporary accounts as this:

> . . . In the military camp, in the crowded streets of the city when the troops march to the front, in the ballroom, in the concert hall, at the seaside and in the mountains, go where you may, you hear Sousa, always Sousa. . . . It is Sousa in the band, Sousa in the orchestra, Sousa in the phonograph, Sousa in the hand organ, Sousa in the music box, Sousa everywhere. . . . As a conductor, Sousa is of the people and for the people. . . . The influence of his concert work among the masses is incalculable and the Sousa Band is ever the pioneer in the cause of good music.[2]

Sousa made his mark in the world not only as a composer but also as an entertainer. He spurned the opportunity for a musical education in Europe and chose instead the world of entertainment. By the time his band had made its early twentieth-century tours of Europe, the name Sousa was a household word on two continents. Today it may seem incredible, but for a short period he was actually the best-known musician in the world and was regarded as one of the most important musical figures.

By the late 1890s Sousa was recognized as much more than a popular composer; he was considered one of the most polished conductors of the Western world. Because of his broad understanding of the classics, he towered head and shoulders above other band conductors. The fact that he was the conductor of a concert band instead of a symphony orchestra had little apparent effect on his status. Successes in the field of operetta gave him a further measure of respect. He electrified his listeners with his style of conducting and inspired his musicians to greater efforts. Other evidences of his prestige as a conductor were seen in the countless imitations of him by vaudeville comedians.

It can be said that he developed his natural gifts to the greatest degree. He composed without a piano or the aid of any other musical instrument or device, something which the layman might think impossible. Throughout his life he emphatically stated that his music came not from within, but from another source. His willing submission to this "higher power" will be discussed in chapter 4.

THE LEGACY OF JOHN PHILIP SOUSA

There were four major turning points in Sousa's life. The first was at the age of thirteen, when his plans for running away with a circus band were interrupted by his father, who enrolled him as an apprentice in

[2] "The Era of Sousa," *Musical Courier*, July 4, 1898.

the U.S. Marine Band. The second, at age twenty, was when he decided against a European musical education after his release from the Marine Corps. The third was when he was appointed to the leadership of the Marine Band at the age of twenty-five, after seemingly being headed for a career in theater music. The fourth came after twelve years as leader of the Marine Band, when he resigned to organize his own band. If he had chosen an alternative at any of these critical times, the world would have seen a different John Philip Sousa.

The Sousa the world did see left a heritage of martial music. He standardized the march form as it is known today. At a time when countless thousands of marches competed for the public's favor, Sousa's outdistanced the competition. He was exceptionally inventive within the restrictive bounds of the common march and added colorful and imaginative titles as a bonus. While some countries seem to prefer the music of their native march composers and while the quality of certain individual marches may be debated, the fact remains that Sousa composed a far greater number of marches of enduring quality than any other composer.

The distinguished music critic Olin Downes once stated that Sousa could put more ideas into fewer measures than any other composer.[3] More astonishing than this was his resourcefulness. He repeated himself only in style; his marches differ from one another to such a degree that defining this style is an onerous task. "The Washington Post" remained foremost among marches, its name being synonymous with the two-step, until the two-step was supplanted by the fox-trot about the time of World War I. Sousa considered "Semper Fidelis" his finest march, but his public has decided upon "The Stars and Stripes Forever" as his masterpiece. It has been said by many writers that he would have achieved immortality had he written no other march than this.

THE PROLIFIC SOUSA

The volume of Sousa's works is impressive indeed. His total production dwarfs that of nearly every other American composer, as seen in Table 1, a summary of his works. Though it is not generally realized, he was creative in many areas. It seems incongruous that his name is identified exclusively with the march, since his marches, in fact, represent only a fraction of his entire output. If all his works could be played in sequence without interruption, the marches would consume only about 30 percent of the time. He was one of the few American composers who could present a varied program entirely from his own compositions.

[3] *Boston Post,* September 17, 1922.

TABLE 1. THE WORKS OF JOHN PHILIP SOUSA

Category	Number
Operettas	15
Marches	136
Suites	11
Descriptive pieces	2
Songs	70
Other vocal works	7
Waltzes	11
Dances	13
Humoresques	14
Fantasies	27
Incidental music to stage productions	6
Overtures	4
Concert pieces	2
Instrumental solos	4
Trumpet and drum pieces	12
Arrangements and transcriptions	322
Books	7
Magazine and newspaper articles	132
Letters to the editor	20

Table 1 includes Sousa's literary efforts, most of which have fallen by the wayside, except for purposes of scholarly research. He loved to write, and his daughter Helen always insisted that her father would have been a newsman had he not chosen to be a musician.

SOUSA'S FAR-REACHING INFLUENCE

Sousa made an indelible impression abroad, moving the Old World toward recognition of America's progress in the arts. The Sousa Band made four tours of Europe between 1900 and 1905, and then a tour around the world in 1910-1911. The band's excellence caught Europe by surprise, and in all probability it did more to further American prestige than any other organization of its time, musical or otherwise. The news media of the day carried stories to the effect that the Sousa Band was doing more to create international goodwill than a whole corps of diplomats.

At home the influence of Sousa and the Sousa Band was even greater. The band was on a par with the country's leading symphony orchestras, partly because Sousa had enticed some of the finest symphony and opera musicians to his own band. Together they made more of a contribution to the advancement of good music than any symphony orchestra in the New World before the advent of radio. As a touring organization they brought classics to remote areas of the country and to hundreds of towns where people had never heard a symphony orchestra.

By bringing a first-class musical organization to the American people, Sousa was dissolving the long-held notion that only European musicians could be competent. Before his time, there existed a strange but highly effective prejudice against American names in music; American composers and performers had to have European names to be accepted by the American public. American conductors took the brunt of this discrimination because they had difficulty securing important positions. Sousa helped their cause by outperforming the favored Europeans.

A PHENOMENON OF THE ENTERTAINMENT WORLD

Sousa's name was magic; he was one of the greatest drawing cards of the concert stage anywhere. Few entertainers in the history of show business—and indeed, few international figures of his time—appeared personally before more people.

To understand the unprecedented success of the Sousa Band, several factors must be considered. The Sousa Band rode a peak of interest in bands which took place roughly between 1890 and 1910. This undoubtedly would have occurred without Sousa, but the movement would not have been as spectacular or as widespread.

In those days music was a personal thing. At the turn of the century, practically every home had a piano, and people were playing mandolins, zithers, guitars, banjos, and an assortment of other instruments. Home entertainment was the fashion, along with the hometown band, because there were few methods of relaxation more fulfilling. There was no radio or television; no movies, no automobiles. And the phonograph was just coming into use. One could scarcely walk the distance of a city block without hearing a Sousa march being played on a piano or some other instrument.

It is little wonder, then, that when the Sousa Band came to town, other activities ceased. Businesses declared a holiday, schools were dismissed, flags were flown, and people came for miles around to see the man called the "March King." Sousa was often presented the key to the city, and it was "Sousa Day." This tradition was, to a lesser extent, carried on through the 1920s. When the train bearing the Sousa Band pulled into the railroad station, it was greeted by community bands, school bands, Boy Scouts, Girl Scouts, town officials, and all manner of dignitaries.

If ever there were an American institution, it was the fabulous Sousa Band. For a period of nearly four decades, when railroads were the fastest means of transportation, and without the benefit of modern communication available to present-day entertainers, the Sousa Band generated a success story which stands alone in musical history. According to Sousa's formula, it was produce or cease to exist, and Sousa produced. He had the instinct

The Sousa Band traveled over a million miles and was the best-known musical organization in the world before the advent of radio. At Hamburg, Germany, in 1900, the band sported a new instrument called the sousaphone (back row, left of center), which the bandsmen dubbed ''raincatcher.''

and stage presence of a great showman. His style of programming was unique, and no one has since duplicated it with such astounding success.

The Sousa Band was not a marching band, as people are prone to imagine, but rather a concert band. In fact, it marched only seven times in its history. It was a band of artists, for several established performers were with the band every season. Besides the usual stellar band instrumentalists, Sousa always featured a well-known soprano, often an operatic personality of considerable stature, such as Estelle Liebling. He usually engaged a renowned violinist as well, as in the case of Maude Powell. Comparisons with a symphony orchestra were justifiable. As Sousa put it, "In dynamics, I have never heard any orchestra that could touch us."[4] The symphony men who played under him were of the same opinion.

The Sousa Band traveled over a million miles by land and sea. Its accomplishments are nothing short of miraculous when one realizes that it operated without one penny of governmental—or other—subsidization. And Sousa became a millionaire in the process. He played his way into the hearts of the masses by appealing to their tastes and by giving them liberal doses of classics, unabashedly mixed with stimulating march music, a little humor, and variety, variety, variety. To his credit is the development and use of the type of whimsical collocation known as the humoresque, a unique form of musical presentation which was seldom successfully imitated. For thirty-nine years it was usually "standing room only" for Sousa. No other American composer ever met with this acclaim.

Why did John Philip Sousa, a reasonably accomplished violinist and orchestra leader with a promising future, choose the band as his career? Simply because he chose to entertain rather than to educate. This is seen in surveying the titles of his compositions, arrangements, and transcriptions, and in studying his literary works and concert programs. His decision was a sound one, and he carefully weighed the possibilities when forming his own band in 1892:

> I had before me four distinct bodies, comprising the instrumental combinations, to select from. First, the purely brass band. Second, the so-called military band, differing in its composition in every country. . . . Thirdly, the beer hall or casino string band . . . and fourthly, the symphony orchestra, containing all the essentials for a perfect performance of the classical writers. I realized that each of these musical bodies was hemmed in by hide-bound tradition and certain laws as unchanging as those of the Medes and Persians. I carefully weighed the conditions surrounding these musical bodies and their governing influences and concluded to form a fresh combination in which I would be untrammeled by tradition and in a position to cater for the millions rather than the few. . . .[5]

[4] "Sousa and His Mission," *Music*, July, 1899.

[5] "Why Is Sousa?" *Adelaide* (Australia) *Advertiser*, quoted in *Musical Courier*, August 10, 1911.

The Sousa Band was in actuality a compromise between a band and a symphony orchestra. Sousa's demonstration that a concert band could play many classical selections as well as a symphony orchestra was a revelation to those who heard his band. This was well illustrated by several of his sopranos whose first reaction, when approached with the possibility of singing with the Sousa Band, was "What! *Me* sing with a *band*?" After listening, they promptly signed up.

THE PATRIOT

Few musical works were ever conceived with nobler emotions than John Philip Sousa's marches, which were some of the most distinctive patriotic inspirations of the time. His name was linked to the assertiveness and

Entertainment, not *education*. . . . "To cater for the millions rather than the few. . . ." This was the formula of the most successful bandmaster of all time. He contradicted himself in this statement, for he did indeed educate his audiences.

energy of the United States, in whose capital he was born, for he endeavored to write music which would make people stand erect and be proud to be called Americans. Even a casual perusal of the titles of his marches is enough to convince one that they could have been written only by one passionately devoted to his native land: "Hail to the Spirit of Liberty" . . . "The Invincible Eagle" . . . "The Liberty Bell" . . . "The Stars and Stripes Forever." These and others were intended to inspire fighting men on to greater efforts and to instill in fellow citizens the loyalty and enthusiasm which he himself felt.

In times of war, the pulse of Sousa's marches fired the hearts of his countrymen. This was especially true during the Spanish-American War, when he composed the pageant *The Trooping of the Colors* and stirred multitudes to a patriotic frenzy in a tour of the larger cities. This was a strange action for one whose father had been born in Spain, but he left no doubt about his sentiments. His patriotism was even more evident during World War I, when his country was at war with Germany, the land of his mother.

He spent over nineteen years in military service, serving the Marine Corps and the navy and twice attempting to enlist in the army. During World War I, he shortened his highly profitable band tours to enlist in the U.S. Navy at the grand salary of one dollar per month. He was sixty-two years old at the time. Many still recall the moving sight of the white-bearded Sousa, sword in hand, marching at the head of his 300-piece "Jackie" band in Liberty Loan parades. He too was moved, and many times told how the memorable Liberty Loan parade in New York City gave him the greatest thrill of his life.

His fiery and contagious patriotism sprang from the city of his birth, where troops and bands of the Civil War made a profound impression on him. This outward passion for his native land was evident throughout his life, and at his death a volume of editorials appeared which would have done justice to the greatest of national heroes. One in particular would have made him proud by referring to him as the "Pied Piper of Patriotism."[6]

INFLUENCE ON BANDS

Sousa's influence on the development of bands throughout the world was monumental; few composers have had a more profound impact upon any musical medium. The excellence of the Sousa Band, even from its earliest days, provided inspiration for the formation and betterment of bands of every character and level of proficiency. Wherever the Sousa Band traveled, its reputation preceded it. It was the acknowledged model of perfection.

[6] *New York Herald Tribune*, March 7, 1932.

War Department General Staff

The composer of "The Stars and Stripes Forever" was appropriately called the "Pied Piper of Patriotism."

Sousa's contribution to band betterment began not with the Sousa Band but with the U.S. Marine Band, which he raised from mediocrity to one of the finest military bands anywhere during his twelve years of leadership. When his dream came true—a band of his own—he began to set standards which were, for all practical purposes, unattainable by others.

In addition to enriching the band's literature by his own compositions, he led the way to finer band arrangements and transcriptions. As a transcriber he was ahead of his time. His principles of instrumentation and tone coloring are taken for granted today and were said to have influenced certain classical composers. The vocal soloists of his band were duly inspired by his delicate transcriptions of operatic excerpts, and this stimulated many writers to refer to the Sousa Band as a "wind symphony." He campaigned for the standardization of band instrumentation on an international basis, but the results of his efforts would be difficult to ascertain, and no one else is ever likely to accomplish this task because of national traditions.

He gave freely of his time to further the cause of school bands, which benefited immeasurably by his example, and in many other ways his unassuming prominence encouraged the maturity of the school band movement in the United States.

The musical instrument known as the sousaphone was, of course, named after Sousa. The first one was built to his specifications, but who actually constructed it is debatable. According to one of Sousa's few references to it, it was built by J. W. Pepper, a Philadelphia instrument manufacturer and music publisher.[7] Another story comes from the Conn Corporation, whose instruments Sousa endorsed for many years. They claim credit for building the first sousaphone. The Pepper sousaphone, allegedly built around 1892, was evidently used very little and was not widely publicized. Conn's first sousaphone was built in 1898 and was widely promoted. In 1908 Conn introduced a model in which the bell pointed forward, and this model is in common use today. The bell-front design reverted to the directional sound that Sousa was trying to avoid, so he never used this type of sousaphone.

It would be futile to attempt to enumerate the countless tributes that Sousa received from bands and band directors during his lifetime in the form of medals, trophies, compositions written in his honor, testimonial dinners, parades, and so forth. It is understandable that when the highly respected American Bandmasters Association was formed, John Philip Sousa was elected as its first honorary life president.

[7] *Christian Science Monitor*, August 30, 1922.

Sousa was a catalyst in the jazz movement from the earliest ragtime days, as this music publisher's advertisement attests.

Courtesy T. H. Corrie

CONTRIBUTION TO OPERETTA

The influence of Sousa was definitely felt in the field of operetta; he was one of the pioneers of the American musical theater. Nine of his fifteen operettas were produced, and eight were published. *El Capitan* (1895) was very successful until after the turn of the century. All of his later operettas fared well, but they could not replace the perennial Gilbert and Sullivan favorites and were soon eclipsed by those of Victor Herbert and others. Early in his career Sousa contributed orchestrations and other musical theater offerings and was active in arranging and writing incidental music for various stage productions.

IMPACT ON JAZZ

Another of Sousa's contributions to the world of music, strange as it may seem, was in the field of jazz—not so much because of his original compositions as because of his use of jazz material in his band programming. His interest began with one of jazz's forerunners, ragtime. He programmed ragtime sparingly during the late 1890s in the United States and found that the populace loved it. A sprinkling of Sousa Band recordings of ragtime tunes appeared on the market, but these were of little significance. It was Sousa, however, who was initially responsible for the popularity of ragtime in Europe. When the Sousa Band made its first tour abroad in 1900, the people of Paris were unexpectedly enthusiastic over the ragtime tunes they heard. In practically no time, ragtime was the rage. It is unlikely, with at least some sheet music and a scattering of crude recordings available, that Sousa's performance of ragtime was the first ever heard in Europe, but it was he who set Europeans afire with tunes such as "Smoky Mokes," "Whistling Rufus," and others. He was enthusiastically acclaimed all over Europe, and his judicious—if meager—programming of ragtime endeared him even further.

He did not go overboard with popular music, because this was not in character with his philosophy of music. When dixieland and hot jazz made their debut a few years later, Sousa first viewed them with disgust. It was understandable, because the first dixieland bands were not manned by polished musicians. He expected jazz to die a quick death, believing that the public would not stand to see its youth corrupted by what he erringly construed as lack of talent. He made a few statements which he probably wished later he had not made. His chief objection was the borrowing of classical melodies by jazz bands, which he considered blasphemous.

The public did not ridicule the new jazz as Sousa had predicted, because musicians of higher caliber quickly joined the ranks. It assumed an inevitable refinement, and Sousa was quick to realize his mistake when he saw jazz take on semiclassical proportions. He joined a few classical composers who experimented in the new medium by composing a "dance hilarious" called "With Pleasure" (1912) and a concert piece which leaned toward a fox-trot, "Willow Blossoms" (1916). After these pieces he abandoned dance music and wrote practically nothing but war-oriented songs for two and one-half years.

When he took to the road again in 1919, he had decided that the public wanted lively music. He concocted a humoresque entitled "Showing Off Before Company" in which individual players or groups "showed off." Certain of his players with experience in jazz were instructed to present just that to the audiences. This innovation in the programming of a highly respected concert band caused quite a bit of comment among reviewers. The public reacted as Sousa had expected; they thought that if the highly regarded Sousa Band was playing jazz, jazz must be acceptable.

Therein lies the contribution of Sousa to jazz—when it was suspended between Tin Pan Alley and the concert stage, he contributed to its acceptance. Correctly gauging the public's grasp of jazz, he went on to incorporate jazz tunes into some of his fantasies, most notably "Jazz America." He also included some syncopated movements in his suites. Meanwhile, the humoresque "Showing Off Before Company" became a trademark of the Sousa Band, and they were sometimes presenting nearly half an hour of jazz on their programs in the mid-1920s.

IMPACT ON THE RECORDING INDUSTRY

Sousa's contribution to music through the media of recordings was made via the back door. He had expressed vigorous opposition to the phonograph for many years, but a good grade of music was nevertheless introduced to many through recordings fallaciously labeled "Sousa's Band."[8] It was Sousa who coined the term "canned music" in 1906 when he was waging a campaign against the phonograph industry's abuses of composers' rights. He was reconciled with the recording industry in time, but only because the industry yielded to what he considered a composer's constitutional guarantee of his privileges. His concern carried considerable weight because he was, and always has been, the most frequently recorded band composer. Records of "The Stars and Stripes Forever," for example, sold more copies than any other composition for many years.

[8] Sousa seldom participated in the recording sessions of the studio bands called "Sousa's Band." His name was used with some justification, however, because most or all of the musicians employed for the recordings were current or former members of the Sousa Band.

ON THE RADIO

Sousa's token contribution to music through a new and upcoming means of communication called radio was also made via the back door. He needed the rapport of a live audience to be at his best and felt that he would be completely out of his element in the soundproofed radio studio—as in the soundproofed recording studio. At first he did not yield to requests for broadcasts. By the time he had received over 10,000 letters urging him to broadcast, however, he reconsidered. Finally realizing radio's potential, he consented to broadcast a series in 1929 and another in 1931.

THE PRACTICAL COMPOSER

Sousa thought melody was the basis of all popular appeal and used it in practical ways. He was not as idealistic as some composers, because he would not permit himself to compose music which he did not expect to become popular. The one apparent ambition he had for his music was to make it acceptable to the public. Some of his failures were revised several times before he finally gave up on them. So much the better if his compositions brought wealth, but this was of secondary importance. It is strange that he did not express hopes that his music would prove to be of such character that it would be preserved for posterity, but perhaps this was unnecessary. No doubt he realized that at least some of his works had achieved immortality. This was obvious to him when he saw multitudes rise to their feet when they heard "The Stars and Stripes Forever," as though it were the national anthem.

By no stretch of the imagination could Sousa be called a commercial composer, because he seldom composed music on order. Unlike many of the classical composers whom he idolized, he seldom accepted commissions. He received requests, but most were not granted. His spirit of independence and pride left him free of obligations. He began and ended his career as a composer of entertaining music.

HONORS

Sousa's memory is preserved in many ways, and this will be discussed in chapter 6. The hundreds of citations, trophies, medals, flags, and other honors bestowed upon him during his lifetime are not well known, however, so it is well to reflect on them.

Many poems and musical compositions were written in his honor, and a collocation of these would be almost impossible. Among his other distinctions were three honorary chieftainships of Indian tribes, and many

Some of Sousa's favorite medals were, from left to right: The Victory Medal of World War I (1918); the Military Order of the Veterans of Foreign Wars (1919); the Palmes d'Officier d'Academie (1901) with the Rosette of Officier de L'Instructeur Publique of France (1904); the Victorian Order from King Edward VII of England (1901); the Cross of Artistic Merit of the First Class from the Academy of Arts, Science and Literature at Hainault, Belgium (1900); and the Emblem of the Sixth Army Corps of the United States (1900).

honorary memberships in civic and private organizations. If he were to have worn all the medals he received, one could not have seen his uniform through the maze of precious stones, metal, and ribbons. Several were cherished above all others; he had inexpensive imitations made and locked the originals in a New York vault.

John Philip Sousa—known throughout the world as the "March King"—remained a modest man until he drew his final breath. When asked his occupation, his typical reply was "Salesman of Americanism, globetrotter, and musician."

2
Biography of John Philip Sousa

CHILDHOOD IN WASHINGTON, D.C.

John Philip Sousa was born in Washington, D.C., on November 6, 1854. The birthplace was a modest house at 636 G Street, SE, in a section of town known then as the "Navy Yard." The home was one and a half blocks west of the Marine Barracks and half a mile north of the Anacostia, the eastern branch of the Potomac River.

He was the third of ten children, four of whom died in infancy. His father, John Antonio Sousa, was born in Spain of Portuguese parents who had fled their country during an uprising. His mother, Maria Elisabeth Trinkhaus, was born in Bavaria. Being the oldest boy, John Philip probably received his first name from his father and paternal grandfather. His middle name was most likely derived from both his mother's brother Philip and his father's brother Filipe.[1]

John Antonio Sousa, who usually went by the name of Antonio Sousa, came to Brooklyn while serving as a musician in the United States Navy and there met Maria Elisabeth while she was visiting an uncle. They were married there in 1848 or 1849. Their first child, Catherine, was born late in 1850 and the second child, Josephine, was born sometime between 1851 and 1854.

The Sousas moved to Washington in early 1854, and Antonio enlisted in the U.S. Marine Band as a trombonist. The infant Josephine apparently died about the time of John Philip's birth. Up until that time Antonio was of the Catholic faith. Marie Elisabeth was a Lutheran, and Antonio was converted to that faith shortly after the death of Josephine. John Philip was baptized in the Concordia German Evangelical Church, a

[1] Another possibility is that his father named him for a Portuguese ruler named John who once defeated a Spanish ruler named Philip and restored Portuguese independence.

Defense Department (Marine Corps)

The birthplace of John Philip Sousa is a landmark in the southeastern section of Washington, D.C.

Defense Department (Marine Corps)

The father and mother of John Philip Sousa were American immigrants. His kindly father, Antonio, was born in Spain of Portuguese parentage, and his mother, Elisabeth, was a hardy and deeply religious Bavarian. Both were of middle-class families. Antonio, however, was apparently descended from nobility.

Courtesy Concordia United Church of Christ

At the age of three weeks John Philip Sousa was baptized in this Lutheran church in the northwest section of Washington, D.C., by the Reverend Samuel D. Finckel. The church, then known as the Concordia German Evangelical Church, was rebuilt in 1892, underwent changes of denomination, and is now known as the Concordia United Church of Christ.

Lutheran church on the corner of Twentieth and G Streets, NW, on Sunday, November 26, 1854.[2]

In the early part of 1855 the Sousas moved one block farther west on G Street where two more children, Ferdinand and Rosina, were subsequently born. Ferdinand lived only two months, and Rosina two years. The Sousas purchased their first property in the United States, an L-shaped lot the southeast corner of Seventh and E Streets, SE, in the spring of 1858. Antonio divided the lot three ways, keeping the corner lot to build on and selling the others within days. Thereafter this was the family home, where Antonio and Elisabeth spent the remainder of their lives. Construction on the house was probably begun during the

[2] Baptismal record, in German, of the (present) Concordia United Church of Christ. In several of Sousa's writings, he refers to this church as "Dr. Finkel's [sic] Church."

Antonio Sousa built this home in 1858. He and Mrs. Sousa lived in it for the remainder of their lives, and to John Philip it was always home. It was originally a frame house.

last half of 1858, and this was the house which John Philip was to hold dear as his boyhood home in Washington.[3] Another child, George, was born there in February, 1859.

Very little is known about the first four years of John Philip's life. When he was five he exhibited the intense determination for which he

[3] The house number is listed in various Washington, D.C., directories as 500, 502, 527, or 528 Seventh Street, SE.

was to be recognized in manhood. He deliberately soaked himself in a cold rain in protest against his mother's refusal to give him his fill of doughnuts. The resulting pneumonia rendered him an invalid for over a year and a half. Toward the end of this illness, his schooling was begun by his father, mother, and sister Catherine, who taught him to read and write.

It was probably during the autumn of 1861, or the end of his sixth year, that he received his first musical instruction. This was from an elderly Spaniard, John Esputa, Sr., who gave him evening solfeggio lessons in the home. John Philip was unable to cope with the teacher's quick temper, however, so the lessons lasted only for a brief period.

His formal education began first with short periods in two small neighborhood private schools. Next entering the public school system, he was apparently passed beyond the primary ("second secondary") level by examination and into Secondary School No. 7, where he spent one or two years. After this he was enrolled in an intermediate school for two years and then attended Wallach Grammar School for two more. All the above schools were located within blocks of his home.[4]

Sometime during his stay in the secondary school, probably 1863, a third sister, Annie Frances, was born. She lived only two years, being the fourth and last of the children to die in infancy.

Before John Philip's formal education began, he was enrolled in a newly established evening conservatory of music operated by John Esputa, Jr. (1830-1882), the son of the solfeggio teacher. The school was located in Esputa's home at 511 Eighth Street, a short block from the Sousa home. This was late in 1861 or early in 1862. Esputa was a prominent violin and viola teacher and also had the reputation of being a fine cornetist. Like his father, he was short of temper. Taking cognizance of this, John Philip kept his distance while quietly absorbing a wealth of knowledge on musical subjects. Despite John Philip's reticence, Esputa eventually realized that he had an extraordinarily gifted pupil on his hands. He found that the young Sousa could read music on sight with unusual accuracy and had perfect pitch. Moreover, he had won several medals when examinations were held at the end of the third year. He had really won all of them, but Esputa refused to give them all to one student.

The caliber of instruction at Esputa's sixty-pupil conservatory was remarkable for that period in America, providing John Philip with a more than adequate foundation in music theory and harmony, as well as performance on several instruments. Esputa published his own textbook. John

[4] Students enrolled in Washington public schools during the 1860s attended "grammar" school for a total of eight years. These eight years were divided into two years each in primary, secondary, intermediate, and grammar levels. (Ref. J. Ormund Wilson, "Eighty Years of the Public Schools of Washington—1805 to 1885," in *Records of the Columbia Historical Society*, Vol. 1, October 30, 1896.

Philip was enrolled for nearly four years and studied voice, violin, piano, flute, cornet, baritone, trombone, and alto horn. He was encouraged by his father, who gave him additional instruction on the trombone, the instrument which gave the young Sousa more difficulty than any other. His trombone practicing was reputed to have been the cause of consternation in the neighborhood.

Esputa was harsh in his treatment of male students, and John Philip never adjusted to this. Trying to be creative, he composed a piece called "An Album Leaf" and took it to Esputa for an evaluation. Esputa crushed him by tossing it over the piano and calling it "bread and cheese." "An Album Leaf" is the first known Sousa composition, but it may be lost forever because no manuscripts are known to exist.

Pencil rendering by Charles G. Hood

At the age of ten "Philip," as he was called by his family, was a quiet, industrious student.

Courtesy Col. Osmund Varela

After school hours Sousa received excellent musical training in a private conservatory established by John Esputa, Jr. (1830-1882). Esputa is shown here with his family and several of his pupils. Sousa, aged eleven, is left of center in the back row.

A row with Esputa at the end of the third year nearly ended John Philip's musical career before it started. In a quarrel resulting from an apparent misunderstanding in the interpretation of Esputa's instruction on bowing the violin, they nearly came to blows, and John Philip hastily decided to drop music. After discussing it with him, his father found him an all-night job in a bakery—while he continued his schooling in the daytime. John Philip was exhausted after the second night, and his father suggested that he make his peace with Esputa and abandon thoughts of becoming a baker. With Antonio negotiating, they settled their differences and were on good terms from that time on. Toward the end of their musical association, Esputa asked him to perform a violin solo at a concert given by his students at a government mental institution, and Sousa jokingly referred to this in later life as his first "professional appearance."

Almost coincidental with John Philip's years in Esputa's school was the American Civil War. The horrors of war were impressed upon him as he accompanied his parents on visits to wounded men in hospitals and by the nearness of battles outside Washington. Also impressed upon him, however, was the sound of the military bands which found their way to Washington, and this contributed to what was to become a great passion for band music. Antonio continued in active service with the Marine Band, and John Philip, at the age of ten or eleven, was permitted to attend rehearsals with his father and play cymbals, triangle, and alto horn.

John Philip Sousa's natural talent, coupled with the stimulating environment in which he was raised, has caused historians to remark that his development as the prime example of a musical patriot was a natural one and that he was obviously born at the right time and place in American history. In retrospect, he often referred to this as being raised "in the shadow of the Capitol dome."

The Sousa family lived in an unassuming manner, and John Philip's childhood was an exceptionally happy one. In his youth he was called Philip by his family, and this name was thereafter used by his intimate friends. Evidently he was the favorite of his mother, who was almost totally unmusical, and he would compose short tunes for her amusement. Unfortunately, none of these has been preserved. This early maternal favoritism may have been the seat of resentment among his brothers in later life, when he had reached the pinnacle of success.

His father was dignified, of a pleasant temperament, and much loved by his neighbors, friends, and musical associates. John Philip thought of him not only as a parent but also as a companion. In addition to his service with the marines, Antonio also did upholstering and cabinetry work and built a shed on the northeast corner of the lot to carry on these trades. The influence of both his industrious mother and his gentle, intellectual father was evident in the John Philip Sousa of later years. When asked to reflect on his upbringing, he would usually reply that his energy was inherited from his Bavarian mother and his temperament and burning desire for knowledge from his father. In southeastern Washington, it was a common sight to see the young Sousa with an armload of books or his violin wherever he went.

His thirst for knowledge was no impediment to a normal childhood. Once the effects of the earlier siege of pneumonia were outgrown, he was not much different from any other American boy except for his mental endowment. He was a brilliant child but not known as a prodigy in either his schoolwork or his musical endeavors. He learned to love competitive sports, primarily baseball and boxing. He also loved hunting, fishing, and boating. To raise money for materials to build a sailboat, he once earned the sum of eight dollars by catching and selling fish and by carrying coal and water for neighbors.

The Sousas changed their church affiliation sometime between 1855 and 1863, undoubtedly for reasons of convenience. The Concordia Lutheran Church was a three-mile walk or ride, so they transferred to Christ Episcopal Church on Sixth Street, a mere two blocks from their home. The first record of this move is found in the 1865 church obituary record of their infant daughter, Annie Frances. The birth of the last Sousa daughter, Mary Elisabeth, in December, 1865, is also documented by a church baptismal record of 1866.

At eleven John Philip demonstrated an ability to organize by forming a dance, or "quadrille," orchestra. With seven grown men, he performed regularly at dances sponsored by a Professor Sheldon until the men duped him into asking for more money, and he alone was dropped by Sheldon. Sheldon operated a local academy for dance instruction and promoted it by sponsoring dances.[5] John Philip also did some minor solo work as a violinist at concerts, but since these concerts were not mentioned in Washington newspapers, it must be assumed that they were informal affairs.

A MARINE AT THIRTEEN

In John Philip's twelfth year he was presumably still in attendance at Wallach Grammar School, but nothing is known of his musical training at that time. In his thirteenth year his younger brother Antonio was born. And in this year two events molded his musical career. The first was his enlistment in the U.S. Marine Corps as an apprentice musician, and the second was the beginning of the study of harmony, composition, and violin with George Felix Benkert.

[5] The school was advertised in Washington newspapers of 1871-1872 as "Professor Sheldon's Fashionable Dancing Academy."

Washington D.C.
July 8" 1872.

I hereby give my consent to the enlistment of my son John P. Sousa, as a 3rd class Musician in the Marine Band, U.S. Marine Corps, for the term of five years.

Antonio Sousa
Musician Marine Band.

Witness—
Wm. T. Daly.

Defense Department (Marine Corps)

After an absence of six months from the Marine Corps, Sousa reenlisted as an apprentice musician. As with his first enlistment, the consent of his father was necessary.

The enlistment in the Marine Corps was not planned, and one of Sousa's favorite stories was the account of how it came about. He had been practicing his violin at home and was approached by the leader of a circus band who had been listening to his playing from outside. The flattering bandleader persuaded him to join his troupe secretly for a tour starting the next day. Circus life would be attractive and exciting, John Philip thought, having visions of being the leader of a circus band himself some day. The plot was discovered by his father, however, who arose before the scheduled departure time and casually escorted him to Marine Corps headquarters. Arrangements had already been made with the commandant, and on Tuesday, June 9, 1868, John Philip Sousa was enlisted as a "boy," or apprentice, in the band of the U.S. Marine Corps for the tentative period of seven years, five months, and twenty-seven days.

This period of his Marine Corps service was to last nearly seven years in two separate enlistments, and in this time his instruction was probably limited mostly to instrumental performance and some theory.

One dollar per month was deducted from his pay for schooling and another two dollars was deducted for musical training. His schooling, technically, was for the purpose of learning to "read, write and cypher as far as the single rule of three," and in his musical training he received instruction on the trombone, drum, fife, and clarinet. Father and son were serving together.

In his off-duty hours, the private study with George Felix Benkert was inspiring. Benkert's approach was completely different from Esputa's in that he gently encouraged the young Sousa. Whereas Esputa had given the future "March King" a bad start by belittling his first composition, Benkert offered only constructive criticism. Once, when Benkert and Sousa were discussing an Offenbach operetta, Benkert calmly predicted that Sousa would someday write a better one. Benkert was apparently one of America's better musicians, one who unfortunately died at an early age. He was a local orchestral conductor who also taught music. For a while his small symphony orchestra presented monthly concerts, with Sousa playing violin in the orchestra, or "Orchestral Union."[6]

Although himself an outstanding pianist, Benkert gave Sousa some unusual advice. He recognized Sousa's extraordinary talent in composition and declined to teach him piano. His reasoning was that it would interfere with Sousa's composing, because if he composed at the piano, his fingers would fall in familiar places. The individuality seen in Sousa's compositions lends weight to the proof of Benkert's theory. The youthful Sousa idolized Benkert and spoke highly of him for the remainder of his life.

Sousa's teen-age years were different from those of other young men in that they were spent in military service. By day he was a marine musician, and in the evenings he was an eager civilian musician, performing professionally at every opportunity. He also may have been teaching part time in Esputa's conservatory.[7] Socially, he mixed well with those of his age group, particularly in the northwestern section of town, the center of Washington's culture. The population of Washington was only slightly in excess of 100,000 in 1870, and it could not offer a cultural atmosphere comparable to that of Philadelphia, New York, or Boston. Sousa made the most of it, however.

Louis Sousa, the last of the family, was born in January, 1870. Catherine, the oldest, was married by this time, and the other four children living at home at the time of John Philip's sixteenth birthday were George, eleven; Elise (Mary Elisabeth), four; Tony (Antonio), two; and Louis, not yet one. John Philip celebrated his sixteenth birthday by smoking his first cigar and becoming violently ill.

[6] "Orchestral Union" was apparently a nickname, as mentioned in Sousa's autobiography, *Marching Along*, p. 28. Benkert's programs were billed as "classical chamber concerts" or "classical concerts" in Washington newspapers of 1874-1875.

[7] "The March King," *Every Ladies Journal* (Melbourne, Australia), July 8, 1911.

The first published Sousa composition appeared in 1872, "Moonlight on the Potomac Waltzes." It was frivolously commissioned and published by a friend who wished to win a young lady's favors by presenting her with a composition dedicated in her honor. The piece was assigned the notation "opus 3," but Sousa never revealed what the first two opus numbers might have been. A galop, "Cuckoo," appeared in the summer of 1873, concurrently with the first Sousa march, "Review." These were sold to a Philadelphia publisher for 100 printed copies of each. "Review" was called "opus 5." These numerical designations were given only sporadically for the next seven years with no suggestions as to what the missing numbers might have been. Thereafter they were not listed.

Whereas nearly all his later compositions were signed "John Philip Sousa" with a date and a place, his early works were signed "J. Philip Sousa" or "John P. Sousa." How he was compensated is unknown in most cases, but some of his works were sold for as little as five dollars. He was unconcerned about the money; what was important to him was that his first creations were accepted by publishers and that he was totally engulfed in the art of music.

Two incidents in 1873 changed Sousa's perspective on life. The first was a tactless rejection by an unnamed girl friend whom he had escorted to a dance—only to have her leave with another. The humiliation he suffered in this, his first apparent romance, spurred him on to success purely out of spite. The second incident took place in early September. Sousa had composed a march, "Salutation," to honor Louis Schneider, who had just assumed leadership of the Marine Band. The band was playing the new march on the parade field as Schneider approached, and, when he learned that it had been written by a low-ranking young bandsman, he ordered it off the stands. Sousa thought little of Schneider from that time on and did not serve out his full enlistment. How these incidents affected his life is explained in chapter 3.

CONDUCTOR OF THEATER ORCHESTRAS

By the time Sousa was twenty, his formal musical training was coming to an end, and he was playing the violin professionally. In addition to his appearances with Benkert's small symphony orchestra, he performed in the orchestras of Ford's Theatre (Ford's Opera House) and the Washington Theatre Comique (Comique Summer Theatre). His position at the Washington Theatre Comique was that of conductor and first violinist, a position he accepted readily even though the fare was vaudeville. It was his first regular conducting experience.

His various musical exploits attracted the attention of the Honorable William Hunter, who later became somewhat of a patron. Hunter, an assistant secretary of state, invited Sousa and three others to perform informally as a string quartet each week in his home. To keep the quartet active and modern, Hunter obtained music from Europe. Seeing possibilities in Sousa, he tried to send him to Europe for further musical study. An interview was arranged with the famous Washington philanthropist William W. Corcoran, who questioned Sousa and asked for time to consider the matter. Corcoran would likely have consented, but Sousa felt a compelling need to help support his family and preferred not to be obligated to anyone. He did not return to learn of Corcoran's decision but showed his appreciation several years later by composing the march "Corcoran Cadets" in his honor.

On May 18, 1875, Sousa received a special discharge from the Marine Corps. His decision was influenced by the earlier slight by leader Louis Schneider. Secretary Hunter arranged for the discharge. Sousa began a private teaching practice and continued to work evenings in the orchestra at Ford's Theatre.

At the same time, he was in love with a girl named Emma M. Whitfield Swallow, whom he may have met in an amateur literary club called Vis-a-Vis. With Emma he collaborated on several songs, the total number of which is unknown. Vis-a-Vis had its own periodical, but copies are nowhere to be found today. Sousa wrote some verse for this periodical, which obviously had a very limited circulation.

While courting Emma late in June, 1875, he had another opportunity to conduct, this time as a substitute at Ford's Theatre. The celebrated American actor Milton Nobles was starring in the play *Bohemians and Detectives* (also known as *Jim Bludso*), and Sousa impressed him favorably. Upon learning that Nobles was planning to tour with the show, Sousa applied for the job of musical director and composed "The Bludso March" ("The Phoenix March") to convince Nobles of his versatility. The position had already been filled, however. Later, in Chicago, Nobles needed a change of conductors and wired Sousa offering him the position. The wire arrived just after Sousa had proposed marriage to Emma. Meanwhile, a complication arose.

Emma's stepfather, Benjamin Swallow, was a clerk-treasurer in a local business and a part-time minister of a small church.[8] Word of Emma's engagement to Sousa had somehow reached him, and he disapproved on the grounds that Sousa was a musician and would therefore be notoriously poor. When Sousa confronted the Reverend Mr. Swallow, there was a comical but brief exchange of words. Thinking of Milton Nobles's offer from Chicago, Sousa informed Swallow that he would leave town immediately and prove that one could make a respectable living as a musician. He proposed to return after two years to marry the girl with or without her father's consent. With that, he left for Chicago.

[8] Sousa often referred to Benjamin Swallow as Dr. Swallow. The term "doctor" was at that time politely used in addressing clergymen and was not necessarily associated with earned degrees. Swallow is listed in Washington, D.C., directories of 1870-1879 as reverend, clerk, or clerk-treasurer.

At twenty-one Sousa settled in Philadelphia for four years, after having traveled as orchestra leader with two theater companies. There are conflicting dates on the autographed copies of this picture, which was made when Sousa was between the ages of nineteen and twenty-one.

He met the Nobles troupe in Streator, Illinois, and journeyed with the tour as far west as Nebraska, then through the South, and back to Washington. Arriving in the winter of 1876, he was reemployed as violinist in the orchestra of Ford's Theatre until early April when the vaudeville show *Matt Morgan's Living Pictures* came to town. This was a series of still poses, or tableaux, presenting nude girls. The show went on the road, and Sousa was asked to accompany it as leader of the orchestra. While on the road he composed a set of very short descriptive pieces accompanying the scenes in which the girls posed.

Matt Morgan's Living Pictures evidently made little impression on Washington, but there was adverse public reaction in other eastern cities.[9] Sousa narrowly avoided arrest in Pittsburgh, but others in the company were less fortunate. After the eastern tour they headed westward. Sousa left the company in the Midwest, however, because he wanted to be in Philadelphia for the hundredth anniversary of America's independence.

OPPORTUNITIES IN PHILADELPHIA

Arriving in Philadelphia early in June, 1876, Sousa had difficulty securing a job. He took the opportunity to hear the orchestra of Theodore Thomas and the band of Patrick S. Gilmore. Both groups deeply impressed him, and he later adopted some of the conducting styles of both men. He auditioned for Simon Hassler, a music jobber, who promptly placed him in the first violin section of the official centennial orchestra, or International Exhibition Orchestra, which Hassler conducted. The fact that Hassler had heard of Sousa's work in Washington was of some benefit.

For two weeks commencing June 19, the guest conductor was the French composer Jacques Offenbach.[10] There is some evidence that Sousa may also have made a short tour of the East with Offenbach but not with this same orchestra, which remained in Philadelphia. Sousa was never introduced to Offenbach while playing in the orchestra, but during one performance Offenbach requested an impromptu medley of international airs, and Sousa was asked to supply it. He responded with his first fantasy, "The International Congress." It did not become overly popular, perhaps because it was overshadowed by a composition written expressly for the centennial by Richard Wagner, the "Centennial Inauguration March."

When Offenbach left, Sousa was undecided about going to New York to seek a career there, returning to Washington, or staying in Philadelphia. Hassler solved this problem by offering him a position as

[9] The show was not reviewed by either the *Washington Post* or the *Washington Star*.
[10] This two-week period is confirmed by advertisements in the *Philadelphia Public Ledger* and other Philadelphia newspapers. In numerous stories written about Sousa it has been incorrectly reported that Offenbach conducted the orchestra for several months and even that Sousa accompanied this orchestra on tour.

violinist in the Chestnut Street Theatre. The orchestra there was excellent, and the theatre was one of the best equipped in the world. The play *Our Boys* ran for 174 nights, ending November 18, and Sousa continued with the orchestra after that.

He composed several short pieces in 1876 and 1877, mostly for use in Philadelphia theaters. In addition, he resumed private teaching. He also worked part-time for the W. F. Shaw Publishing Company correcting proofs under the direction of Thomas à Becket, the distinguished Philadelphia editor, pianist, and music educator. The spring of 1877 found him playing in Hassler's Permanent Exhibition Orchestra on the centennial grounds, and in the summer season he was conducting a vaudeville orchestra at Cape May Point, New Jersey, a fashionable summer resort.

One day late in September he accidentally (?) met his fiancée, Emma Swallow, on a Philadelphia street. She was accompanied by her stepfather, and after dining the three of them went to the Swallows' hotel. The Reverend Mr. Swallow was evidently convinced that Sousa was doing well as a musician because he invited him to Washington to discuss the long-awaited marriage with Emma. It is likely that Sousa and Emma did have some contact in the two years they were separated, because he set one of her poems, "Song of the Sea," to music in 1876.

After the Saturday night theater program, Sousa left for Washington, attending church with the Swallow family the next day. Then, in an interview with Swallow, the marriage was approved. Sousa received quite a shock, however, when Emma's mother told him privately that her daughter was also being courted by an older man, a former Confederate Army officer. Upset because Emma had not told him of this, Sousa immediately left the house and returned to Philadelphia. Emma was puzzled at this sudden departure, and the explanation was left to Mrs. Swallow. Emma's letters to Sousa went unanswered, and she married the Confederate Army officer in less than two weeks.[11]

Shortly after this romantic setback, Sousa left the orchestra of the Chestnut Street Theatre and joined the one at Mrs. Drew's Theatre. The reason for the change is not known, but perhaps it was because it provided a better opportunity to score music for the stage productions. One of the things he wrote there was a complete orchestration for Gilbert and Sullivan's *Sorcerer*, which he did in the spring of 1878. He was also associated with some of the Philadelphia minstrels. One comical song, "Mavourneen Asthore," was composed for the Carncross and Dixie Minstrels, a company which lampooned serious stage works. Another of his songs in this vein was the nearly uncouth "Smick, Smack, Smuck," which together with "The Free Lunch Cadets" and " 'Deed I Has to Laugh," were probably written specifically for minstrels, perhaps all for Carncross and Dixie.

[11] An announcement of Emma M. Whitfield Swallow's marriage to J. P. Bartlett on October 3, 1877, was given in the *Washington Star*, October 6, 1877.

Also starting in the fall of 1878 was his employment with still another Philadelphia music publisher, J. M. Stoddart and Company. For them he arranged a group of fourteen medleys (fantasies) for piano, based on popular operas and operettas. This work stretched out until the time he left Philadelphia, nearly two years later.

Antonio Sousa had retired from the Marine Band, and John Philip was supplementing the family income. He felt that his family deserved a better house and offered to help with the financing, but Mrs. Sousa was sentimental about the old one and preferred not to leave the

". . . a cloud of chestnut hair. . . a remarkably pretty girl with the loveliest complexion I had ever seen. . . ." This was Sousa's description of the girl who became his wife, Jane van Middlesworth Bellis of Philadelphia.

neighborhood. As a compromise, it was agreed that John Philip would pay for having the outside of the house remodeled. So a brick facing was added over the existing frame construction, probably in the fall of 1878.

Another opportunity to work as an arranger came early in 1879 when he was again engaged by the W. F. Shaw Company, this time to compile a book of eighty-seven solos for violin and piano. The volume was called *Evening Pastime*, and many of the selections received original treatment by Sousa. He was then asked to revise and shorten it, and it was reissued as *Evening Hours*. The two volumes sharpened his skill and widened his reputation as an arranger.

Sometime during 1879 Sousa apparently completed his first operetta, *Katherine*. It was a collaboration with Wilson J. Vance, a Washington journalist and government clerk. The work was never produced and was withheld from the public except for rare performances of the overture many years later by the Sousa Band.

Gilbert and Sullivan's *H.M.S. Pinafore* had become immensely popular in the United States by this time. Practically every amateur or professional operetta company in Philadelphia was obliged to produce it. New companies were formed, including children's companies, an all-Negro company, and many others. It was so much in demand that even the minstrel companies were doing excerpts and were spoofing it as well. One exceptionally fine new company, the Amateur Opera Company, needed a musical director, and Sousa was selected. Under his alert and demanding direction, the company rapidly took shape and produced several fine performances. His masterful orchestration contributed to its success. After two weeks in Philadelphia the company changed its name to the Church Choir Company and traveled to New York for a successful season of seven weeks at the Broadway Theatre.[12] The production was favorably commented upon by Gilbert and Sullivan, who attended one of the performances. The company then returned to Philadelphia for a run of four more weeks at the Academy of Music.

[12] A confusing account of the New York engagement is given on p. 63 of Sousa's autobiography, *Marching Along*. The wording is ambiguous, leading the reader to believe that his *Pinafore* company played first at the Broadway Theatre and then at Daly's Theatre. There is no record of the *Pinafore* company playing at Daly's. What he undoubtedly meant was that the Broadway later became Daly's. According to advertisements in the *New York Times*, the company played at the Broadway Theatre from March 10 to April 26, 1879, and at the Broadway Opera House from November 10 to 29, 1879. Also on p. 63 of the autobiography, Sousa calls the company the Philadelphia Church Choir Company. Actually, its various other names (Amateur Opera Company, Church Choir Company, and Gorman Original Philadelphia Church Choir Company) were learned from advertisements, announcements, and reviews in Philadelphia and New York newspapers and by comparing the names of soloists and chorus members.

MARRIAGE

During a rehearsal of the *Pinafore* company on February 22, 1879, Sousa met his wife-to-be, Miss Jane van Middlesworth Bellis, the daughter of a Philadelphia carpenter. She was celebrating her sixteenth—or possibly seventeenth—birthday.[13] "Jennie," as he always called her, was a beautiful girl, and it was love at first sight. How long she stayed with the *Pinafore* company is not known, but she was probably with it in November, when, as the Gorman Original Philadelphia Church Choir Company, they played three weeks at the Broadway Opera House in New York. Although many of the amateurs were replaced with professionals, Sousa probably saw to it that his sweetheart stayed on. She was only an understudy and not a gifted vocalist, but this was surely overlooked. The company changed its fare from *H.M.S. Pinafore* to *The Contrabandista*, Sousa providing the orchestration, and moved northward into New England territory. The new operetta was not well received, and they returned to Philadelphia in less than a month.

On Tuesday, December 30, 1879, John Philip Sousa was married to Jane van Middlesworth Bellis by the Reverend W. S. Roberts, a Baptist minister, in a semi-private affair at her home.[14] She was sixteen (or seventeen), and he was twenty-five. Jennie had not completed her schooling and knew little about such things as cooking, but to Sousa these things were almost totally unimportant.

Following the wedding Sousa worked as a substitute violinist in several theaters around Philadelphia. Between jobs he completed the fantasies for piano which he had been preparing for Stoddart. Toward spring he was asked to compile and compose music for a variety show, *Our Flirtations*, and this was accomplished while on a vacation at nearby Cape May. The show was produced at the Park Theatre in Philadelphia during the last part of August and the first part of September, and then it went on tour.

CONDUCTOR OF THE UNITED STATES MARINE BAND

Our Flirtations was playing in St. Louis when Sousa learned by telegram that he was being considered for leadership of the U.S. Marine Band. A series of telegrams between him and his father resulted in his father accepting the position by proxy, although John Philip had difficulty securing his release from the show. Sousa and his wife arrived in Washington

[13] See Appendix 2.
[14] Announcement of the marriage is given in the *Philadelphia Public Ledger* and other Philadelphia newspapers.

Shortly after his marriage in December, 1879, Sousa grew his famous beard and retained it until World War I.

on the last day of September, 1880, and the next day he enlisted in the Marine Corps. Technically, this was his third enlistment.

According to family stories, Sousa's father did carpentry work for the commandant of the Marine Corps and managed to keep in touch with those in charge of the band after his retirement. It was no doubt suggested that John Philip Sousa, as a former member of the Marine Band and now widely experienced as a conductor, composer, and arranger, would be an ideal replacement for the departing leader. The commandant had seen him direct *Our Flirtations* in Philadelphia and was inclined to agree.

John Philip Sousa thus became the fourteenth leader of the U.S. Marine Band and the first to be American born.[15] He replaced none other than Louis Schneider, the leader who had earlier ceased the playing of his march "Salutation" and who had been discharged as "unfit for service."[16] Sousa accepted Schneider's position at an actual loss in salary, but in so doing he gained a measure of retribution.

[15] Three previous leaders and served twice. If counted in this manner, Sousa would have been the seventeenth.

[16] "U.S. Marine Band Chronology from 1798" (record kept by the U.S. Marine Band, Washington, D.C.). Entry for October 1, 1880.

In taking command of the Marine Band, Sousa found himself conducting a military band for the first time. Not having been trained as a military bandmaster, he approached musical matters entirely differently from most of his predecessors. The library consisted mostly of hackneyed music, and much of this was replaced immediately. He also was dissatisfied with the instrumentation, and this too was changed.

More difficult were problems among the players, but within a year conditions were greatly improved. The pay was low, and the main source of the men's income was not their military pay but outside musical engagements. Sousa encouraged the men to continue this practice and made it easier for them to find extra work simply by improving their musicianship. Rehearsals became exceptionally strict, and less competent players gradually fell by the wayside. He smoothed the way for the departure of dissatisfied players by arranging for their immediate discharge upon receipt of written requests, something previously not permitted.

The band was approximately forty strong at the time of Sousa's appointment. During the first year the number had dropped to nearly thirty before the band was restored to the original strength. Most of the bandsmen had been European, but the band cultivated a snappy image with young American replacements. It is probable that Sousa did considerable recruiting among young musicians of his own acquaintance in Washington and Philadelphia. He spent some time in Philadelphia right after signing his enlistment papers, ostensibly for that purpose. Sousa's brother George was a percussionist in the band, but whether or not he was recruited at this time is uncertain.

Sousa augmented and improved the library by adding some of his own transcriptions, and during the year 1881 he also added six new marches of his own. The revitalized Marine Band made its first appearance under his direction at a White House reception on New Year's Day, 1881.

As a reformer he was quite successful. Whereas the band had previously played for relatively unsophisticated crowds, the concerts began to attract discriminating audiences. As a marching unit they showed much improvement, and their reputation spread rapidly.

In Sousa's twelve years as leader, he served under five presidents, three of them during his first year. President Hayes was just leaving office and was succeeded by Garfield. Garfield was assassinated shortly after taking office and was followed by Arthur. Sousa wrote two marches in honor of Garfield: "President Garfield's Inauguration March" and "In Memoriam," marking the beginning and the end of the President's short tenure. The Marine Band's first trip under Sousa was its journey to Cleveland to accompany Garfield's remains to the burial place.

Although Sousa had little opportunity to become acquainted with President Garfield, he felt a special kinship because they were both Masons. Sousa became a Third-Degree Mason by being "raised" on

November 18, 1881, and was taking his preliminary work when Garfield was assassinated. Earlier, while a congressman in Washington, Garfield had become a member of Columbia Commandery No. 2, Knights Templar.[17] Sousa was later to take his Knights Templar work in that same lodge.

In those days the importance of Masonic membership to American military bandleaders cannot be overemphasized. It was almost an unspoken requirement, but today the tradition is diminishing. Masonry—especially the Masonic marching units—was very popular around Washington in the 1880s. Rivalry was keen, and drill competitions were held among the Washington organizations and with those of other cities. Bands were needed for parades, so the Marine Band was called upon frequently. Sousa, by having charge of this band, became increasingly popular with Masons in many other cities. These ties with Masonry held fast until his death half a century later.

For a brief period after moving from Philadelphia to Washington, the young Sousas lived with John Philip's parents at the old homestead. But they were soon living alone in a rented house near the Marine Barracks. Their first child came in the spring of 1881—John Philip Sousa, Jr. The second, daughter Jane Priscilla, was born in the fall of 1882, and with her a family tradition began. Her initials, J. P., were the same as those of her father and brother. From that time on, at least one member of nearly each family of direct descendents has had the initials J. P. and has been named either John Philip or Jane Priscilla. The third and last of the Sousa children, Helen, was not born until 1887.

HIS FIRST PUBLISHED OPERETTA

The Marine Band's reputation was spreading, and its services were much in demand. One noteworthy engagement away from Washington was a series of concerts given at Cape May, New Jersey, from August 20 to 27, 1882. Sousa composed a march called "Congress Hall" and dedicated it to the proprietors of the Congress Hall Inn there. His first published operetta, *The Smugglers*, was produced that same year. After a very short run, it was abandoned. Sousa was greatly disheartened, but within days he commenced work on another operetta, *Desiree*. This was apparently started early in 1882, completed late in 1883, and finally produced in the spring of 1884. It made only a ripple in the operetta world but was more successful than *The Smugglers*. The librettist was Edward M. Taber, with whom Sousa later collaborated on several songs, most of which were comical. Much of the success of *Desiree* could be attributed to comedian De Wolf Hopper, who made his debut in comic opera.

[17] Charles E. Baldwin and J. Harry Phillips, *History of Columbia Commandery No. 2, Knights Templar 1863-1963*, p. 32.

Defense Department (Marine Corps)

In less than two years the U.S. Marine Band, under Sousa, had grown from a military band of little distinction to a band of renown. Its first important engagement outside Washington was at Cape May, New Jersey, in 1882, where the band played beneath what was probably the first electric arc-lamp ever used to light a bandstand.

The first of a new type of composition for Sousa was written in 1885—the humoresque. It was called "A Little Peach in an Orchard Grew." Sousa's humoresques were similar in form to his fantasies but had a humorous flavor, and they became a trademark with him. They were eventually so successful that it is now difficult to realize that he did not piece together another for six years after the first one. Perhaps he thought they were not in character with a military band, but later, when he had his own band, he used them freely.

SOUSA'S FIRST NOTEWORTHY MARCH

The march which established Sousa in military band circles, "The Gladiator," was written in 1886. "The Rifle Regiment," one of his most interesting marches, was also produced that year. He realized that he had made his mark when he observed other bands using "The Gladiator." He often mused that he knew his "time had come" when he heard it played on a hand organ. The success of "The Gladiator" was primarily due to the quality of the march itself, but there was considerable publicity by the publisher, Harry Coleman. Sousa had published with several other firms before 1885 and continued to do so, but he did most of his business with Coleman for a period of seven years. He was paid from twenty-five to thirty-five dollars each for his marches. This price included payment for a complete band score and a reduced score for piano.

There were other works of 1886 which tended to increase Sousa's stature as a composer. The stately "Presidential Polonaise," composed to fulfill a request of President Arthur before he left office, was written for indoor affairs at the White House, and "La Reine de la Mer Valses" was dedicated to Mrs. William C. Whitney, wife of the Secretary of the Navy. And of no little consequence was his first published book, *The Trumpet and Drum*, a handbook of instruction, which contained eight short original trumpet and drum pieces. In addition to his military assignments, Sousa was also moderately active in Washington theatrical circles about this time. He composed overtures to two plays, and it is possible that he wrote incidental music or overtures for several others.

Eighteen eighty-eight was the year of another of Sousa's lasting marches, "Semper Fidelis." Its name was taken from the Marine Corps motto and was eventually adopted by the Marine Corps. Also that year, the operetta *The Wolf* was evidently completed, but it was never published or produced.

FIRST CALLED "MARCH KING"

Sometime between 1889 and 1891 a "March King" was born, probably shortly after an event taking place in Washington in 1889 on the Smithsonian grounds. The proprietors of an enterprising newspaper, the *Washing-*

ton Post, asked Sousa to compose a piece to promote an essay contest they were sponsoring. He responded with a march he called simply "The Washington Post." It was premiered at the Smithsonian grounds on June 15, when the contest winners were announced, and it caught the public's fancy. The march was adopted by dance masters and identified with a new dance called the two-step. "The Washington Post" spread quickly and was soon the number one hit tune in both America and Europe. The newspaper for which it was written was vaulted into prominence.

As conductor of the U.S. Marine Band from 1880 to 1892, Sousa served under Presidents Hayes, Garfield, Cleveland, Arthur, and Harrison.

Defense Department (Marine Corps)

In 1889, the year of Sousa's second greatest march, "The Washington Post," the Marine Band's portrait was as above. The musician in the upper-right-hand corner is William H. Santelmann, who became its director in 1898.

A remark in a British band journal reached the sharp eye of Harry Coleman, who published the march. The author suggested that since Johann Strauss, Jr., was called the "Waltz King," the American bandmaster Sousa should be called the "March King."[18] Coleman made maximum use of this in his advertising, and the regal cognomen has persisted ever since.

Sousa took great pride in serving the presidents of the United States. He collected a large number of international melodies which he kept ready when foreign dignitaries visited Washington. That he was performing his job well by being prepared for any occasion was noted by those in authority. Benjamin F. Tracy, the Secretary of the Navy, decided to expand Sousa's collection and directed him to compile a volume for official use. A year later, *National, Patriotic and Typical Airs of All Lands* was completed. It was an objective, scholarly work and more comprehensive than any such volume previously published in America. It also received a respectable distribution overseas. The depth of research was well illustrated by the background notes on the compositions, many of which Sousa was obliged to harmonize himself. The volume was a landmark in books of its kind; Sousa thus established himself as a writer as well as a composer.

In the fall of 1889 Sousa experienced what was probably his most vivid lesson in the art of playing on the emotions of a crowd. The Secretary of the Navy had ordered the Marine Band to play in Fayetteville, North Carolina, for a four-day celebration of the hundredth anniversary of the ratification of the United States Constitution by the state of North Carolina.[19] Sousa led the Marine Band in several concerts and parades and at the grand finale, the Centennial Ball. He knew that since Civil War days, the one song dear to the hearts of Southerners was "Dixie." He used it with superb showmanship. The band played "The Star Spangled Banner" and other patriotic airs, North Carolina's governor made a speech, and the crowd settled back to hear a concert by the Government band from Washington. Sousa whispered "Dixie" to his musicians. Within seconds pandemonium broke loose. Among the rebel yells former Confederate soldiers hugged one another, hats flew into the air, and the spontaneous, wild uproar brought tears to Sousa's eyes.[20] He himself said that the effect was indescribable. What would otherwise have been an icy reception was transformed into a frenzied wave of enthusiasm that

[18] The exact source is unknown. At the author's request, a search of remaining band journals of 1889-1892 was made by several British scholars in 1967 and 1968. It is tragic that a considerable number of historical documents were destroyed in bombing raids of World War II, particularly in London.

[19] Sometimes referred to as the Mecklenburg Declaration of Independence.

[20] From an unidentified 1892 Chicago newspaper, quoted in the *Fayetteville* (North Carolina) *Observer*, February 24, 1957.

lasted for nearly twenty minutes.[21] From that moment on John Philip Sousa knew the value of playing what his audiences wanted to hear.

The trip to North Carolina doubtlessly whetted Sousa's appetite for showing off his band in other parts of the country, but travel was restricted by the commandant of the Marine Corps. Sousa's requests for extended concert tours were denied, and except for officially sanctioned appearances, the band could not leave Washington for periods of more than twenty-four hours. This restriction limited out-of-town appearances to cities such as Philadelphia, where they played three times a year.

Sousa had to be content with whatever travel was allowed, but in 1890 the Marine Band's reputation was furthered by a new gadget called the phonograph. A small Washington company known as the Columbia Phonograph Company sought a military band to record, and the Marine Band was selected. They began by making approximately sixty cylinders, which were released in the fall of 1890, and within two years well over 200 were released.

Sousa was becoming increasingly aware of the popularity of his marches and was eager to have them perpetuated by this novel invention. "The High School Cadets" and "Corcoran Cadets," which were written in 1890, were among the first pieces recorded. The cylinders were crude at best, and the recording process was laborious because mass production was unknown. To produce even a small number of recordings it was necessary to repeat the selection over and over again, using as many of the bulky recording machines as could be gathered around the players.

The infant recording industry had graduated from voice dictation to music. But the music was extremely coarse when played back through the ear tubes in the "nickel-in-the-slot" parlors that were springing up around the country. The playing time of the brittle wax cylinders was two minutes at the most, and about the only music that could be heard above the scratchy sound was that of a loud military band. Among the companies producing cylinders, the Columbia Phonograph Company was the leader. The recordings made by the Marine Band, unrefined though they were, became the most popular recordings in America. Sousa's music was getting exposure, but he soon saw the futility of it all. The recording sessions were boring and tiresome. Because of the nature of the compositions recorded, a conductor was not a necessity—only someone to start and stop the players at the proper times. Sousa delegated this to an assistant and was absent when most, or perhaps all, the recordings were made.

The Marine Corps commandant who had opposed Sousa's requests for concert tour of the band became ill and was relieved of his post.

[21] *Fayetteville Observer*, January 17, 1965. The paper states that this account was originally published in an 1892 issue of the *Saturday Evening Post*.

The Library of Congress

Before the days of microphones, only a limited number of players could be crowded within range of the mechanical recording machines. Several machines were used, and to produce recordings in quantity it was necessary to play a given selection repeatedly. Thus, to produce 400 cylinders, ten machines were used, and the selection was played forty times. Notice that Sousa is not present at this recording being made by members of the U.S. Marine Band. This photograph, one of the first of a recording session, was published in the *Phonogram*, October, 1891.

Defense Department (Marine Corps)

Under Sousa's leadership the U.S. Marine Band had reached the highest standard ever attained by an American military band. The band made its first two concert tours in 1891 and 1892, the second extending to the West Coast. Sousa's assistant conductor was Salvadore Petrola, a noted arranger and a former member of La Scala Orchestra of Italy.

Seeing his opportunity, Sousa conferred with the Secretary of the Navy and was advised to appeal directly to the President. In a subtle move, he spoke first to President Harrison's wife and was shortly summoned to the President's office and given official sanction for a Marine Band concert tour.

There were few musical organizations of the Marine Band's caliber touring in the United States at that time. In fact, the Marine Band was often referred to as the National Band. The most active was the band of Patrick S. Gilmore, who was known as the "father of the concert band in the United States" and who had won international acclaim as the organizer of the colossal Peace Jubilees. The manager of several Gilmore Band tours, David Blakely, was engaged for the Marine Band tour. Blakely had followed Sousa's progress closely, and it is probable that he had applied pressure on Sousa to petition for a tour.

A five-week tour was arranged for the spring of 1891. The concerts began in New England, continued through the Midwest, and ended in Pittsburgh. Public reaction was gratifying, but the tour had been strenuous. Upon arriving in Washington, Sousa suffered what was evidently a nervous breakdown. The Marine Corps surgeon sent him to Europe to recuperate.

The voyage to Europe was hardly conducive to recuperation, for the ship Mr. and Mrs. Sousa sailed on was first tossed about in a violent storm and then caught fire. The crew battled burning cotton in the hold, and the ship eventually made it safely to England. After visiting friends in England, the Sousas sailed to France and then traveled to Germany to attend the Bayreuth Festival. Before returning to America, Sousa made a special effort to visit the grave of the composer he respected above all others—Richard Wagner.

Not long after his return from Europe, plans for a second Marine Band tour were being made, no doubt promoted by both Sousa and Blakely. Sousa must have had to convince his superiors that he would pace himself this time and not end up in poor physical condition. Permission was granted for a seven-week tour extending to the West Coast from March through May, and it was even more successful than the first tour.

Toward the end of the tour, in Duluth, Minnesota, Sousa received a telegram from one of his brothers in Washington informing him of their father's death and stating that the funeral would be postponed until he could return to Washington. Antonio Sousa had been proud of his son's musical accomplishments, and it is a pity that he could not have lived for three more days to learn of a surprising offer made to his son, which was to lead to successes overshadowing all previous triumphs. In Chicago Blakely approached Sousa with the idea of resigning from the Marine Corps and organizing a civilian concert band. Sousa had dreamed of having his own band some day, so the words did not fall on deaf ears.

He was cautious, however, realizing that if the new venture failed, he would be ruined.

Blakely made a strong case. He had managed the Gilmore Band with great success before breaking with it. In looking for another conductor to promote, he had traveled to Europe and had found none with Gilmore's unique talents. In watching Sousa's rise to fame both as a conductor and a composer, he was convinced that he had found his man. He was prepared to offer Sousa four times his Marine Corps salary plus a percentage of the profits. A few days later, when the band arrived in Washington, Sousa had made his decision and requested his release from the Marine Corps. He was asked to invest $1,000 in stock, and a contract was signed by both parties on May 27, 1892.

ENDING HIS MARINE CORPS CAREER

Sousa's acceptance of Blakely's offer brought a storm of protest from Washingtonians who appreciated his efforts in building a peerless musical organization in the nation's capital. They feared that Sousa would take the better musicians with him, leaving the Marine Band in the condition in which he had found it twelve years earlier. The newspaper editors also had their say. The *Washington Post* printed a sarcastic editorial under the heading "Washingtonians Amazed at the Presumption of Chicago," which was directed at Blakely's interests in Chicago, where the headquarters of the new band were to be located.[22]

On July 29, 1892, with two days of his military service remaining, a testimonial concert was given in the National Theatre. Vice-President Levi P. Morton and Speaker of the House Charles F. Crisp were among those making addresses, and congratulatory messages were sent by Secretary of the Navy Benjamin F. Tracy and hundreds of others. The theater was packed, and Sousa showed his appreciation by playing many of his own compositions.

The following afternoon, July 30, a farewell concert was held on the White House lawn. It was a rainy day, but a huge crowd was on hand, including President Benjamin J. Harrison. The *Washington Post* described the scene as follows: "It looked as if an army of black mushrooms had camped out on the green lawn while the heavens wept, presumably with sorrow. . . ."[23] At the conclusion of the concert, the bandsmen presented Sousa with a handsome engraved baton. It was presented by Walter F. Smith, his first cornetist, who was resigning with him to join the new band. Sousa made no speech but responded with an encore. A reception was held after the concert, and Sousa formally received his discharge.

[22] April 18, 1892.
[23] July 31, 1892.

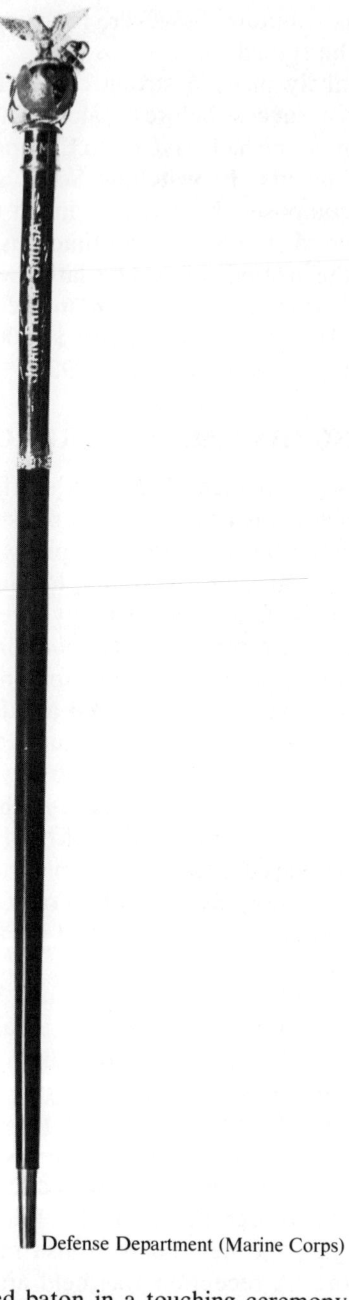

Defense Department (Marine Corps)

Sousa was the recipient of this engraved baton in a touching ceremony at his farewell concert with the Marine Band, attended by President Benjamin J. Harrison. The 17 1/8-inch baton is capped by the Marine Corps' globe and eagle emblem, and the inscription reads: "John Philip Sousa—Presented by members of the U.S. Marine Band as a token of their respect and esteem. July 29, 1892." It was returned to the Marine Band in 1953 by Sousa's daughters.

The rank which Sousa held as leader of the Marine Band has been lost in the record books, but his enlistment papers of 1880 and 1885 refer to him as a private. Later his rank was sergeant major, and before his discharge it was warrant officer.[24] Although technically a private, he had certain privileges as "principal musician." His official title was "Leader," later changed to "Director." Neither is his salary known for certain, but at the time of his discharge he was reportedly receiving, with allowances, the pay of lower-grade commissioned officers. It is estimated that his highest rate was between $1,200 and $1,800 per year.

The salary he was to receive as conductor of his own band was certainly an incentive for leaving, but there were other reasons as well. One thing that disturbed him was the fact that he was never made a commissioned officer. He thought his position was worthy of a commission and resented those who outranked him ordering him to play their own preferred numbers at any time.[25] His successors did receive commissions. He was also anxious to have the pay of his musicians increased[26] and was especially provoked at ambiguous legislation which inadequately defined the salaries of the bandsmen.[27] When he asked for clarification, no action was taken. These things were doubtlessly considered when he made the decision to separate.

Filling Sousa's position was difficult. The man who replaced him, Francesco Fanciulli, played very little of Sousa's music, either at concerts or in parades, and this pleased neither the Washington populace nor certain Marine Corps officials. In 1897 Fanciulli was arrested for refusing to obey a superior's order to play a Sousa march and was subsequently court-martialed.[28] He noted that Sousa took his scores with him and interpreted this to mean he did not want his music played by his successors, but others interpreted Fanciulli's actions as sheer jealousy.[29]

In nearly twelve years with Sousa, the Marine Band had become America's premier military band, an organization comparable to those of long tradition in Europe. Sousa himself proclaimed it to be the finest marching band in the world. Both he and the band gained by his Marine Corps career. On the one hand, the director's position attained new dignity, and on the other, it is doubtful that Sousa would ever have become

[24] Testimony before the House of Representatives Committee on Military Affairs, January 18, 1927.

[25] Testimony before the Senate Subcommittee on Military Affairs, January 26, 1928.

[26] Letter from Sousa to U.S. Marine Corps commandant, May 20, 1890.

[27] Letter from Sousa to the Second Comptroller of the Treasury, September 16, 1891.

[28] Harry H. Thompson, "The Marine Band—The Washington Post." *Marine Corps Gazette*, August, 1932.

[29] It is interesting to note that Fanciulli, like Sousa, wrote a march for the *Washington Post*. Fanciulli's was entitled "The Daily Post March" and was first played at a White House concert on August 24, 1895. After his discharge in 1897, Fanciulli had a distinguished music career. His path crossed Sousa's several times, but there is no evidence of friction.

known as the "March King" without the opportunities provided by the Marine Corps. It is safe to speculate that he would be proud if he could see the present-day Marine Band in all its glory, knowing that he was initially responsible for its rise to prominence.

Sousa looked back on his Marine Corps career philosophically:

> Apart from the musical opportunities, it was a great experience for the development of character. In official life a man has to stand right up to the job. He makes his mark or he fails. The temperamental "flowing-tie variety" of musician could not exist under these circumstances, and sometimes I think it would be a very good thing for the world if he couldn't exist anyway. The discipline is invaluable. One learns that whether he will or not he has to adjust to the workings of a great organization, and I don't know any experience that better enables a man to find himself, if he hasn't already done so, than just that. . . .[30]

The disciplines he learned were to be applied to his civilian band for the next thirty-nine years.

FORMATION OF THE SOUSA BAND

Sousa went to Philadelphia to recruit musicians. He contracted with approximately twenty there and went on to New York. Headquarters were set up there instead of in Chicago, as had originally been planned. Both he and Blakely were determined to sacrifice nothing in the way of quality, and it was well over a month before rehearsals began. The combination of Sousa's reputation and Blakely's promotion attracted some of the finest players in America, a great percentage of whom had been established European artists. For Sousa, the band was to be much more progressive than the one he had left behind. For Blakely, it was to be the equal of any European band, and it was to surpass the organization of Patrick S. Gilmore, the enterprising Irish-American bandmaster. Sousa had heard Gilmore's splendid band many times and knew the competition. He openly had great respect for Gilmore, but he also had confidence in his own ideas. A competition between Sousa and Gilmore never materialized, however; Gilmore died unexpectedly in St. Louis just two days prior to the Sousa Band's first concert.

After rehearsing for two weeks in New York, the initial Sousa Band concert was presented at Stillman Music Hall in Plainfield, New Jersey, on Monday evening, September 26, 1892. Out of respect for Gilmore, Sousa quickly made an arrangement of Gilmore's "The Voice of a Departing Soul" ("Death's at the Door"). The program was solemnly begun with this composition, all the musicians standing.

A youthful American soprano, Marcella Lindh, fresh from Europe, was engaged as soloist for the first tour. An Italian baritone named Antonio

[30] *Boston Post*, September 17, 1922.

Galesei was also to appear, but his ship was quarantined in port. The concert was received enthusiastically, and the band which was to grace the American scene for nearly four decades was successfully launched.

Before the short tour was completed, Sousa had contracted with several of Gilmore's former musicians, and nineteen of them eventually joined Sousa. Among the nineteen were Herbert L. Clarke, who was to become the world's foremost cornet soloist, and E. A. Lefebre, the renowned saxophonist whom Gilmore had advertised as the greatest of all time. Meanwhile, the Gilmore Band was revived under the baton of David W. Reeves, and there was considerable rivalry between the Gilmore musicians and those who had joined Sousa. Several heated letters between the two factions appeared in the pages of the *Musical Courier*. The Gilmore men repudiated those who had deserted, and the Sousa men retaliated by announcing that the rehabilitated Gilmore Band was as good as dead. Sousa wisely elected not to become involved, and both parties respected his detachment.

Incidentally, the name of the new band was "Sousa's New Marine Band," a name chosen by Blakely against Sousa's wishes. This was quickly abandoned, however, because of criticism from Washington. The band wound its way westward to Chicago, playing at the World's Fair for two weeks, and there it was temporarily referred to as the "World's Fair Band."

At the fair the band played a joint concert with the Theodore Thomas Orchestra to dedicate the new buildings, and the two conductors became warm friends. They had many things in common, both personally and artistically. Thomas was in charge of musical activities at the fair, and he arranged for another appearance of the band the following spring.

From Chicago the band traveled eastward through New York City and into the New England states. This portion of the tour unfortunately had been arranged by two of Blakely's inexperienced assistants, and the concerts were held mostly in small towns where Sousa was relatively unknown. Attendance was spare, and Blakely came to Boston to inform Sousa that he was cancelling the remainder of the tour. Shocked by Blakely's hasty decision, Sousa demanded that the tour proceed as scheduled. It did, and business picked up. The tour ended successfully in mid-December with a final concert in New York.

In 1892 and 1893 Sousa learned many business lessons. His near disaster at Blakely's hands instilled in him a basic distrust of managers, and he was more aware of business dealings from that time on. Blakely was later to regret his lack of faith in Sousa after he saw that the band's successes were exceeding even his wildest dreams. Also in those two years, Sousa was breaking off with the publisher Harry Coleman—and little wonder. Coleman had purchased Sousa's marches outright; royalties did not go to Sousa but rather to Coleman, who profited enough on

Defense Department (Marine Corps)

In less than a year the newly formed Sousa Band was the most sought-after musical organization in America. Here they are at the St. Louis Exposition in September, 1893.

the Sousa marches alone to buy two musical instrument factories. Sousa contracted with the John Church Company of Cincinnati next, and this relationship was infinitely more satisfactory. The first of his marches to be published by Church was "The Liberty Bell." Whereas such famous marches as "The Thunderer," "Semper Fidelis," and "The Washington Post" earned Sousa $35 each from Coleman, "The Liberty Bell" alone netted him over $40,000 in less than seven years.

UNPRECEDENTED SUCCESS OF THE SOUSA BAND

The new band's fame had spread. Except for the first quarter, 1893 was a year of steady employment. During January through March, while the band was not on call, Sousa was busy preparing a number of band transcriptions and the suite *The Last Days of Pompeii*. Meanwhile, Blakely was inspired to greater efforts in promotion. The 1893 season was unusual in that the band toured very little, playing a string of lengthy engagements. In New York a joint concert was presented by the Sousa Band and the New York Symphony Orchestra under Walter Damrosch. After more concerts in New York, the band moved on to Boston for the Columbian Festival and then to Chicago for a repeat engagement at the World's Fair (Columbian Exposition). At the twenty-seventh Saengerfest in Cleveland, Sousa conducted a chorus of 4,000 children. In July and August the band played the first of what was to become a very popular stay each year at the fashionable Manhattan Beach in New York, and while there Sousa composed one of his most enduring marches, "Manhattan Beach." Most of September and October were spent at the annual St. Louis Exposition, where the band was a spectacular success. After a tour through the Midwest, the band ended the year back in New York.

Eighteen ninety-four was another year of almost constant booking. After a five-week engagement at San Francisco, the band toured across the country and played another five weeks at New York's Madison Square Garden. Then came return visits to Manhattan Beach and the St. Louis Exposition. For the Board of Directors of the Exposition Sousa composed the march "The Directorate." The Sousa Band season ended with another tour through the Midwest.

Blakely was elated with public acceptance of the Sousa Band. Eighteen ninety-five, another highly successful year, saw him make Sousa an equal sharer in the profits. Between road tours, the band again played at Manhattan Beach and at the St. Louis Exposition. They also played at the Cotton States Exposition in Atlanta. For this occasion Sousa composed the lively march "King Cotton."

A TRIUMPH IN OPERETTA

By 1895 Sousa had hit his stride as a march composer. Still, there was something bigger he longed to conquer: operetta. Conquer it he did in 1896. De Wolf Hopper, who had made his comic opera debut in Sousa's *Desiree* eleven years earlier, now had his own comic opera company and invited Sousa to write the musical score for an operetta to be called *El Capitan*. Charles Klein had written the libretto. Sousa completed the score at Manhattan Beach in the summer of 1895. The work was first presented in Boston and was an immediate success. For a period of four years it was one of the most popular operettas being produced on this side of the Atlantic. While *El Capitan* was reaching its zenith during the first half of 1896, the Sousa Band was making its second coast-to-coast tour. It traveled into Canada for the first time and completed the season with its fourth engagement at Manhattan Beach.

The Sousas sailed to Europe for a vacation, visiting in England first and then in France, Germany, Austria, Switzerland, and Italy. They attended many concerts and music festivals, and Sousa was studying the culture with a possible future tour of his band in mind. He was pleased to note a general enthusiasm for his marches there, and while in Germany he was guest conductor of the Berlin Philharmonic Band at the Berlin Industrial Exposition.[31]

The vacation ended abruptly in Italy when word came that David Blakely had died on November 7 in his Carnegie Hall office. The Sousas sailed for home immediately. While in Europe and on the ship coming home, Sousa conceived his greatest work: "The Stars and Stripes Forever." His own accounts of its inspiration reflect a passionate love for his homeland. The end result was a precious expression of patriotism which would have done justice to any composer of any era.

THE FIGHT WITH THE MANAGER'S WIDOW

Back home Sousa tended to the business of the next tour, but he encountered difficulties which were to lead to the most distasteful relationship of his life. The widow of deceased band manager, Mrs. Ada P. Blakely, could not come to terms with him. Sousa believed that his contract with Blakely, signed in 1892 but later modified, terminated automatically upon Blakely's death. Mrs. Blakely thought otherwise.

A tour extending into the spring of the following year had been previously arranged by Blakely, and through an oral agreement with Mrs. Blakely, the band began this tour. It was an ambitious one, extending

[31] October 11, 1896.

as far west as San Diego and as far north as Washington, back through the Midwest, and up into the New England states. The financial terms were entirely unsatisfactory to Sousa, and it was only a short time before serious trouble arose. Mrs. Blakely did not pay Sousa any part of the net profits as her husband had done, insisting on paying only $115 per week.[32] After two months Sousa demanded and received $2,500 from the temporary manager. At that time the band was playing in Denver. He made an identical demand five weeks later and was again paid. While the band proceeded on its tour, many strongly worded letters and telegrams were exchanged among attorneys, Sousa, Mrs. Blakely, the temporary manager, and other concerned parties. The situation reached a climax on April 8, 1897, the date of the last engagement arranged by Blakely, at which time Sousa declared himself no longer obligated to account to the Blakely interests.

The Sousa-Blakely contract of 1892 was unique in that it had been founded upon personal considerations; neither could have made the contract with anyone else. Blakely had assumed all financial responsibilities, including all risks of loss. Sousa had been in charge of musical details, but technically he was Blakely's employee. In return for a guaranteed salary and a percentage of net profits, Sousa had agreed to split the royalties of his musical compositions. Blakely owned the music, and, because of a peculiarity in the contract, this included Sousa's own compositions written during the term of the contract—even his own original manuscripts. One complication came from something that had never been put into writing: a profit split that ignored the percentages stipulated in the contract. The actual profit split had been agreed upon verbally, and Blakely had neglected to revise the contract.

Another oddity of the contract was that it allowed Blakely to assign a name to the band, so long as "Sousa" was in the name. This issue, plus the issue on royalties, was the substance of Mrs. Blakely's contention. Believing the original contract no longer valid, Sousa did not divide royalties with Mrs. Blakely.[33] After the incident of April 8, Mrs. Blakely took the matter to court. In court the Blakely attorneys argued that Sousa should account for all receipts of the band, all royalties received from his publisher on music composed during the term of the contract, and all of the band's music library. In an astounding move, Mrs. Blakely contended that Sousa had no right to use his own name in connection with the band founded by her husband; she asked that Sousa should forever be deprived of the use of his own name in connection with any future musical enterprise.

[32] Evidently based on the salary of $6,000 per year, as stipulated in the original Sousa-Blakely contract, which was signed six years earlier.

[33] Sousa had an independent contract with his publisher, the John Church Company, but was obligated to divide his royalties with Blakely, per their contract.

The litigation was to last three years, after which time the Supreme Court of Pennsylvania reached a decision, and Mrs. Blakely's appeal was denied.[34] The court ruled that because of the distinctly personal services offered by both Blakely and Sousa, their contract terminated with Blakely's death.[35] But Sousa was obliged to surrender the band library as well as ownership and royalties of music he had composed during the period of the contract and to account for receipts of the band up to the end of the tour previously contracted for by Blakely. On the matter of the use of Sousa's name, the court was sharply critical of Mrs. Blakely's intentions, holding that an artist's name could not be regarded as a trade name and was therefore not saleable. They added that the name "Sousa" implied Sousa's own skill, science, and art and that an attempt to assign his name to another would be to deceive the public.

THREE MORE SUCCESSES IN OPERETTA

The spring tour of 1897 continued, managed by Sousa's appointees: Everett Reynolds and his assistant, Col. George Frederick Hinton. Starting in the New England states, the band toured through the eastern part of the United States and on into Canada. Most of the summer was spent at Manhattan Beach, and another tour through the East followed. It was during this year that Sousa completed another operetta, *The Bride Elect*. Although this was less successful than *El Capitan*, Sousa turned down an offer of $100,000 for it—a decision he would later regret.

Plans were being made for a European tour in 1898 or 1899, but these were dropped at the outbreak of the Spanish-American War. The war motivated Sousa to compose a patriotic pageant called *The Trooping of the Colors*. The band made a tour of the larger cities, and the composition was used in conjunction with large choruses. With a war in progress, the patriotic fervor created at some of the concerts actually bordered on bedlam.

Sousa tried to reenlist in the Marine Corps, but there were no suitable positions for him.[36] He then volunteered his services as a bandmaster in the Sixth Army Corps, completely without remuneration, with the understanding that he be permitted to complete two tours for which he was already committed.[37] A recommendation that he be granted the rank of captain was made to President McKinley, but he was not destined to see army service. In June, at the end of the first tour, he was on

[34] *State Reports, The Supreme Court of Pennsylvania at July and October Terms*, Vol. 197, 1900.

[35] The court held that Blakely's "successors," as mentioned in the contract, implied a corporation which was later to be formed, not Blakely's heirs.

[36] "John Philip Sousa," U.S. Marine Corps release, n.d.

[37] Letter from Sousa to Assistant Adjutant General, June 6, 1898.

the verge of a nervous collapse and was advised by his physician to take a complete rest. At the end of the second tour, in December, he was striken with typhoid fever, and his condition was complicated by pneumonia. He lay near death for twelve weeks, and the war had ended by the time of his recovery.[38] He was later presented with a medal in appreciation of his intentions. His total army service consisted mostly of the donation of some music and a letter giving suggestions for the improvement of army bands.[39]

While resting at the end of the first 1898 tour, Sousa leased a farm in Suffern, New York, for the summer. There he completed the operetta *The Charlatan*. It was another collaboration with Charles Klein, and again De Wolf Hopper played the title role.

Eighteen ninety-nine was another year of strenuous cross-country touring. Much of the summer was spent in Manhattan Beach, where Sousa completed another operetta, *Chris and the Wonderful Lamp*. On October 30, during the portion of the tour following the Manhattan Beach engagement, the band marched in Admiral Dewey's victory parade in New York. After the completion of the tour, the Sousas enjoyed a lengthy vacation in Mexico.

THE FIRST EUROPEAN TOUR

To begin the twentieth century, Sousa revised *Chris and the Wonderful Lamp*. He composed the march "Hail to the Spirit of Liberty" and took the band on another cross-country tour. At the completion of the tour a farewell concert was held in New York at the Metropolitan Opera House on April 22, and the band sailed for Europe. One of Sousa's most challenging dreams was becoming a reality. A last minute development, however, nearly wrecked plans. Everett Reynolds, the band manager, pressed Sousa for an extension of his existing contract and balked at traveling to Europe without it. Sousa could not see the necessity of such an extension; he explained that if Reynolds did not benefit from the tour abroad he would be given an opportunity to recover any losses by another American tour. Sousa considered the demand an affront to his honor, and they could not come to terms. Letters of credit were obtained, and the band sailed without Reynolds.

The European tour of 1900 was a memorable event in the annals of American music. Never before had an American ensemble of this caliber toured Europe with such success. Sixty-three strong, the Sousa Band brought both American music and the American flag to European communities where neither had previously been known.

[38] "With Sousa at the Beach," *Criterion*, July 8, 1899.
[39] Letter from Sousa to Major General James H. Wilson, January 12, 1899.

Named the official band at the Paris Exposition in 1900 by Commissioner General Peck of the United States, the Sousa Band epitomized New World vitality.

One purpose of the European trip was to represent the United States at the Paris Exposition. In impressive ceremonies celebrating the independence of both France and the United States, the band played for the unveiling of a statue of Washington on July 2 and for the unveiling of the Lafayette Monument on July 4. For the latter occasion, the march "Hail to the Spirit of Liberty" was given its first public hearing. After the ceremony the band made one of its rare marching appearances by parading through the principal streets of Paris escorted by mounted units of the Garde Républicaine. This was the first time an American organization had been given this honor.

From Paris, the Sousa Band toured Europe. An enthusiastic reception was experienced in France, where outdoor audiences sometimes danced to the ragtime tunes. The French were almost of one accord in their praise, but Sousa's spell wore off more quickly there than in other countries. Initially the Germans were less impressed, perhaps because the precision of Sousa's Band merely reminded them of the precision for which their own military bands were known. But eventually they were won over, and critics compared Sousa's Band to a great orchestra because of its smoothness and the technical excellence of the individual musicians. Featured on the programs were two men whom Sousa considered the world's finest on their respective instruments: cornetist Herbert L. Clarke and trombonist Arthur Pryor. In Britain Sousa found that newsmen were unaccustomed to such vigor in a military band. At first they were slow to accept his style of programming, but they were soon compelled to accept the people's wholehearted approval. Despite the scattered criticisms of a few reviewers, Sousa's individuality was universally acknowledged throughout Europe. The band played a total of 175 concerts in thirty-four European cities.

While the Sousa Band was playing in Paris, Sousa made his presence known in other ways. He wrote articles for the *Paris Herald* decrying governmental subsidization of the arts. This was reprinted in other papers, causing considerable comment. Then too he raised eyebrows by playing the German patriotic song "Die Wacht am Rhein" in Paris, much to the discomfort of German officials, because of current anti-German feelings.

For his outstanding performance Sousa was decorated by the Belgians after the tour of that country. The band then returned to America. Nearly four months had been spent in France, Germany, Belgium, Holland, and England. As they embarked on September 1, Sousa was already planning another trip to Europe. At home the band appeared at expositions in Pittsburgh and Boston and then disbanded until the end of the year.

THE "S.O., U.S.A." LEGEND

The band's inventive promotion man, Col. George Frederick Hinton, had been in Europe prior to the tour. Publicity had come easy for the band in America, where it was well known, but Hinton needed a gimmick to create interest in Europe. He thought of one, but it was to plague Sousa until his dying day. In England Hinton slyly started the rumor that Sousa was really an English immigrant named Sam Ogden whose initials and destination were printed as "S.O., U.S.A." on his luggage. It was a fascinating story, although false, and it made good copy at no cost to Hinton. It was perhaps the most effective advertising Sousa ever had. In France a variation of the rumor was that Sousa was actually

In 1900 Col. George Frederick Hinton, the Sousa Band's publicity manager, originated an "S.O., U.S.A." cognomen, which still persists.

a Frenchman named S. Oulette, again with his luggage marked "S.O., U.S.A." Likewise in Germany it was Sigismund Ochs or Siegfried Otz. Hinton apparently stopped there because the rumor was well on its way by itself. Other versions found their way to many countries for years to come. In Greece, for example, Sousa was said to have originally been a Greek named John Philipso, whose baggage was marked "John Philipso, U.S.A." And so forth. Sousa mused that he had been called upon to deny the story in every country on earth. Surprisingly, the story still persists today.[40]

THREE MORE EUROPEAN TOURS

Another coast-to-coast tour occupied the Sousa Band during the months of January through May, 1901. After this they played the first of many memorable engagements at Willow Grove Park in Philadelphia. Engagements there were highly desirable because the park was developing into the most important summer music center in America. For the Pan-American Exposition at Buffalo, which followed, Sousa composed the march "The Invincible Eagle," and the stay at Buffalo was followed by three two-week engagements at Manhattan Beach. Then came the Pittsburgh Exposition and the Indiana State Fair. After a farewell concert in New York, the band embarked for its second tour of Britain.

Arriving in London on October 4, the band gave several concerts there and then traveled to Scotland for a month at the Glasgow Exhibition. Many of England's major cities were visited during the next three months, but the highlight of the season was a command performance at Sandringham on December 1. At the conclusion of this concert, Sousa was presented with the Victorian Order. He asked if he might reciprocate in his own way, and this eventually led to the march "Imperial Edward," dedicated to King Edward VII.

Two tours of the United States and several amusement-park engagements in 1902 were anticlimactic after the visits to Europe. In January, 1903, Sousa's Band went abroad for the third time. After a second command performance, this time at Windsor Castle on January 31, Sousa was hospitalized briefly with a "chill on the liver." He soon recovered and embarked on an extensive tour of Europe. Concerts were given in England, Ireland, Scotland, Wales, France, Germany, Czechoslovakia, Poland, Russia, Austria, Sweden, Holland, Belgium, Bohemia, Norway, and Denmark. The tour lasted thirty weeks and totaled 362 concerts.

Nineteen four was another year of touring in the United States. The summer was occupied by long engagements at amusement parks and fairs. "The Diplomat" was Sousa's march effort for the year, and

[40] The author has been "informed" countless times, by well-meaning persons, of the origin of Sousa's name. Even former members of Sousa's Band have asked him if evidence had not been uncovered which would substantiate the story.

he seemed to be tapering off on his composition. He was instead concentrating on literary endeavors. The success of his first novel, *The Fifth String* (1902), led him to write a semiautobiographical novel, *Pipetown Sandy* (1905). Once this was completed, he began making preparations for a fourth European tour.

The 1905 season saw the Sousa Band once again in Britain. He noted that composers, especially those from foreign countries, lacked protection against the sale of bootleg copies of their compositions. He wrote strongly worded letters of appeal to three London newspapers, the *Times*, the *Daily Mail*, and the *Daily Telegraph*. The letters created much interest, and a reform was soon underway.[41] All was not well in Sousa's own country as far as composers' rights were concerned, and he was soon to be engulfed in the most involved controversy of his career.

Once back in America, with four tours of Europe behind it, the band enjoyed considerable prestige. The management could virtually name its price at expositions and fairs. There were dreams of a tour around the world. Such a plan was on the docket for 1906, but it did not materialize for another four years.

CAMPAIGNING FOR COMPOSERS' RIGHTS

The jovial operetta *The Free Lance* was completed late in 1905 and produced in 1906, the year in which Victor Herbert and Sousa were marked as men willing to fight for composers' rights. A congressional committee held hearings on proposed revisions to the existing copyright law. Herbert, Sousa, and others were instrumental in the proceedings, and their influence was seen in the eventual passing of new legislation in 1909.

For years composers believed they were entitled to royalties on music which was mechanically reproduced. But they had received nothing from the manufacturers of phonograph records and piano rolls, who profited by the fruits of their labor. With prompting by President Theodore Roosevelt, the Copyright Division of the Library of Congress drafted a new bill which would allow royalties on recorded music as well as on printed works. The phonograph and piano-roll industry lobbied effectively against passage, but composers were not well represented. However, when Herbert joined in the proceedings, followed by Sousa, the picture changed.

Herbert and Sousa testified at the hearings, which commenced June 6. They viewed the mechanical reproduction of music as an ominous threat to live performance and chided phonograph and piano-roll manufac-

[41] Letters to the editor of the *Times* and the *Daily News*, written on the same subject while on the 1903 tour of Britain, apparently created little attention.

turers for ignoring the ethical questions involved. Vigorous debate followed. No definite legislation was drawn up as a result of the first round of hearings, and Congress adjourned for the summer. Taking cognizance of the opposition's staggering power, Sousa used the recess to good advantage. He wrote the most outspoken magazine article of his career, "The

"'There is a man in there playing the piano with his hands!'"

The Library of Congress

This cartoon was one of several used in Sousa's 1906 article in *Appleton's Magazine*, "The Menace of Mechanical Music," attacking the recording industry. The phrase "canned music" was coined by Sousa in the article.

Menace of Mechanical Music," for *Appleton's Magazine*. He blasted the recording industry in no uncertain terms and was obviously soliciting public support for the forthcoming hearings. The article brought stinging criticism, but it also drew much praise for bringing the subject into the open. Another article, "My Contention," was written for *Music Trades*, and this was followed by a satirical piece called "The Year in Music" for *Town Topics*.

Sousa testified with renewed vigor when the hearings reopened in December, and Victor Herbert lobbied tirelessly behind the scenes. The legislation which eventually passed would have been much less favorable to composers had it not been for the energetic campaigning of Herbert and Sousa. When the Authors' and Composers' Copyright League of America elected its officers in 1907, Herbert and Sousa were named president and treasurer, respectively.

After passage of the copyright bill, Sousa's attitude toward the recording industry changed. In addition to his usual business with the Victor Talking Machine Company, he contracted with Thomas Edison's National Phonograph Company for a limited number of recordings. During the hearings, Victor's representatives had been somewhat sympathetic with Sousa's viewpoints, while Columbia's representatives seemed to antagonize him. He had previously done a considerable amount of recording business with Columbia, but after the congressional hearings relations were permanently severed.

No outstanding marches were written in the four years leading up to a tour of the world in 1910-1911, except for "The Fairest of the Fair" (1908) and "The Glory of the Yankee Navy" (1909). It was business as usual for the Sousa Band, which now had an enviable reputation on two continents and was clearly in a class of its own among commercial traveling bands. Sousa toyed with the idea of writing a grand opera, but the closest he came was his "all-American" operetta *The American Maid*. First known as *The Glassblowers*, it was begun in 1907 and completed in 1909, but it was not produced until 1913. It was his last operetta to be published or produced.

Sousa's mother died in Washington on August 23, 1908, while the Sousa Band was playing at Willow Grove. She was eighty-two, and Sousa had visited with her for two weeks shortly before her death. Although she had been able to attend only one Sousa Band concert in sixteen years, she had been a constant source of inspiration to him.

THE WORLD TOUR OF 1910-1911

In the autumn of 1910 the Sousa Band began its most extensive undertaking: a trip around the world, traveling from west to east. The tour started with a dubiously named "farewell" concert in New York, then a tour through New England and the southern part of Canada and back to New York. It was off to a shaky start, however, owing to Sousa's illness. Earlier, he had been the victim of the mosquito in a hunting trip through southern Maryland and was overcome by malaria at the beginning of the New England tour. He was carried from a Yale University stage on a stretcher and to a New Haven, Connecticut, hospital. After being incapacitated for thirteen days he rejoined the band in Montreal.

The Sousa troupe sailed from New York on December 24, 1910. The first stop was Great Britain, where, for two months, they appeared in England, Ireland, Scotland, and Wales. They sailed southward, and after concerts in the Canary Islands, they traveled to South Africa for a stay of four weeks. Crossing the Indian Ocean, they played nearly four months in Australia and New Zealand. They moved northward through the Pacific Ocean, with stops in the Fiji Islands and the Hawaiian Islands, and then moved on to Canada, ending with a tour across the United States. A final concert was held at the New York Hippodrome on December 9, 1911, and the band was dismissed until the following March.

Counting the rehearsals and the "farewell" tour that preceded the actual embarkation, the world tour lasted one year, one month, and one week. It was an outstanding artistic success, but financially the proceeds were merely adequate. It is ironic that in Australia and New Zealand, where receptions were the warmest, they actually lost money. The Sousa Band was not the first musical organization to travel around the world, but it attracted widespread attention and encouraged others who followed.

Three noteworthy musical products of the world tour were the *Tales of a Traveler* suite, inspired by events of the tour; the *Dwellers of the Western World* suite; and the march "The Federal," which was dedicated "to the Australasians." Sousa had also completed another book just before the tour, *Through the Year with Sousa*.

At the completion of the world tour, Sousa relaxed by indulging in the sport of trapshooting, a pastime which had been consuming much of his leisure time in recent years. His passion for trapshooting and horseback riding presented him to the public in a different light, and these activities are discussed in chapter 3.

FORGING AHEAD

The years between the global tour and America's entry into World War I were years of varied activity for both Sousa and his band. They crisscrossed the country each fall, winter, and spring, and the summers brought several engagements at fairs and expositions. Willow Grove Park in Philadelphia had become a regular stop. Engagements there lasted three weeks or more.

In a bold and almost unprecedented venture, the Sousa Band traveled around the world in 1910-1911. The tour covered nearly forty thousand miles. The band is shown here in Johannesburg, South Africa, with violinist Nicoline Zedeler and soprano Virginia Root. Sousa's wife and two daughters also made the trip.

Sousa and the French composer Camille Saint- Saëns struck up a cordial friendship at the Panama-Pacific International Exposition in 1915. Both dedicated compositions to the Exposition.

Nineteen fifteen was particularly eventful. From May until July the Sousa Band played at the Panama-Pacific International Exposition in San Francisco. For this Sousa composed the march "Pathfinder of Panama." The Exposition inspired still another composer to write music, of a more elegant nature; Camille Saint-Saëns wrote his grandiose *Hail California* for orchestra, band, and organ. Although it was given a resounding premiere by the combined efforts of the Exposition Orchestra, Sousa's Band, and an organist (all conducted by Saint-Saëns), the work did not become popular. For that matter, neither did Sousa's new march, even though it had the advantage of having been recorded by members of Sousa's Band.

Sousa and the aging Saint-Saëns became friends and were seen together frequently during the Exposition. The genial Frenchman thought highly of both Sousa and his band, as evidenced by his spontaneous endorsement at one particular concert. At the conclusion of one of Herbert L. Clarke's cornet solos, Saint-Saëns rose from his seat. Much to everyone's surprise, he came to the stage and proclaimed that he had never heard such a magnificent performance on either a trumpet or cornet in all his eighty years. Both the band and the audience broke into applause.

After the Exposition the Sousa Band toured through the Northwest and Midwest and then played a month at Willow Grove and another two weeks at the Pittsburgh Exposition. They then moved into the New York Hippodrome to create a record of sorts for musical organizations in New York by performing at the *Hip Hip Hooray* extravaganza for a period of eight months. They acted in the dual capacity of playing regular concerts onstage and replacing the traditional orchestra in the pit for the remainder of the show. During this time Sousa composed his popular "New York Hippodrome" march and completed his last operetta, *The Irish Dragoon*. *Hip Hip Hooray* closed for the season in early June, 1916. Sousa then made a 1,000-mile journey through New Jersey and Pennsylvania on horseback and took part in trapshooting tournaments. Ever eager to help Uncle Sam, he volunteered to serve as an army bandmaster near the Mexican border when friction arose between the United States and Mexico as a result of Pancho Villa's raids. The crisis was short lived, however, and he was not called to active duty. The United States was soon to be involved in a far more serious conflict, however, and this time Sousa's offer to serve his country was accepted.

A NAVY RECRUIT AT SIXTY-TWO

For the 1916-1917 season the *Hip Hip Hooray* show left the New York Hippodrome and took to the road for engagements lasting from several days to several weeks in major Eastern and Midwestern cities. The Sousa Band added to the success of the show, as might be expected. The troupe

After living in New York hotels for over twenty years, the Sousa family bought this mansion at Sands Point, Long Island, near Port Washington. It overlooks Manhasset Bay and was affectionately called "Wildbank." The three-acre estate included the eight-bedroom house and a two-story apartment garage. Sousa added a wing to the house, which was designed by the noted architect Alexander B. Trowbridge.

disbanded just as America entered World War I, and the Sousa Band adjourned until midsummer.

In May, 1917, Sousa was approached by the American composer John Alden Carpenter regarding the possibility of a special enlistment in the navy to train young bandsmen at the Great Lakes Naval Training Center. A meeting was arranged with Capt. William A. Moffett, Lt. James M. Bower, Carpenter, and Sousa. Moffett was commander of the base, and Bower, a member of his staff, happened to be the husband of Sousa's younger sister Elise. Sousa was asked if he would accept a commission as a lieutenant in the navy and be administrator of the newly formed Band Battalion. With the understanding that he would be granted leave during the summer months of 1917 and 1918 to fulfill engagements of the Sousa Band for which he had already been committed, he accepted.

Sousa enlisted on May 31, 1917, and was assigned the rank of lieutenant in the U.S. Naval Reserve Force. As a lieutenant, he was the first

NAVY

WASHINGTON, D.C.

38466

Treasurer of the United States

AUG.15,1917

15-51

PAY One DOLLARS

TO THE ORDER OF JOHN PHILIP SOUSA,
GREAT LAKES, ILL.

SOUSA, J.P. 4-NCDR $1#

OBJECT FOR WHICH DRAWN
NAVAL RESERVE FORCE
RETAINER PAY

50043

PAY INSPECTOR, U.S.N. 59013

"I joined the Reserves on the last day of May;
I gave up my band and a thousand a day.
A dollar a month is my government pay—
My God, how the money rolls in!"

navy musician to be a commissioned officer. He joked about his age (sixty-two) and was the oldest man ever to enlist in the navy up until that time. At his own insistence, his salary was set at one dollar per month.

He reported to the Great Lakes Naval Training Station near Chicago and went to work organizing the band corps and assisting in recruiting. That summer he took leave from July until mid-September for performances with the Sousa Band. Once back at Great Lakes, he took a select group of bandsmen on a short tour around the Midwest to promote Liberty Loan bond sales.

With Sousa at the helm, young musicians rushed to volunteer for service. He subdivided the organization into smaller units for assignments aboard ships and at various naval stations, and formed a large band for special events. At times its membership numbered 350. This hugh band was used for tours of major cities in the East and Midwest, for marching in parades, and for performing at rallies to support Liberty Loan bonds, the Red Cross, navy relief, and recruiting programs. They were most effective at rallies where pleas were made for the purchase of bonds. Sousa would put one of his batons up for bids, and the band would play request numbers, patriotic songs, and plenty of Sousa marches. The Band Battalion raised over $21 million.

The spirit of the large "Jackie" band, as it was called, was high. Sousa endeared himself to his men by marching every step of every parade at the front of the band and by eating and sleeping with the men. The average age of the bandsmen was twenty, but the white-bearded Sousa was "one of the boys." The long parades were very tiring for him, but his men would have been the last to know. He did not insist on strict discipline because it was not necessary; the men tried diligently to please him and kept their affairs in order.

Courtesy M. Emmett Wilson

Sousa's 300-piece "Jackie," or "Bluejacket," band of World War I, which traveled more than three thousand miles by special train, thrilled millions in war-bond and Red Cross rallies. Drum major Micheaux F. Tennant, strutting at the head of the band, was called "the peacock of the navy." Here they are seen marching down High Street in Columbus, Ohio, on September 28, 1918.

Feeling the need to identify with his youthful bandsmen, Sousa shaved off his famous beard. He jokingly remarked that this single act caused Germany to surrender, explaining that Kaiser Wilhelm realized that a nation made up of men willing to make such sacrifices could not be defeated.

Defense Department (Marine Corps)

While at Great Lakes, Sousa was music editor of the *Great Lakes Recruit*, a monthly magazine. One of his most popular contributions was "What Constitutes True Beauty in a Woman."

Sousa was on leave again from June 24 until September 8 to fulfill the second and last of the Sousa Band engagements for which he had contracted. Returning to Great Lakes, he prepared the band of sailors for an arduous tour in which they played for audiences in twenty-six cities in twenty days. Returning to the station in mid-October, Sousa developed a painful ear infection, and his activities were curtailed for three weeks.

On November 9, the band left for Toronto to assist the Canadians in their Victory Loan campaign. The parade there on November 10, in which many amputee war veterans appeared, was described by Sousa as one of the most moving experiences of his life.[42] The Armistice was declared on the eleventh, and the following day the band was in downtown Chicago for a gala celebration.

Immediately after the Chicago parade, Sousa caught influenza and was sent to his home at Sands Point to be attended by his own physician. The Band Battalion had been very fortunate all during the war in that they did not lose a single man in the tragic flu epidemic of that period. They had taken every precaution, arming themselves with antiseptics and even carrying a special hospital contingent aboard their special eight-car train.

Sousa was relieved of active duty in late January, 1919. He had twice refused promotions, believing that he could perform his duties sufficiently as a lieutenant.[43] However, he was promoted to lieutenant commander a little later while on inactive status. He was proud of having been an officer and often remarked privately that he regretted not having that status in the Marine Corps many years before.

Throughout the war newsmen sought the "great war song," some predicting that Sousa would write it. He composed several brilliant marches during that period, but an inspiring song was needed, not a march. Sousa did compose the music for several war songs, but none proved to be worthy competition for such favorites as George M. Cohan's "Over There." Three of his wartime marches were truly outstanding and have retained their popularity over the years. They are "U.S. Field Artillery," "Sabre and Spurs," and "Solid Men to the Front."

THE POSTWAR YEARS

It was not Sousa's nature to retire upon leaving the navy after World War I, although many thought he would. Instead, the Sousa Band was regrouped, and the indomitable Sousa continued as though there had been no interruption. Changing times brought some changes in the band's format, but the programs continued mostly in the usual tradition. While

[42] "Band Battalion Makes Big Hit in Toronto," *Great Lakes Bulletin*, November 14, 1918.
[43] According to a story in the printed programs of the 1919-1920 Sousa Band tour.

A lieutenant in the navy, Sousa twice declined promotions but was promoted to lieutenant commander after his release from active duty. More than three thousand bandsmen were trained under his supervision.

Sousa was proud of his navy lieutenant-commander's uniform and wore it at most concerts in the 1920s.

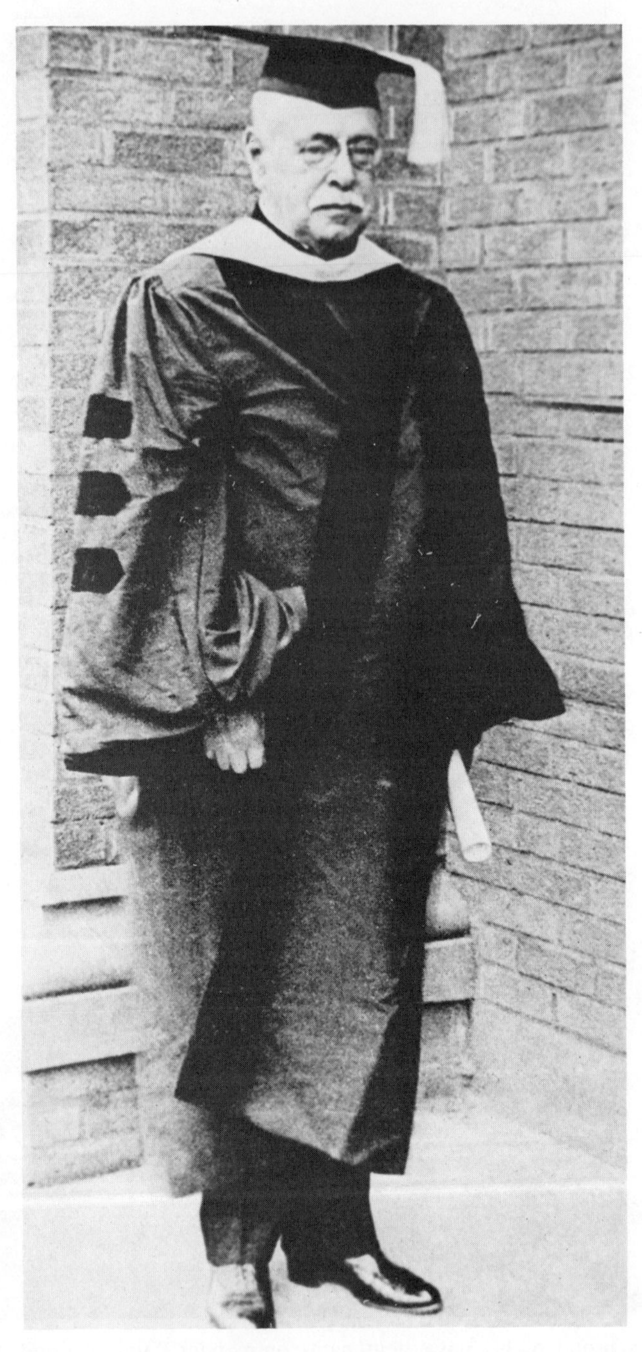

Honorary Doctor of Music degrees were conferred on Sousa by the Pennsylvania Military College and Marquette University.

United Press International

Three Indian tribes named Sousa honorary chief. The English equivalents of his Indian names were "Great Music Chief," "Chasing Hawk," and "Chief Singer."

most other touring bands went out of business in the Roaring Twenties, the magic name of Sousa drew capacity crowds wherever he went.

Except for a short visit to Cuba in February, 1922, and an occasional jaunt into Canadian territory, the band did not leave the United States after the war. The tours did not shorten until after the 1925-1926 season. The Willow Grove engagements were discontinued after 1926, but these were supplanted by engagements at the Steel Pier in Atlantic City. The tours dropped off sharply in 1929, primarily because of the depression.

Except for his marches, the volume of Sousa's compositions diminished during the 1920s. There were no more operettas and few compositions of any consequence except for the humoresques and fantasies, which temporarily pleased the public. Almost all his works during his last five years were marches. Among the more outstanding marches of his last decade were "The Gallant Seventh" (1922), "Nobles of the Mystic Shrine" (1923), "The Black Horse Troop" (1924), "The Pride of the Wolverines" (1926), "Golden Jubilee" (1928), "George Washington Bicentennial" (1930), and "The Northern Pines" (1931).

With more than four decades of entertainment behind him, it is little wonder that the postwar years brought considerable recognition from his countrymen. He was literally an American institution, as the press consistently proclaimed, and few musicians have ever been held in such high esteem. His honors ranged from being granted honorary Doctor of Music degrees to being named honorary Indian chief. Honorary doctorates, not awarded freely in those days, were conferred on him by the Pennsylvania Military College on February 27, 1920, and by Marquette University on November 26, 1923. The first Indian honor came from the Star Blanket tribe of the Fire Hills Indian Reserve in Saskatchewan, Canada, on July 30, 1925. They named him Kee-Too-Che-Kay-Wee-Okemow, meaning "Great Music Chief." The second was from the Ponca tribe in Oklahoma, who named him Dah-Wah-Nar-Gee-Thar, or "Chasing Hawk," on October 12, 1928. The third came from the Pawnee tribe, also of Oklahoma, who named him simply "Chief Singer" on May 16, 1931.

During this period Sousa became increasingly interested in the development of school bands and orchestras. He gave many loving cups and trophies to outstanding school bands and often invited them to perform during intermissions of Sousa Band concerts. He was much in demand as a guest conductor and did not refuse a request if conditions permitted. He was much sought after to adjudicate band and orchestra contests. He obliged but was reluctant to give unfavorable grades. It was a joy to him to see the founding of the National High School Orchestra and Band Camp at Interlochen, Michigan. He was guest conductor there during the last two summers of his life and dedicated the march "The Northern Pines" to them, donating the royalties to a scholarship fund.

An event of some historical significance took place in May, 1923, when Sousa and Thomas A. Edison came face to face in a meeting arranged by the editor of *Etude* magazine. Edison was the inventor of the phonograph, the machine which had alienated Sousa almost from its introduction. Sousa's views had changed considerably since the copyright legislation of 1909, however, and the meeting produced only a fraction of the fireworks it could have. Sousa praised Edison liberally and related that listening to Enrico Caruso and other artists of the past thrilled him. He had finally been won over by the realization that Edison's invention had made possible the immortality of many great performing artists.[44]

[44] "A Momentous Musical Meeting," *Etude*, October, 1923.

By this time it was not the phonograph but the radio which troubled Sousa. In the spring of 1924, he once again found himself allied with Victor Herbert, this time to combat bills put before Congress by interest groups of the radio industry who were attempting to exempt the industry from royalty payments. Herbert and Sousa were part of a contingent from the American Society of Composers, Authors and Publishers (ASCAP) who defeated the proposed bills. They not only objected to

U.S. Department of the Interior, National Park Service, Edison National Historic Site

"I am different from you, Commander Sousa. You know music in one way and I know it in another."

"You have made the art of the musician immortal, Mr. Edison."

Sousa's career paralleled the growth of the recording industry, but for many years he saw the phonograph as a threat to live music.

United Press International

Victor Herbert (right) and Sousa were good friends and twice joined forces to fight for composers' rights when important bills were before Congress. They are seen here with Gene Buck, president of ASCAP, at the Capitol Building in Washington just before Herbert's death in the spring of 1924.

the loss of income which would result if the bills were passed, but they also noted that steady playing of popular tunes over the radio diminished the popularity of the music before sheet music had a chance to sell in quantity. Herbert died shortly after this trip to Washington, and Sousa, who had been a charter member of ASCAP, succeeded him as a vice-president.

Sousa appeared before Congress twice more, for another cause, in January, 1927, and January, 1928.[45] He had no personal interest at stake but came to give testimony in behalf of army bandmasters. A bill was being introduced to raise army band standards through higher pay and by commissioning army bandmasters. He first appeared before a House committee with the noted conductor Walter Damrosch and several others. He said it was outrageous that army bandleaders were not the social

[45] Hearings before the Committee on Military Affairs, House of Representatives, 69th Congress, Second Session, on H.R. 444, S. 2337, January 18, 1927; Hearing before a Subcommittee of the Committee on Military Affairs, Senate, 70th Congress, on S. 750, January 26, 1928.

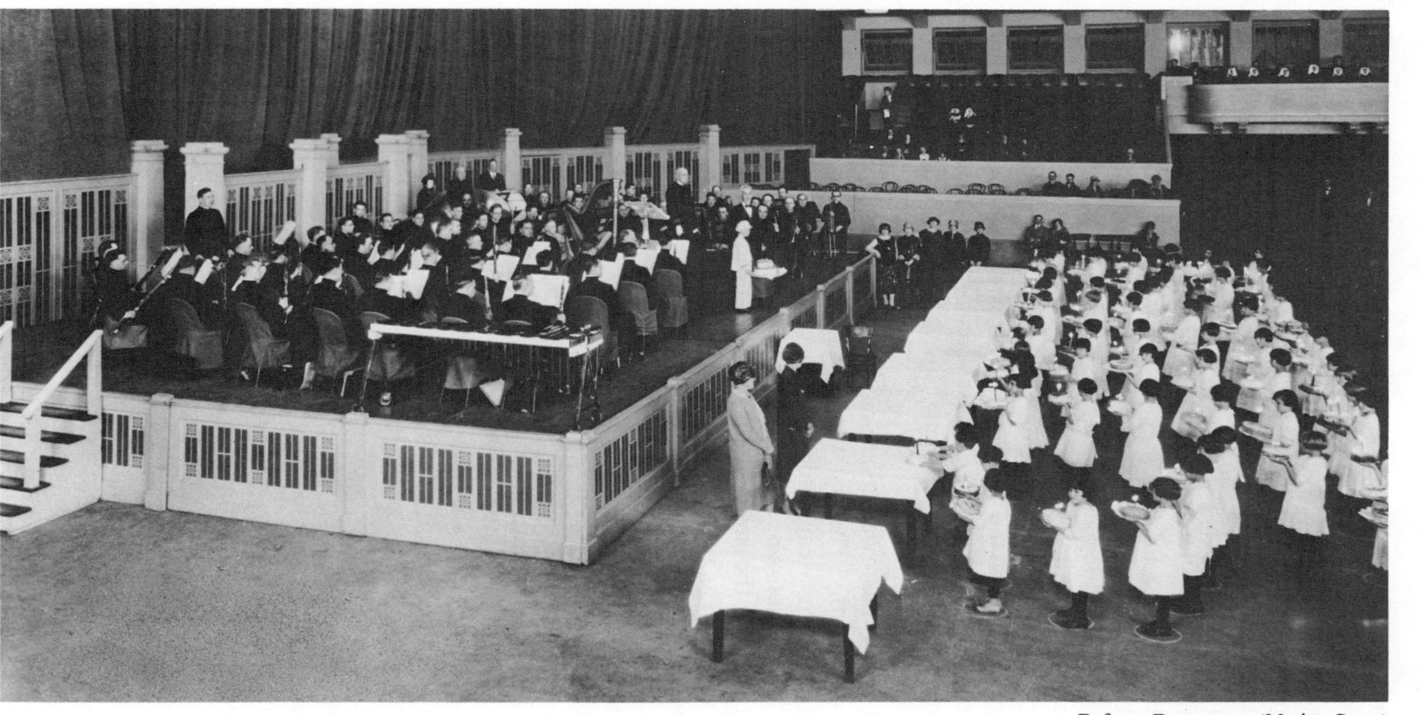

Defense Department (Marine Corps)

Regardless of his whereabouts, his public always remembered Sousa's birthday. On his seventy-second birthday in 1926, seventy-two Milwaukee children presented cakes, each with a candle on it.

equal of regular officers and that the U.S. Army lagged behind European military organizations in this respect. He pointed out that the situation was not in accord with the musical stature afforded to civilian conductors. He also appeared before a Senate subcommittee, again stating that the noncommissioned rank of army bandleaders was an outrage and adding that this was a species of snobbishness not equalled in other countries. Under questioning, he bluntly pointed out that the intelligence required of army musicians was far greater than that of the average soldier and that the subordinate position of army musicians had resulted in their bands being inferior to high school bands in the United States.

Nineteen twenty-nine marked the first Sousa Band radio broadcasts. These were hour-long programs, from New York in the General Motors "Family Party" series on the National Broadcasting Company's network. What listeners heard was not the Sousa Band which toured but a band made up mostly of current and former Sousa Band musicians who lived in the New York area.[46]

Among honors bestowed upon Sousa during his final years, two were particularly noteworthy. The first was being named honorary life president of the prestigious American Bandmasters Association at its first annual convention in Middletown, Ohio, on July 5, 1929. Of significance was the fact that three of the nine bandmasters who founded the ABA were Sousa Band alumni. The second honor was being asked to travel to Britain, where he presented the score of his "Royal Welch Fusiliers" march to the organization of that name on June 25, 1930. This march had been written at the request of United States Marine Corps officials to commemorate a long association between the fusiliers and the marines. On disembarking after his return to New York, he fell on the gangplank as he turned to give his autograph to a passenger. He received a deep cut on his head which required several stitches. The ship's captain pointed out that what might otherwise have been a routine docking would now be given considerable publicity. In his characteristic humor, Sousa assured the captain that he was "glad to oblige."

Suffering from the effects of a fall from a horse ten years earlier, Sousa entered John Hopkins Hospital in Baltimore in January, 1931, to see if measures—perhaps surgery—could be taken to restore the use of his left arm. Nothing could be done, but he was, as always, determined that death alone could end his active participation in music.

THE END OF AN ERA

Eight weeks after a final two-week tour of the Sousa Band in 1931, Sousa celebrated his seventy-seventh birthday in grand style. At an all-Sousa

[46] A total of twenty-one broadcasts of the Sousa Band were made on the following dates: May 6, 13, 20, 27, June 3, 10, 17, 24, July 1, October 7, 14, 21, 28, and November 4, 1929; October 31, November 3, 10, 17, 24, December 1, 8, 1931.

program broadcast by the Goldman Band in New York, he sliced a huge birthday cake with a sword and shared the podium with Walter Damrosch, Edwin Franko Goldman, Arthur Pryor, and others. He spoke of having just completed some lengthy compositions and remarked that he wished to live to 100 and write more marches.

The last two weeks of his life were eventful, as he would have wished. On February 22, 1932, he conducted the combined bands of the army, navy, and Marine Corps in front of the Capitol building in a performance of the "George Washington Bicentennial," a march written for the 200th anniversary celebration of George Washington's birth. Five days later, on the twenty-seventh, he participated in his final concert, conducting the orchestra of the U.S. Marine Bank in his march "Hands across the Sea." The occasion was the annual dinner of the Military Order of the Caraboa. Gen. Douglas MacArthur, Chief of Staff of the U.S. Army, presided. Witnesses said that the performance was inspired and that tears were visible in the eyes of several musicians. Was there something about Sousa's manner which caused them to sense that the end was near?

Sousa was active until the end, which came quickly. He had been invited to direct the Ringgold Band of Reading, Pennsylvania, in a concert commemorating their eightieth year on Sunday, March 6, 1932. On the preceding Friday he had gone to Philadelphia to visit a close friend and associate, James Francis Cooke, the editor of *Etude*. He was accompanied by his secretary, Miss Lillian Finegan, and soprano Marjorie Moody. After checking in at his hotel, he went directly to Cooke's office. There, his peculiar behavior suggested that he might have had a presentiment of death. Upon arriving he asked Cooke if he believed in God. He then complained that much modern music would fail; it lacked inspiration because many foolish composers did not believe in God. He made declarations of his own beliefs and elaborated on his oft-expressed statement that he composed only with the help of a "higher power." In the following twenty-four hours he returned to this subject four more times. Each time he went into greater depth, as though he were making one last effort to clarify his innermost religious convictions.[47]

That evening he dined at Cooke's home, and together they went to a performance of the play *If Booth Had Missed*. The next morning he arose early and asked Cooke to take him to the Theodore Presser Home for Retired Music Teachers. He was in a happy mood but seemed to be in frail condition. Lunching at the Penn Athletic Club, he ate very little and complained of a cold. After a long nap he bought a cough syrup and then boarded the train for Reading.

He was met at Reading by members of the Ringgold Band, friends, and a group from Gregg Post No. 12, of the American Legion. He was escorted to the Abraham Lincoln Hotel to register and then to Legion

[47] Eulogy by James Francis Cooke, *Etude*, June, 1932.

Courtesy Bert K. Warrek

Just hours before his death, Sousa (left) posed for his last photograph with Eugene Z. Weidner, director of the Ringgold Band.

headquarters for a rehearsal with the Ringgold Band. The concluding number—and the last composition ever played under his baton—was his own immortal "Stars and Stripes Forever."

After the rehearsal a banquet was held at the Wyomissing Club. Two hundred people were present. Sousa again ate sparingly and appeared tired, but he gave a short, witty speech. Afterward he autographed many menus. He was taken to the hotel about 11:30 p.m., accompanied by Albertus Meyers, formerly of the Sousa Band and director of the Allentown (Pennsylvania) Band. In Sousa's room he and Meyers conversed until after midnight. About half an hour after Meyers left, Miss Finegan, who was in an adjacent room, heard severe coughing. She arose, went to his door, and knocked but got no reply. She went to summon a physician but for naught. At approximately 1:30 on the morning of Sunday, March 6, 1932, John Philip Sousa was dead of a heart attack.

The body was taken to the Auman Funeral Parlor in Reading and was attended by an honor guard from The American Legion. In the afternoon the honor guard and the Ringgold Band accompanied the coffin to the railroad station. The band played a funeral dirge in the rain and wind as crowds lined the streets. Sousa's son-in-law, Hamilton Abert, escorted the body to Washington together with Sousa Band manager

Courtesy Charles S. Bisbing

While at Reading, Pennsylvania, to conduct an anniversary concert of the Ringgold Band, Sousa died in his room on the fourteenth floor of the Abraham Lincoln Hotel on Sunday, March 6, 1932.

Harry Askin, the legion honor guard, an honor guard from the Pennsylvania National Guard, and other individuals from Reading.

On Monday and Tuesday family members arrived in Washington. John Philip Sousa II had come from his home in California. Meanwhile, black drapes were hung in the windows of the Sousa home at Sands Point. On both days the U.S. Marine Band broadcast memorial programs. On Wednesday both houses of Congress paused to pay tribute, and the Senate appointed a committee to attend the funeral. President Hoover designated a party to represent the White House. The body was removed from Gawler's Undertaking Establishment in Washington and taken to the Marine Barracks. There, from 3:00 until 10:00 p.m., the body lay in state at the Marine Band Auditorium, attended by a marine guard of honor. The bronze casket, placed among palms and draped with the flag Sousa loved so well, was opened for public viewing. Sousa was clothed in his blue U.S. Navy lieutenant commander's uniform. That evening the Marine Band participated in a third memorial program, this one narrated by a young announcer destined to become one of America's favorite radio personalities: Arthur Godfrey.

Underwood and Underwood

A Marine Corps honor guard was in attendance as Sousa's body lay in state at the Band Auditorium of the Marine Barracks in Washington, D.C.

United Press International

The U.S. Marine Band played Sousa's "Semper Fidelis" in dirge time as his caisson was drawn by eight white horses to Congressional Cemetery.

The funeral was set for 3:00 p.m. on Thursday, March 10, a cold but beautiful day. The short service included no eulogy. It was held in the Marine Band Auditorium and was aired by the Columbia Broadcasting System. Among the honorary pallbearers were several notable musicians: George M. Cohan, Sigmund Romberg, Henry Hadley, Arthur Pryor, Edwin Franko Goldman, A. A. Harding, and Gene Buck. There were other honorary pallbearers, and at least three different sets of names appeared in the news media.

Sidney K. Evans, Chief Chaplain of the U.S. Navy, and the Reverend Edward Gabler of Christ Episcopal Church, Washington, D.C., officiated at the service. Music was provided by a male quartet from the Gridiron Club, which sang "Jesus, Lover of My Soul" and "Abide with Me." Companies of marine and navy men waited outside on the parade ground. As the casket was removed from the building, the Marine Band played "The Son of God Goes Forth to War" and "Nearer My God to Thee."

Inscribed on Sousa's grave marker is a fragment of his greatest march, "The Stars and Stripes Forever." Other graves in the plot are for his wife and three children.

"If, out of the cadences of Time, I have evoked one note that, clear and true, vibrates gratefully on the heartstrings of my public—I am well content."

Eight white horses drew the black caisson to the final resting place in Congressional Cemetery, seven blocks to the southeast. As the procession began, the band played Sousa's "Semper Fidelis" in dirge time. Between cadences of muffled drums, the strains of two of Sousa's dirges were heard: "In Memoriam" and "The Honored Dead." Thousands lined the streets to pay their last respects. At the cemetery inadequate police protection resulted in confusion and some delay. The graveside ceremony was brief but meaningful. The Marine Band played "Lead Kindly Light," Masonic rites were held, a prayer was offered, and a navy firing squad gave a salute. "Taps" was sounded by a solitary marine bugler.

An era had ended.

3
The Gentle Man

A HAPPY, ACTIVE LIFE

Basically a simple, unassuming man with an unbounded optimism, John Philip Sousa sincerely believed that his success was due to hard work, not to a superiority over others, and during his adult years he was always "able to wear the same size hat."[1]

Beneath that hat, size 7¼, was a man of medium dark complexion, 5 feet 7½ inches tall, and averaging 180 pounds. He had the same build and general appearance as his father Antonio, but unlike Antonio, he wore a heavy beard much of his life; and whereas Antonio had a bass voice, John Philip spoke in a tenor voice with a slight croak in it. His small hands and feet were no indication of his muscular body and manly bearing. He had black hair and penetrating dark brown eyes. Because of nearsightedness he wore pince-nez glasses with thick lenses, without which he felt insecure.

Like many other notable composers and conductors, he was blessed with an extraordinary memory and constantly astounded friends and acquaintances with his recall. He had a seemingly insatiable curiosity, partly satisfied by being an inveterate reader. The library of his Sands Point home contained over 3,000 volumes, covering everything from light poetry to scientific subjects. Home after a tour, he could hardly be torn away from the rare book catalogues which had arrived during his absence.

Sousa was a busy man all his life. As such, he was happily at peace with himself and would have traded places with no one. From his earliest years he was exceedingly active, making efficient use of his time. Each day was judiciously planned, including times of leisure. While a violinist

[1] John Philip Sousa, "Keeping Time" (part 6), *Saturday Evening Post*, December 12, 1925.

in Washington and Philadelphia theaters, he preferred working on his compositions to relaxing with his fellow musicians during intermissions or after performances. He was of the opinion that a creative man was obliged to present all of his talent to the world and should therefore have a capacity for unlimited work.

He steadfastly proclaimed that he would never retire or give a "farewell" concert. When newspaper reporters sensed the end of his career and asked the inevitable question, his ready reply was, "When you hear of Sousa retiring you will hear of Sousa dead!" He was sensitive to even the most subtle hints of feebleness and secretly had his conducting

When the self-made millionaire Sousa permitted himself the luxury of relaxing, it was usually among books. He was well informed on many subjects. He is seen here on the front porch of his Sands Point home, "Wildbank," with one of his many dogs.

podium lowered inch by inch so that his lack of agility would not be obvious. One could arouse his anger by offering to help him board a train. This token pride may be overlooked, because in all other respects he aged gracefully. He always kept himself physically fit, even when on tour; conducting four to six hours per day was physically exhausting, and he certainly did his share of walking between train stations, concert halls, and hotels.

He was so busy that he was never very close to many members of the Sousa clan. To his nieces and nephews he was "Uncle Johnnie," "Uncle John," or "Uncle Jack," but he seldom saw them. Though he was fond of his oldest sister Katherine and his youngest sister Elisabeth, he had little contact with his brothers. Strangely, of his five sisters and four brothers, he mentioned only Catherine in his autobiography.

Some of his happiest times were spent with his wife and children at home between tours, and among his most pleasant recollections were the times spent around the dinner table when all indulged in conversations on nearly every imaginable subject. He had the knack of drawing out their innermost thoughts, and they all cherished these moments.

No one in the family traveled with him in later years, but during the first years of the Sousa Band's existence Mrs. Sousa or one of the children often accompanied him. They were also together during extended engagements at parks or expositions. The question naturally arises as to Mrs. Sousa's reaction to being left at home for periods of many months. She endured this, but there were strained relations at times, particularly in his later years. Because few knew of this, the rare disagreeable episodes never created a false public image. All things considered, Sousa's wife and three children brought him many supremely happy years.

Morally, Sousa was a man of the highest of ideals. This was revealingly and succinctly stated by one of his former managers, who observed that Sousa gave the general impression of one trying diligently to be the most honorable man who ever walked on the face of the earth.[2]

Obscenities were repulsive to him. He would not tell an off-color story and would simply leave the company of those who did. He often just stared them down. He disliked profanity and was known to use it himself only under extreme provocation. It was a mark of distinction for one of his bandsmen to be able to say he had heard Sousa utter a "Christ and all His brethren!" or a "Christ Almighty!" in the strictest privacy.

His noticeable respect for women in general no doubt stemmed from his relationship with his mother, whom he revered. She pleaded with him to remember her teachings, and he always acknowledged her gentle influence. She had been especially firm in her conviction of honoring

[2] Interview with Mr. William Schneider, traveling manager of the Sousa Band, 1919-1929, on September 15, 1968.

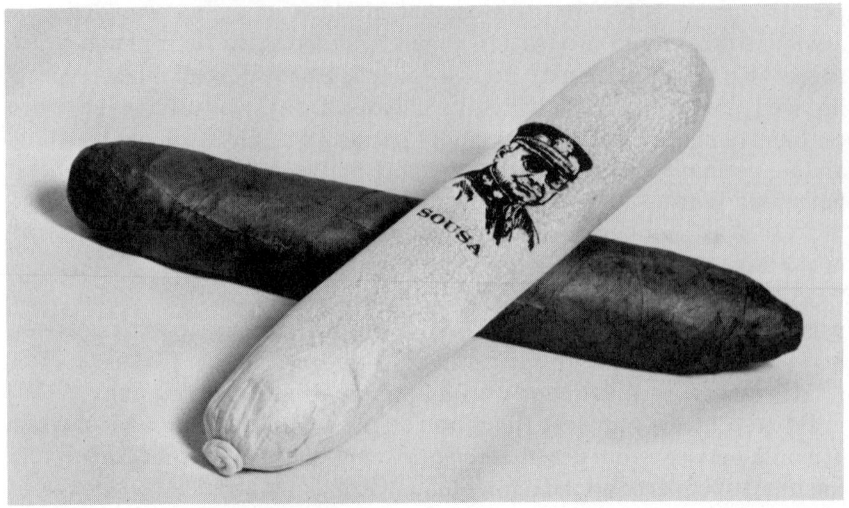

Courtesy Elbert Severance

Sousa's specially made Havana cigars were these Fonseeka "McKinleys." Except for the wrapper, they were identical to those made for Adm. George Dewey.

the Sabbath, and he respected her wishes by not composing on that day. He put together several medleys of well-known hymns, and these were reserved exclusively for Sunday use. It should be noted that he wore a white uniform on Sunday, while on weekdays he usually wore black. Once when some local ministers halted a Sunday concert, Sousa indignantly commented—in all seriousness—that there was more inspiration in his marches than in their sermons.[3]

Inasmuch as Sousa did not attend church regularly in adulthood, especially while on the road, it would appear that he was not a religious man. He was, however, very much in tune with the Divine. Close friends often observed—quite accurately—that his music was his religion. He sincerely believed that, facilitated by music's universal appeal, a sermon could be preached with music as well as with words. He not only believed that his own melodies were divinely inspired but that the "unseen helper" also prepared the way for them by touching the public heart. This will be discussed in the next chapter.

Sousa was tolerant in his concepts of religion, and religious bigotry was unthinkable. He was known to have dismissed members of his band for ridiculing the religious beliefs of other bandsmen. Specifically he was an Episcopalian, but his beliefs were broad. He believed in evolution, but not as set forth by Darwin. Although he put little stock in literal

[3] At a concert in Binghamton, New York, November 12, 1922. His retort was carried widely by the press.

interpretation of the Bible, he felt this served a purpose for those who were not intellectually inclined. In his opinion, Jesus of Nazareth was a great intellect and the foremost teacher of all time, but he did not believe in the virgin birth.

It might well be imagined that Sousa led a disciplined life in order to keep pace with the everyday developments of his travel. He lived

Courtesy Nora Fauchald Morgan

Few pictures were ever taken of Sousa smoking. This one was presented to soprano Nora Fauchald in 1926.

temperately. While he was pleased with food well prepared, he was not a fussy eater and enjoyed this and other fine things of life in moderation. He had enough self-control never to let a habit—for example, smoking—get out of hand. He had no use for cigarettes or pipe smoking, but he did find a solace in tobacco by smoking cigars after concerts. He never smoked in the morning, and when he did smoke, he indulged in expensive cigars that were custom made. He took pride in these and sued the P. Lorillard Company for $100,000 in May, 1925, when they introduced, without his knowledge, a cheap cigar with his picture on the label.[4]

He found little use for liquor but did partake occasionally at meals. Drunkenness disgusted him, but he saw nothing wrong with moderate drinking. He spoke out strongly against Prohibition, decrying its tragic failure in the United States. He was better informed on this subject than most because wherever the Sousa Band toured, he noted that bootleggers were making a mockery of the Eighteenth Amendment. He felt that most beers and some light wines should have been classified technically as nonintoxicants. As for Prohibition, he thought a more practical solution would have been to have liquor dispensed by state stores to licensed patrons whose licenses would be subject to revocation. In a humorous vein, he once testified before Congress that Prohibition was causing the decay of operetta because the inspiration for the typical drinking song was becoming extinct.[5]

Had one peered into one particular drawer of Sousa's personal trunk during the 1920s, he could easily have gotten the wrong impression—the drawer contained forty small vials of Scotch whiskey which his valet kept full. (Where the Scotch came from during Prohibition days was obviously not discussed.) He nipped at this sparingly before meals, on the advice of a doctor, to help kill the constant pain in his neck and left shoulder which was the aftermath of the broken neck he suffered in 1921. In all his life he was never publicly seen under the influence of alcohol, and, from all indications, this never occurred privately.

Sousa was a veritable fountain of sparkling humor, as might be expected of an operetta composer. His wit was of the wry, subtle variety. Because he seldom gave a hint of his humor except through the twinkle of his eyes, the uninitiated victims of his wit were unable to tell whether or not he was serious. For instance, he often capitalized on his wife's youthful appearance by introducing her and the three children as "my four children by my first wife." Many of his bandsmen never saw him laugh aloud, but a few well remember the time he unexpectedly broke into laughter when one of his bass players split his trousers fielding a

[4] Supreme Court, State of New York. The matter was settled out of court.

[5] Statement made before the House Patents Committee on May 6, 1924, when he was testifying against a bill which would have relieved broadcasters of paying royalties to owners of music copyrights.

baseball during a game. His type of humor was well described by the girls of a high school journalism class, who reported the following after an interview: "He wasn't a bit hard to talk to, although he did look real serious. He could say the funniest things, and never crack a smile."[6]

One of Sousa's humoresques, "The Mingling of the Wets and Drys," gave rise to an incident which pointed up his sense of humor. For several years the Sousa Band had played at Ocean Grove, New Jersey, a mecca of the Methodists. Upon hearing that Sousa was planning to play a composition based on drinking songs, they protested, whereupon he substituted another humoresque entitled "Follow the Swallow."[7] The Methodists failed to see the humor of it, however, and never invited him back.

Because of his wit and diversified background, he was an engaging conversationalist and an outstanding speaker. He was much in demand for after-dinner addresses and was called upon constantly while touring with the band. He always had a ready anecdote, usually drawn from his own experience, and he had a knack of converting episodes of his travels into fascinating tales. The nature of his talks was very much like his marches: short and well thought out. He spoke deliberately, choosing his words well.

Persons in the public spotlight who travel extensively may be expected to hold regular or honorary memberships in many organizations, and Sousa was no exception. He was affiliated with the American Society of Composers, Authors and Publishers (ASCAP), the American Bandmasters Association, and his Washington Masonic Orders (Hiram Lodge No. 10, Eureka Chapter No. 4, Columbia Commandery No. 2, Knights Templar, and Almas Temple A.A.O.N.M.S.). In addition, he was associated with the Actors' Friends, American Amateur Trapshooters Association, Army and Navy Club, Audubon Society, Authors' and Composers' Copyright League of America, Authors League of America; Benevolent and Protective Order of Elks, Commonwealth Opera Association, French Society of Authors, Composers and Editors; Gridiron Club; Huntingdon Valley Country Club; Indians (trapshooters); Kappa Kappa Psi (music honorary society); Kenlock Gun Club; Lambs; National Association of Shotgun Owners; Lincoln Camp Sons of Veterans; Long Island Good Hearted Thespian Society; Manhasset Bay Yacht Club; Musicians Club; National Geographic Society; New York Oddity Club; Players; Republican Club; Rubenstein Club; Society of American Dramatists and Composers; United States Flag Association; and the Whitemark Country Club. Many of these groups and others have long since lost their identity. The list is by no means complete and does not include the countless local organizations in which he held honorary memberships.

Regarding political views, one could surmise that Sousa was a Repub-

[6] *Ponca City* (Oklahoma) *News*, October 14, 1928.
[7] *New York Times*, May 8, 1927.

TEMPLE BAR 4343

SAVOY HOTEL,
LONDON.

June 26th 1930

My dear Marjorie:
We had a
most pleasant
sailing across the
ocean [illegible]
[illegible] the fog, and
the [illegible] behaved
beautifully.
The great-
day was yes-
-terday. We —
a General
Ten Captains
and a poor
little composer
in a Packard
car, supplied
by the U. S.
Embassy went

Courtesy Marjorie Moody Glines

When writing personal letters, Sousa often used only the extreme right-hand side of the page.

lican because he frequently addressed small gatherings of Republicans in New York City. Then too, he dropped in on the Republican national convention in Chicago in 1924 and led the band in a Sousa march. And when the Sousa Band happened to be in California at the time Herbert Hoover was elected President, it serenaded him at his Stanford University home. But on the whole, Sousa was not outspoken on political matters. Perhaps he thought this would be bad for business.

He had personal peculiarities, but they caused hardships to no one. For instance, he did not carry a watch or matches until his final years. Also, he seldom carried over two dollars on his person. And the personal letters of his late years were written entirely on the right-hand side of the page. His most publicized eccentricities were his use of new white gloves for nearly every concert and his collection of dozens of pairs of custom-made shoes, which he reportedly had insured for $5,000.

But what man of note is not entitled to a few idiosyncrasies?

DETERMINATION AND SUCCESS

If, on the surface, John Philip Sousa appeared to be an uncommonly modest man, how did he achieve such astonishing success in a highly competitive field? The answer lies in his determination—his indomitable will and self-confidence. Beneath his quiet dignity he had a poised fearlessness; nothing was impossible to him. To better understand his determination, it is necessary to analyze several examples of his actions for which there is documentation.

The first evidence we have of his strong will is the boyhood incident mentioned in the previous chapter in which he attempted to punish his mother, who cut off his supply of doughnuts, by soaking himself in the rain and catching pneumonia. Another incident, which reveals a phobia against being ignored, occurred at the age of about sixteen when he was jilted by a girl whom he escorted to a dance. He was secretly in love with the girl, who met another boyfriend at the dance and decided to go home with him instead of the young Sousa. He was at first crushed, but then he decided that he would someday become so successful that she would regret having spurned him for the temporary affection of another. This incident may have had more to do with the molding of his career than is realized. He did not reveal this incident until he was in his twilight years, and then only to his closest friends. A Philadelphia newspaper reporter drew it from him in 1924.[8]

Had he not had great determination when he traveled to Philadelphia in 1876, he might not have found work as a violinist. On his arrival he was informed that there were insufficient jobs for Philadelphia violin-

[8] This poignant and revealing story was printed in the *Philadelphia Record*, August 24, 1924.

ists, let alone outsiders. Undaunted, he sought out the jobber Simon Hassler, auditioned for him, and won a position in the first violin section of the Offenbach orchestra.

Another example of his determination—open, however, to some speculation—is the manner in which he obtained the job as leader of the U.S. Marine Band in 1880. According to written records, he was awarded the position on the basis of his musicianship. This is no doubt true, but how was he, as a candidate, brought to the attention of Marine Corps officials? His father, a retired Marine Corps bandsman, doubtlessly spread the word of his son's successes in other cities. But the young Sousa definitely helped things along and may have actively sought the job in subtle ways.

It must be borne in mind that while he was a member of the band five years earlier, he had been belittled by the leader, Louis Schneider; it was principally because of Schneider that he had secured his military discharge. It is highly unlikely that he forgot Schneider's haughty action, and he probably became very much interested in events transpiring in Washington. Schneider was falling from official grace. Perhaps Sousa anticipated a change in directorship and desired to let it be known that he would be available. At any rate, he made some very interesting moves.

The first was late in 1878 when he composed a march entitled "Esprit de Corps," "esprit de corps" being a term used in connection with military pride and unity, particularly among marine units. Then, in the summer of 1879, he composed another march, this one specifically aimed at the marines because the title was derived from the Marine Corps emblem: "Globe and Eagle." And another that same summer was entitled "On the Tramp" (i.e., "on the march"). And still another, "Resumption March," was dedicated to a Capt. N. K. Nokes of the Marine Corps. Following this up in the summer of 1880, he composed a set of waltzes entitled "Paroles d'Amour," which he dedicated to no less a person than Col. C. G. McCawley, Commandant of the Marine Corps. Why would Sousa have composed these pieces if he were not trying to bring himself to the attention of Marine Corps officials? Shortly after Schneider was discharged from the Marine Corps, John Philip Sousa was named the new leader. Was this a natural sequence of events, or had Sousa been determined to avenge his earlier setback by promoting himself into Schneider's position? The facts would seem to imply the latter.

Still another example of Sousa's strong will is seen after the humiliating failure of his first published operetta, *The Smugglers*. The company folded up in Philadelphia, in debt, after a very short run. Sousa was overcome by grief. His brooding was short-lived, however; within days he was earnestly at work on another operetta, *Desiree*.

Managers of the Sousa Band quickly learned of Sousa's determination. One incident, and by far the most significant incident involving managers, came when David Blakely elected to close down the first Sousa Band tour in 1892 after concluding that receipts would fall below his expectations. But he had not taken into account the stern will of Sousa, who firmly stood his ground and demanded that the tour be completed as scheduled. A second incident occurred when manager Everett Reynolds, thinking that Sousa would surely concede, held out for an extended contract just as the Sousa Band was about to embark on its first European tour of 1900. But rather than yield to Reynolds' demand or cancel the tour, Sousa dismissed him and headed for Europe left almost completely to his own devices and with a band of sixty-three performers on his personal payroll.

Still other evidences of his perseverance were brought out in the 1910-1911 world tour. This tour was undertaken not at the suggestion of the band's manager but at Sousa's insistence. He carried on despite heavy odds. Shortly after the tour began he had a relapse of an earlier siege of malaria, but he sent the band on ahead, catching up with them in a weakened condition and successfully completing this triumphant tour.

As if to prove the old cliché that "the show must go on," it must be recalled that Sousa's determination kept this tradition alive in the Sousa Band. There were countless examples of his making scheduled appearances in spite of sickness and many other personal hardships. The supreme example of his grim will occurred when he appeared before the public only ten weeks after he had broken his neck in 1921—while leading the public to believe that he had suffered only a broken arm or collarbone. It was with great pain that he stood erect. Audiences did not see the perspiration streaming down his face as he conducted, and they were not aware of his state of near exhaustion after leaving the stage. Yet during this period he was composing some of his liveliest music.

Who among the Sousa Band men would not be inspired by such leadership? This brings out a curious fact of the Sousa Band which was generally unknown to the public: it was a mutual admiration society. Each musician of that organization had reached the pinnacle of success through his own individual determination. Sousa fully recognized this quality in others, thus explaining why he had such admiration and respect for his bandsmen; they had achieved their successes in exactly the same dedicated manner in which he had achieved his.

THE SPORTSMAN

> A horse, a dog, a gun, a girl, and music on the side. That is my idea of heaven.[9]

Nowhere was Sousa's determination more evident than in his athletic achievements. From a frail boy of seven he grew to a sturdy man who excelled in several sports.

His favorite noncompetitive sport was horseback riding. He usually kept a stable of several horses at his Sands Point home for his own use between tours. He was frequently seen in the area atop one of his favorite steeds, and it was not unusual for him to ride from his home to the extremities of Long Island. When the Sousa Band played lengthy engagements at Willow Grove, he stabled his horses at the Huntingdon Valley Country Club and took advantage of the afternoon and evening concert arrangement to exercise them—and himself—each morning. He often joked that he kept physically fit by exercising his upper half at concerts and his lower half on the bridle path.

Between tours he sometimes took riding trips of considerable distances. He made at least five trips from Hot Springs, Virginia, to Washington, D.C., and then on to New York. And in 1916 he traveled nearly 1,000 miles entirely by horseback to participate in several trapshooting events. The other members of his family were also good riders, but Mrs. Sousa lost interest in her middle age. His daughter Priscilla once rode from Philadelphia to New York, accompanied by Mrs. Sousa in a chauffeur-driven automobile.

Horses brought him many happy hours, but they also brought him grief. He fell from a horse, Banjo, in October, 1903, sustaining bruises and a scalp wound, but a fall in 1921 nearly ended his career. He had been challenged by a high-spirited steed named Patrician Charley (Patrolman Charley) who "had a humorous gleam in his eye and an almost human quality about him." As he told a reporter of the *Philadelphia Public Ledger* on September 12, 1920: "When I got astride of him the first time, four years ago, I regretted it immediately afterward. For the next fifteen minutes the one thought uppermost in my mind was, 'How am I ever going to get off him without breaking my neck?' " On September 6, 1921, Patrician Charley did indeed break Sousa's neck. Charley had the "blind staggers" and threw Sousa one morning near Willow Grove. An upper vertebra was cracked, and he also suffered painful head and shoulder injuries. He was bedfast for nearly eight weeks, and doctors

[9] This was one of Sousa's favorite sayings. The title of a magazine article he wrote for the *American Shooter* of August 15, 1916, was "A Horse, a Dog, and a Girl."

Sousa had only partial use of his left arm for the last ten and a half years of his life because of being thrown from his favorite horse, Patrician Charley. His public never knew of this affliction.

feared he would never use his arms again. He recovered, but never fully, and had only limited use of his left arm. He could swing his arm to and fro but not outward from his body, severely handicapping his conducting style for the remainder of his career.

His favorite competitive sport was baseball, and to him baseball was the greatest game in the world.[10] He played from the time he was old enough to hold a bat and was an excellent pitcher. The Sousa Band even had its own baseball team, complete with uniforms (see p. 169), and its pitcher was often the black-bearded Sousa himself. He pitched for this team as long as he was able but withdrew from active participation in his forty-sixth year, with the exception of a charity game in 1916. In that game Sousa's Band was beaten by Pryor's Band by the score of 29 to 15; Sousa and Pryor were the opposing pitchers for the first inning. Sousa's march "The National Game" (1925) was, incidentally, inspired by baseball.

[10] The title of one of Sousa's articles was "The Greatest Game in the World." It was published in the February, 1909, issue of *Baseball Magazine*.

Sousa was one of America's best trapshooters. He was also an excellent hunter but was opposed to the shooting of domestic birds for sport.

Other than baseball and horseback riding, Sousa liked trapshooting best. He participated in the national shoots regularly, shooting well over 15,000 targets some seasons. He was enthusiastic about the sport, primarily because he could enjoy it as he grew older. Trapshooting appealed to him because it leveled all ranks, and he wrote several articles on the subject. He was elected president of the American Amateur Trapshooters' Association in 1916 and chairman of the National Association of Shotgun Owners in 1917. He was also a member of the elite "Indians" group of crack shots.

He was regarded as one of the best trapshooters in the country and had many trophies and medals to prove it. His shooting average at meets ranged from 75 to 98 percent. He had a large collection of guns, and the Ithaca Gun Company named one of its models the "Sousa Grade." This particular model was in the $1,000 class. His pictures, as well as quotes on the subject of trapshooting, were featured in DuPont Powder Company advertising.

He was not only an excellent trapshooter, but an excellent hunter as well. Birds and animals he did not shoot in excess, however, for he considered the wholesale slaughter of animals a criminally wicked practice. He had been handy with a shotgun from the days of hunting along the Anacostia River with his father. At different times he was a part owner of a 2,000-acre preserve near Pinehurst, North Carolina, and of a 6,500-acre preserve near Georgetown, South Carolina.

If Sousa had to choose between live birds and clay targets, he would have preferred the clay targets. His proficiency at trapshooting was once misunderstood by an English minister who had read that Sousa had shot a large number of "pigeons." He wrote Sousa urging him to repent and withdraw from his murderous practice. As a joke Sousa sent the minister a box of broken clay targets and suggested that they be broiled before eating.

Sousa was an all-around animal lover, and this was why he looked upon bullfighting as a worthless and unjust sport. He usually kept several dogs at his Sands Point home and, as previously discussed, several handsome horses. When picking up a newspaper, he first read the music news, then the sports news, and then the horse sales.

He also found fascination in the manly art of boxing, and in the late 1890s he sparred regularly at Jack Cooper's Gymnasium in New York City. He was a good friend of heavyweight champion Bob Fitzsimmons and once sparred with him bare-handed.[11] His boxing prowess apparently served him well once when he was reported to have attacked—by throwing from the train—a bandsman who insulted one of

[11] "Sousa As He Is," *Music*, May, 1899.

The "March King" was no John L. Sullivan, but he could handle himself well in the ring.

the lady soloists. Sousa's daughter Helen stoutly denied this, however.[12]

The only other athletic pastimes which interested Sousa were walking and golf, both of which he took up in his advanced years. He spent many hours strolling along the winding, secluded roads near his Sands Point home. As for golf, he often remarked that he would take up this sport when he was too old to participate in any other. So it was, and his scores were so unflattering that they were seldom mentioned.

REGARD FOR OTHERS

Success did not change John Philip Sousa. If anything, it mellowed him. To casual acquaintances he was known as a kindly, tolerant man, magnanimous in every way. To those who knew him personally, he was precisely this same sort of person. In every respect he was straightforward and sincere.

He was a cordial, approachable man, one with a keen sense of justice and democracy who treated all as equals. Both the successful and unsuccessful were at ease in his presence. He made no enemies and was universally loved by people from every strata of society. Even his competitors held him in high regard, partly because he treated them with respect and always had a kind word for them. This was unusual in the competitive world of commercial traveling bands, but Sousa was no ordinary bandleader. He was a showman with a heart, and audiences were his first concern. At the finish of a concert he was often found autographing programs until the auditorium closed. Countless struggling young musicians cherished the memory of having shaken hands with the "March King" and being warmly encouraged.

Punctuality was another of his virtues. This was recognized in boyhood when he received a prize for punctuality (and conduct) in secondary school. Paraphrasing an old quotation, he often remarked that punctuality was the politeness of kings. When a Sousa Band concert was scheduled for eight o'clock, it began promptly at eight o'clock, and when the train pulled out of the station, Sousa had been there waiting for half an hour. The same could not be said for his wife, whom he sometimes referred to as "the late Mrs. Sousa."

To friends and associates Sousa was known as a generous person. He would spare no expense if he thought a cause to be worthy. A good example of this was his action in the Dewey parade of September 30,

[12] One of Sousa's arrangers and copyists, Dr. Peter Buys, while a member of the band, gave an eyewitness account of this fist fight in an article entitled "Recalls Old Days with the March King" in the *Instrumentalist*, January, 1952. It was reprinted in the *Sousa Band Fraternal Society News*, July, 1952. When the story was reported on pp. 52-53 of Kenneth Berger's book, *The March King and His Band*, Mrs. Helen Sousa Abert protested. She told the author that such behavior was beneath her father's dignity and that the incident could therefore not have happened.

When giving an autograph, Sousa often added a musical sketch of one of his marches.

1899. A New York committee had asked the cost of obtaining the Sousa Band's services for the parade, but the band was on tour at the time. Since Sousa had no intention of breaking contracts where the band was already committed, he simply quoted to the committee the actual amount of forfeiture fees plus whatever travel costs would have been involved. Members of the musicians' union in New York somehow gained access to the figures, and not understanding what they included, interpreted the cost to be exorbitant and spread the word that Sousa was trying to scalp the public. Upon hearing this, Sousa was infuriated. He immediately cancelled all engagements, brought the band to New York for the parade, and hired extra men to bring the grand total to over 100—all at his own expense.

A KINDLY EMPLOYER

One standard for comparing the personalities of famous men is to consider their treatment of their employees. Sousa's distinctive relationship with his bandsmen was truly remarkable. He seldom fraternized with them; the social relationship was akin to that of officers and enlisted men. However, the bonds of unity and mutual respect were very real indeed.

The most amazing thing about this relationship was that Sousa never criticized his musicians either publicly or privately. A musician seldom made the same mistake repeatedly. If he did, he was often approached by Sousa inconspicuously and in a polite manner. Sousa would immediately put the errant musician at ease by pleasant small talk and, like a master psychologist, methodically steer the conversation to the man's own personal problems while making no mention of any dissatisfaction in his playing. He was paternalistic in these interviews. Upon determining the source of trouble, he would attempt to offer friendly advice or else give the man a few days off with pay so he could resolve his problems. This indirect method of correction was highly effective and was much appreciated by the bandsmen.

On long train rides, Sousa often strolled through the cars, greeting each individual bandsman, always willing to lend a sympathetic ear. Regardless of age, everyone was "young man." And regardless of how old a musician became, he was welcome to continue with the band so long as he could keep up the pace and play well; there was no mandatory retirement policy.

He was more than fair in the matter of salaries and would generally grant increases when personally requested by the bandsmen. Even when the musicians' union established minimum scales, Sousa's salaries would often exceed the scale. One year the union scales went up after the Sousa Band contracts had been signed, but Sousa raised the salaries proportionately even though he was under no obligation to do so.

His sense of fairness may best be exemplified by the action he took in the autumn of 1921 when he was hospitalized after being thrown from his horse, Patrician Charley. Ten weeks of Sousa Band engagements had to be cancelled. He realized that the misfortune was not the fault of his men, so he paid many of the men's salaries for the entire ten-week period.

It has been said by many that the Sousa Band was the finest of all time. While this may be subject to debate, there should be little doubt that its members shared a devotion to duty such as has never been seen before or since in an organization of its kind. With such a man as Sousa at the helm, it is little wonder.

4
Sousa's Philosophy of Music

I would rather be the composer of an inspired march than of a manufactured symphony.

—John Philip Sousa

This viewpoint was repeatedly expressed by the "March King." Inasmuch as he was one of the most successful of all musicians, his rationale is worthy of critical examination.

It was Sousa's opinion that music for entertainment was of more value to the world than music for education. This concept, which evolved during his early career as a theater musician, led him away from a possible career as a composer or conductor of more serious music. In 1910 he wrote of his "mission in music":

> It seemed to me, in my early life, that the principles of this type of music might be so far elaborated and utilized as to reach the entire world directly and effectively. . . . My theory was, by insensible degrees, first to reach every heart by simple, stirring music; secondly, to lift the unmusical mind to a still higher form of musical art. This was my mission. The point was to move all America, while busied in its various pursuits, by the power of direct and simple music. I wanted to make a music for the people, a music to be grasped at once.[1]

During the period of the Civil War, Washington was alive with military units. The young Sousa had been impressed by the bands he had heard, crude as most of them were. He was particularly awed by the march form. As he put it: "I perceived that such music was closely allied in nature and effect to folk songs and dance tunes; that the universal heart

[1] "Bandmaster Sousa Explains His Mission in Music," *Musical America*, April 16, 1910.

responded easily and always to the simple in art."[2] Sousa's future was thus influenced by his early environment. He had been in pursuit of a career in the theater until his twenty-fifth year, but once given the opportunity to express his individuality through the medium of the band, his destiny was set.

Sousa had a profound understanding of the classics. He was not a conservatory graduate in the modern sense, but his genius more than compensated for this. He vigorously studied great music all his life. He was quick to grasp a reverence for music of the masters through his teachers, and he maintained this level of interest throughout his life. Many shelves of his personal library were filled with the scores of symphonies, operas, string quartets, tone poems, and the like. Certain composers were his favorites, of course, but his tastes were extremely wide in scope. In the company of learned musicians he was eager to discuss the classics, and from memory he could cite examples, give page numbers of the various editions, and clarify minute details. It is interesting to speculate how the "March King" might have turned out had he not declined the opportunity for a subsidized formal music education in Europe.

Critics compared Sousa with the foremost conductors of his time, partly because of his perception of great music. He ridiculed those who belittled bands, proclaiming that there should be no hierarchy in art, and he probably did as much as any other person to win over those who practiced what he called "artistic snobbery."

ON COMPOSING

There were many factors influencing Sousa as a youthful composer, but these merely contributed to the development of his own unique style. He was the product of a young America, and it is safe to assume that his compositions would have taken a different turn had he been born in a different place or at a different time.

He held several composers as ideals. To him, Bach was the greatest of all composers, and he often facetiously remarked that Bach would have thought of him as a lazy apprentice. His adoration of Wagner, whom he regarded as the "Shakespeare of Music," led him to visit that dramatist's grave at Bayreuth when vacationing in Europe in the summer of 1891. Among composers of his own stature, he had a high regard for Victor Herbert, whom he credited with more operettas of high quality than any other composer.

Strangely, his greatest influence came from two men whom he seldom credited with being a controlling element in his own musical cultivation—Gilbert and Sullivan. Their influence is particularly obvious

[2] Ibid.

in his early operettas. There is also a strong similarity in style to certain works of Jacques Offenbach, in whose orchestra he played in Philadelphia.

Sousa made it perfectly clear to the world that if any traces of quality could be found in his music, he could not take credit himself. He had a genuine humility. As documented by journalists all over the world, Sousa acknowledged help from a "higher power." This "higher power," or "somebody," was God. He made few public professions of faith but was emphatic in pointing out his communion with the "higher power" when composing. He believed that atheistic composers could not be inspired to great things. In some of his writings he stated that he merely played one role in the creation and acceptance of his own music. A good example of this is a newspaper interview, which preceded his autobiography by three years:

> The music that becomes valuable in the world's repertoire is formed by the combination of a man with a power beyond himself. . . . First compositions almost invariably show the influence of tradition or environment. It is not until the composer feels that his work must be done with no thought of what others have done that he arrives at the fruition of his genius. Then it will be found that the Unseen Helper not only guides the composer's mind to a successful effort but prepares the ears of the world for its advent. . . . Somebody helps me and sends me a musical idea, and that Somebody helps the public to lay hold of my meaning.[3]

It was Sousa's firm belief that lasting music could come only from inspiration. This was true for him, at least. When uninspired, he could put something on paper, but in most cases he later destroyed it.

Contrary to the theories that composers must be hungry, desperately in love, frightened by a storm, or under the spell of nature, Sousa felt that a composer must lead a contented life. His extemporaneous remarks about his own incentives and methods were surprising and often humorous. An example:

> . . . In the comfort of a good dinner and the companionship of a good cigar, I have accomplished some of the work with which I have been most satisfied. Musical and literary lore is filled with stories of writers who toiled over masterpieces in comfortless garrets while hunger-gnawed. I like to think that their work would have been much greater could it have been performed among the ordinary comforts of life.[4]

Inspirations usually came unexpectedly. He received inspirations from glorious events, beautiful sights, poetry, dreams, while walking or marching, or even on the podium. He could actively seek an inspiration, however, by practicing a sort of self-hypnotism. He mentally projected

[3] *Boston Post*, October 15, 1922.
[4] *Sioux City* (Iowa) *Argus*, November 28, 1923.

"Kill time! That's the way I kill time—by sprinkling gold dust on paper!"

himself into an atmosphere of the particular type of composition he wished to create. When the inspiration came upon him, the melodies often flowed with such alarming speed that it was a struggle to get them on paper. As Sousa described it: "Great ideas come often as surprises, and a musician is awestruck when he gives birth to a melody that he feels is all his own. There have been such times when I have almost been overpowered by a feeling of fright."[5]

History tells us that Sousa's greatest inspirations came when he was in the process of composing a march. The following story is typical of the ones he told on many occasions: "If I want to write a march, I turn my imagination loose among scenes of barbaric splendor. I picture to myself the glitter of guns and swords, the tread of feet to the drum beat, and all that is grand and glorious in military scenes. How these compositions come I cannot tell. It is an utter mystery to me."[6]

He reasoned that marches should basically appeal to the fighting instincts in man, that they should stir his patriotic impulses and "make goose pimples chase each other up and down your spine" or, "make a man with a wooden leg want to step out and march."

As to the aesthetic qualities of a march, Sousa had explicit technical standards. Foremost was simplicity, exemplified by a steady, solid rhythm. He believed that a march should have a logical, clean-cut harmonic structure and a straightforward counterpoint which did not detract from the overall theme of the march. He further believed that a march should be a short masterpiece and that a composer should take the composition of a march as seriously as the composition of a symphony. It is a well-established fact that Sousa did just that; he wrote more marches of high caliber than any other composer.

Sousa had two notable guidelines in composing a march. The first, of course, was inspiration. He did not deny that marches of many classical composers were inspired, but he often stated that they lacked proper environment. One such statement: "Few of the great composers have written great marches because they lived in an atmosphere of peace, away from the barbaric splendor of war and the clash of swords. This exciting quality is missing in their work."[7] The second guideline was to move forward at all times. His own marches, except for some of his earlier ones, illustrate this, with no recapitulation of the earlier sections or return to the original key. He theorized that a march should have a pronounced climax and that this climax should be at the end. This theory was a departure from tradition, and it was perhaps Sousa's most significant contribution to march standardization. The traditional coda was thus eliminated. He believed that the coda was in effect an unneces-

[5] *Pittsburgh Post*, September 12, 1898.

[6] *Boston Post*, October 15, 1922.

[7] John Philip Sousa, *Through the Year with Sousa*, p. 29.

sary announcement that a piece was about to end; when Sousa's marches near the end, it is obvious. It was made even more obvious at Sousa Band concerts when the cornets, trumpets, and trombones came to the front of the stage for the finale.

Regarding the return to the original key, the following is typical of his viewpoint: "The old method ended the march in the tonality of the original key. . . . Speaking gastronomically, when they got to the ice cream, they went back to the roast beef. And the beef had no new sauce on it, no new flavor. . . .[8]

Sousa loved his own marches, of course, but some of his other compositions were actually more dear to him than many of the marches. His songs were especially close to his heart. Most of them do have a simple beauty and are perhaps more reflective of his innermost feelings than is generally known. He was never able to understand why they did not become widely popular. His associates noted that he was visibly saddened by this situation and noted that the person who approached him on the subject of his songs had made a friend for life.

Although he probably had the potential, Sousa did not compose symphonies. The form simply did not appeal to him. Shorter, more concentrated compositions were his forte; he had a robust distaste for padding and suggested that plenty was to be found in existing works. When transcribing orchestral works for his band, he was often heard to mutter such phrases as "My, how he could pad!" He observed that lovers of literature would never deny the greatness of a brief poem and saw no reason why lovers of music should discriminate against shorter works.

Sousa was generously endowed with the faculties common to nearly all great composers. Paramount was his extraordinary gift of hearing a composition upon sight of the music. At an early age his music teacher discovered that he had the rare knack of reading piano scores on sight with unusual accuracy. This eventually developed to the point where he could read and hear several clefs simultaneously on a conductor's score, regardless of whether it was for orchestra or band. Another gift was "perfect pitch." He could identify notes of the musical scale in any register, at any time. Combined with his ability to mentally re-create a score, this pitch orientation enabled him to compose and arrange with uncanny speed. After he had completed a score, it would take four or more copyists the same length of time to extract the parts. When pressed with a deadline, he would sometimes eliminate the conductor's score altogether by retaining a mental image of it and simply writing out each orchestra or band part himself.

Still another gift was his remarkably accurate memory. When constructing a full conductor's score, he would not write out the complete melody line first and then fill in the other parts, as is commonly done.

[8] *Boston Post*, March 10, 1918.

He wrote vertically, a few notes on each line of a score from top to bottom, mentally changing clefs as he went. This mastery in orchestrating astounded the few who were privileged to watch him at work and is almost inconceivable to the musical novice.

His combined talents of "perfect pitch" and being able to hear what he saw enabled him to compose without the aid of a piano or any other musical instrument. Some composers would think this impractical or even impossible, but with Sousa it was a way of life. A piano was totally unnecessary, and even as late as when he was leading the U.S. Marine Band, he did not own one.

He played the piano infrequently and did not consider himself a good player. This was actually a blessing, however, for it was a definite factor in his originality. He said of the ability to hear a piece of music on sight and its relationship to composing:

> I personally can hardly understand how a man can compose original music unless he has this ability. Unless you can imagine yourself away from the keyboard, melody and harmony, you will be in great danger of following the beaten track when you take to formulas. Your fingers will find for themselves secure and pleasant places. A man's musical thought cannot be vital, and his own, if it is bounded north, south, east and west by conventional intervals, scales, and arpeggios.[9]

Only after a composition was finished did he play it on the piano or ask someone else to play it for him. Several of his compositions went to a publisher without his ever having heard a note of them played on any instrument.

Sousa was also aided by an uncommon, but peculiar, power of concentration. He could compose in nearly any environment—on trains, in hotels, in backstage dressing rooms—but a single note of music in the background would seriously distract him. He was known to have composed in his study at the Sands Point home with many guests milling around and was undisturbed until someone drifted to the piano or hummed a melody within the range of his hearing. This broke his concentration.

When compared with the scores of most other composers, Sousa's are conspicuously neat and well organized. He wrote only on one side of a page. As evidence of his methodical and uncluttered thinking, the manuscripts were almost always written in ink. He did not erase, and seldom did he scratch out a passage. His writing was small, perhaps owing to his nearsightedness. Most of his manuscripts are difficult to read, but this may be explained by his great speed in writing them down.

One of the distinguishing features of a Sousa manuscript is his signature on the final page. At the end of a composition, or at the conclusion of one section of a long work, he turned the page sideways and added

[9] *Boston Post*, September 15, 1922.

The Library of Congress

When completing a composition, Sousa would usually autograph the last page vertically in the right-hand margin, adding the date and location. This final page of "The Belle of Chicago" march is now at The Library of Congress and reads, "John Philip Sousa, Washington, D.C., July 23rd 1892."

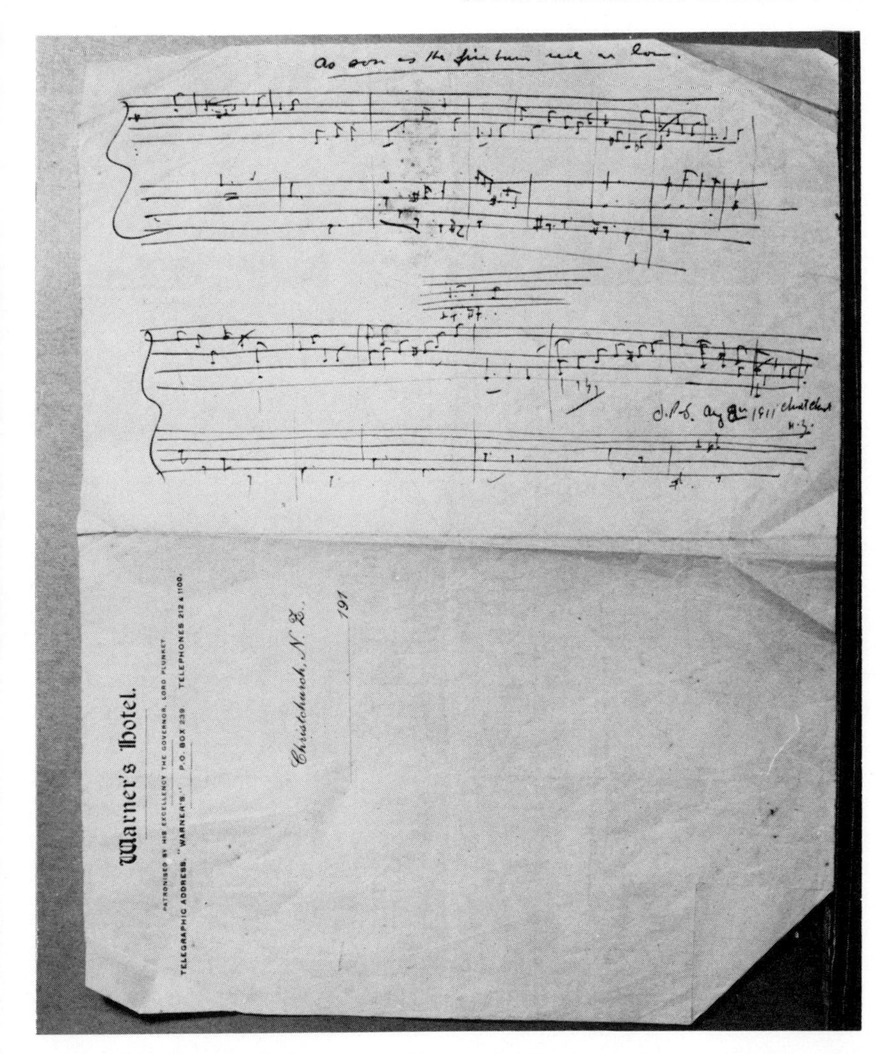

When music paper was not handy, Sousa recorded his random thoughts on any paper he could find. This rough sketch was made on the stationery of a New Zealand hotel in 1911.

to the right hand side, bottom to top, his signature, date, and the place. This was done on most of his original works but was omitted on many of his arrangements and transcriptions. On some of his early compositions, the date was also written on a title page or on the first page of music.

He was seldom without music paper to record random inspirations. In sorting his manuscripts at the Sands Point home in the fall of 1965, the author found hundreds of rough sketches mixed in with other manuscripts, unused music paper, photographs, letters, books, financial documents, and the like. His thoughts took form on individual sheets of music paper, in notebooks, or even on scraps of paper. He would jot down a musical thought and sometimes add his initials and the date after it. He would then start another line with another musical thought. The sketches were sometimes accompanied by a key signature, but other musical notation was seldom given. These sketches were then developed into compositions, often months later. Some were never used. They should prove to be of vital interest to scholars because they represent the formulative history and development of Sousa's music. The analysis of these is beyond the scope of this book.

There has been much speculation about the order in which Sousa made his manuscripts on any given one of his works, particularly the marches. Some say he made a piano part first and developed a band score from that; others say it was the other way around. Actually he did it both ways. Almost always a rough sketch came first. Sometimes he would then write out a piano part to lay out the overall concept and would then build the band score. At other times he would go directly to a band score from a rough sketch or memory and later extract a piano part to be published as such. But because so many of his scores are missing, it will probably never be determined which of the two practices was more prevalent. The extractions were often done by a copyist. Sousa made a few such extractions himself to give out as souvenirs to important people and close personal friends.

Of all the known Sousa scores bearing dates, less than a dozen were dated on Sundays. This bears out his oft-heard story that he did not compose on the Sabbath. Perhaps those few were incorrectly dated, as a few others were, or perhaps he merely checked them over and added his signature on Sunday. According to his autobiography and other writings, the only exception he made was when he arranged Patrick S. Gilmore's "The Voice of a Departing Soul" when Gilmore died in 1892.

Sousa hated to see his music go to waste; when it failed to satisfy the public, he would often revise it and use it again with a new title. Proof of this is in his operettas. Of those which had limited success, fragments turned up in later works. The reverse of this is also true; he used some of his early songs in later operettas. There are also a few examples of his use of the same song in two different operettas. This may have been done more widely than is known, because manuscripts of substantial sections of his early operettas have never been found. He would not let a good march tune go unused, to be certain; probably the only exception to this is the march from the unsuccessful operetta *Desiree*, which was not extracted and used elsewhere.

There are several explanations for the fact that roughly 40 percent of the total estimated number of Sousa's manuscripts cannot be accounted for. Some may not have been returned by the publishers, although those

Sousa kept music paper close by to register themes as they came to him. The author was privileged to search for and catalog the Sousa manuscripts at his Sands Point home in 1965, and the sketches were discovered in unlikely places. These rough sketches, found both on loose paper and in notebooks, stood nearly eight inches tall. From these, many of Sousa's compositions were developed.

of his publishers who are still in business claim not to have them in their possession. Others may have been misplaced by his family, managers, attorneys, or other persons who handled them after they were returned from the publishers. Still others may have been stolen. It is unlikely that Sousa destroyed any of them himself, although it was his practice to destroy rejected manuscripts when he was revising a score.

As previously mentioned, the speed with which Sousa composed was remarkable. He could make a simple woodwind arrangement as an accompaniment for one of his sopranos in two or three hours, and an entire band score for a march could be completed in two days if there were no interruptions. He was proud of having reorchestrated the entire score of Goodwin and Stahl's *The Lion Tamer* (1891) in twenty-two days, but perhaps his greatest achievement in this vein was the complete orchestration of Gilbert and Sullivan's *H.M.S. Pinafore* (1879) in the amazingly short time of forty-two hours.[10] These herculean feats were not the normal procedure, of course. He could develop a band score

[10] *New York Advertiser*, August 27, 1893 (?). (Date faded; clipping in the 1893 Sousa Band press book.)

for a march in three or four days under normal conditions, but most of his operettas were several months in preparation.

In spite of his great speed, the output was not equal to the demand. At the time of his death, he had amassed approximately 500 unfilled requests for marches and was under constant pressure from civic, military, and private organizations. He had a high sense of honor, however, and wrote only as inspirations came to him.

ON CONDUCTING

> Why was Sousa's Band the greatest? Because of its conductor. The band was composed of the finest musicians to be found anywhere. Any conductor could have done well with it, yes, but there was only one Sousa. Mr. Sousa may not have been the best conductor in the world, but he was certainly one of them. He was a small man, not a dashing-dapper-dan who could tower over us. And he had a kind, little old pipsqueeky voice, not a big boomy voice to shout out commands. But when he stepped up on that podium, something happened. I can't explain it; it just happened. We knew we were playing with the immortals, and no one could touch us.[11]

Sousa's brilliance as a conductor can be attributed to his profound grasp of all types of music and to his success in expressing the heart and soul of the music he was conducting. If one adds to this fact that he paid salaries high enough to attract the finest musicians available, it is understandable why his musicians were inclined to make such statements as the one above.

A study of music journals of the late 1890s and early 1900s reveals that Sousa was regarded as one of the greatest conductors of his day, in spite of his being the conductor of a concert band instead of a leading symphony or opera orchestra. His unusual control of his musicians and the complete unity of the band caught the attention of all, but it was his emotional involvement in the music and his individuality of style that put him in the class of the greats. The manner in which he imparted his own inspirations to the music gave audiences the impression that he himself was the very idea he was interpreting and that he was linked to his musicians by some invisible power.

Conductors who communicate their emotions to others in such a spectacular manner are indeed few, but Sousa believed this should be the goal of every serious conductor. As he once told a reporter:

> Is it not the business of a conductor to convey to the public in its most dramatic form the central idea of a composition? And how can he convey that idea successfully if he does not enter heart and soul into the life and

[11] Testimony given by Mr. Edmund A. Wall, early clarinetist with the Sousa Band, to Mr. Vane Kensinger, a clarinetist with the Sousa Band in the 1920s, and related to the author in an interview in June, 1961.

story of the music? How, otherwise, can he give the performers . . . the spirit they require?

When I am directing the alluring, passionate music of Spain and Hungary I feel the warm Southern blood tingling in my veins, and it is my aim to give that life blood to my musicians and my listeners. . . . The movements I make I cannot possibly repress, because at the time I am actually the thing that I am conducting and naturally imagine my players and auditors are the same.

I have it said to me, "When you are conducting, Sousa, it seems natural; in another it would appear incongruous."

One of the most laughable, yet perhaps one of the truest things that has been said of me is that I resemble one of those strolling players who carry a drum on their backs, cymbals on their heads, a cornet in one hand and the concertina in the other—who is, in fact, a little band all in himself. However, that is what I am endeavoring to do all the time—to make my musicians and myself a one-man band. Only, instead of having actual metallic wires to work the instruments, I strike the magnetic ones.

I have to work so that I feel every one of my . . . musicians is linked up with me by a cable of magnetism. Every man must be as intent upon me and as sensitive to every movement of my baton, or my fingers, as I am myself. For my part—though I do not claim to be possessed of supernatural powers—I know precisely what every one of my musicians is doing every second or fraction of a second that I am conducting. I know this because every single member of my band is doing exactly what I make him do.

When I stretch out my hand in the direction of some player I give him the music I feel, and as I beckon to him the music leaps back at me. Again, if I hold up my baton to still the brasses, they are stilled as instantaneously and effectively as though they were mechanical instruments from which, by . . . an electric button, I had cut off the current.[12]

In his early years Sousa was known as a strict disciplinarian. The Sousa Band's accomplishments were testimony to his determination to make his band the equal of symphony orchestras and of any other band in existence. Discipline eventually became almost totally unnecessary because his reputation had spread among professional musicians and they knew what he expected. The amount of rehearsal time before a tour became shorter and shorter as the years rolled by.

Being accepted for membership in the Sousa Band was an honor held by relatively few musicians, particularly during the first fifteen years of the band's existence, and Sousa showed the men his respect in many ways. He had unspoken ways of communicating dissatisfaction. By the same token, his musicians knew when they were pleasing him. He was not overbearing in his own interpretations; if one of his musicians took the liberty of expressing a solo passage in an artistic manner, Sousa

[12] *Hartford* (Connecticut) *Daily Times*, February 7, 1905.

would adopt it. He encouraged this because he thought it good for the morale of both the individual musician and the band and because it was good showmanship.

The subtle ways in which he let performers know that he had heard their mistakes became legendary with the Sousa Band, and those remaining bandsmen greatly enjoy recalling these incidents. Sousa seldom gave the appearance of noticing when a mistake had been made, for it was his

Poetry in motion. "Sousa is the best actor America has ever produced" (Otis Skinner).

theory that the mistake would thus usually go undetected. His usual method of pointing out an error was to wait until the piece was programmed at a later date. At the precise spot where the mistake had been made previously, he would glance at the offending musician, place his hand over his heart, look heavenward, give an understanding smile, and nod his head in the affirmative or flick his ear lightly with his baton. The bandsmen marveled at his ability to single out an errant musician in an entire section, and seldom was the same mistake made twice.

Sousa compared the role of a conductor with the role of an orator. Whereas good orators capture audiences by believing in the parts they are acting, Sousa reasoned that conductors must reinforce their own feelings in order to keep the interest of their audiences. He was more often compared to a good actor than a good orator, however. The great actor Otis Skinner went so far as to refer to Sousa as America's finest actor:

> Talk about Goodwin, Mansfield and the rest of us; why, Sousa is away ahead of all of us. Watch him in his exquisite art of dress, his make-up, his fascinating stage manner, his abandon to the character of the music his band plays and his magnetic capture of his audience. Of course, his band is the greatest on earth and that has something to do with it, but Sousa is the best actor America has ever produced.[13]

Skinner's remark about Sousa's art of dress was a clue to his stage presence. Sousa was insistent upon making the best possible public showing, and he was often accompanied by a valet when on tour. He spent a considerable amount of time in his dressing room preparing for an appearance. His uniforms were neatly tailored, formfitting, and had no pockets to provide bulges. Likewise, his bandsmen were expected to be neat and clean. Prior to about 1910, he was said to have provided shoe shine carts backstage for the benefit of the bandsmen.

The cost of Sousa's white kid gloves was approximately five dollars per pair. He wore them only as long as they were spotlessly clean, and quite often they were discarded after only one concert. This gave rise to the story, which persists even today, that he was superstitious and would wear a pair of gloves but once. At the other extreme, he was reluctant to use anything but an inexpensive baton. In his shipping trunks one could always find a generous supply of plain wooden batons, which he referred to as his "twenty-five cent specials."

Sousa's conducting was characterized by very real toil, and he usually left the stage perspiring. He was forceful yet calm and in complete sympathy with the music at hand. Because he was intensely engrossed in the music, he claimed not to be conscious of his expenditure of energy

[13] Amy Leslie, the *Chicago News*. Undated clipping in the 1895-1896 Sousa Band pess book. Also quoted in a book of testimonials distributed for promotional purposes by David Blakely, Sousa Band manager, 1892-1896.

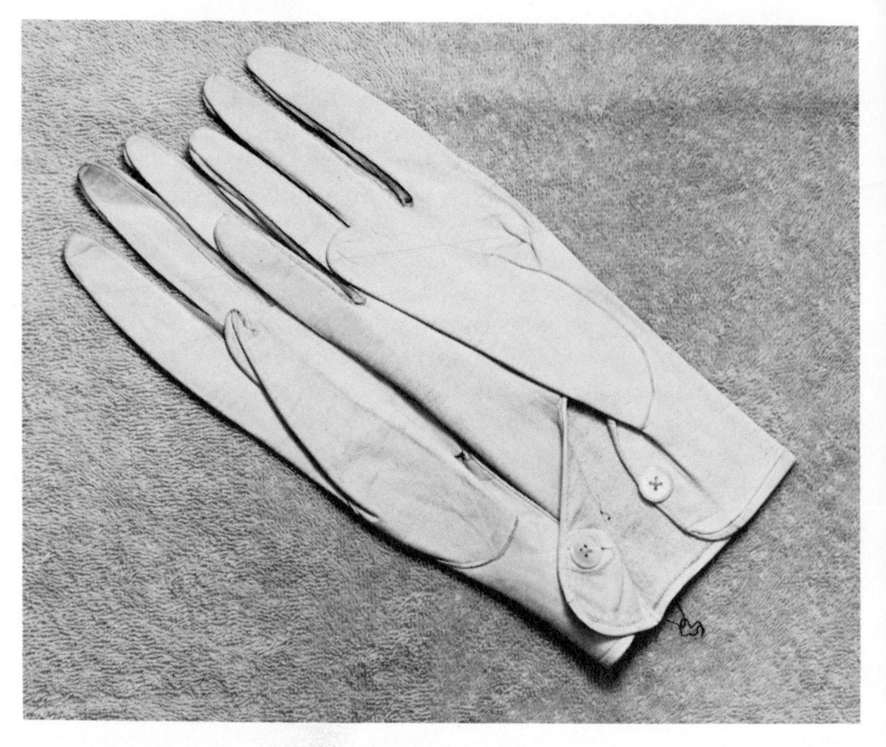

The "March King" was extravagant in his use of white kid gloves for conducting. He wore them only until they showed the slightest sign of soil, and this often occurred by the end of only one concert.

while on the podium. As a composer himself he had an insight into the creative processes of the composers whose music he was re-creating. His personal involvement was an unforgettable experience to his musicians. Only rarely did he speak of this, but he did make a statement in an 1899 interview which revealed his intimacy with music:

> Do you know, I was limp as a rag after "Siegfried" and fairly staggered on my way to my dressing room. People imagine that it is merely a matter of getting up there and beating the time and letting the band do the rest, but to bring out the best work you have to fairly hypnotize the men. In seeking after volume of music in a musical performance you can get a performer up to a certain point all right, but when you go beyond that, if it is a singer, she screeches; if it is a violinist, he scratches, and if it is a brass player he blares. In "Siegfried," where you are seeking after magnificent climaxes with the volume increasing all along, it is a big task to keep all your men at just the right point and not let them step over. Why, when I got through that number I felt as if every bit of that wind had been blown right through me, and I could hardly find my way through the stands to the wings.[14]

[14] "Sousa As He Is," *Music*, May, 1899.

It was his theory that dull performances were accounted for by the lack of inspiration of the conductor. There was seldom a dull performance with Sousa on the podium.

As a young man, Sousa had been active in several sports, and his dignified and eloquent motions on the podium were the result of this background. His mannerisms were not stilted. Rather, his gestures displayed his own sincere expressions of temperament and were in accord with the character of the music. He was a proponent of conducting in circular motions and within a small circle. He believed that angular movements of the baton hand were ineffective, especially in music of a sensuous nature. His style became more reserved with advancing age, but a turning point in his conducting career came in the summer of 1921 when he was injured in a fall from a horse, as described earlier. Even after this he still displayed his splendid physical coordination.

He wasted no motion on the podium. Each of his gestures, which were sometimes almost imperceptible, meant something—the dancing fingers, the delicate hand expressions, the undulations of the wrists, the quick head movements. He swayed gracefully from side to side, leaned forward gently with the tender passages and backward with the strong ones, while his legs remained motionless. When taking a bow, he bent slightly sideways and to the left. His back was firm and straight, and he proudly referred to it as his "military back." He was even accused of wearing a corset, and several times he was called upon to deny this publicly.

Two of his gestures were imitated by several other band conductors. One was the way he held his arms motionless by his sides for several seconds and conducted only by slight movements of his hands. The other was one he used mostly on marches: he would occasionally swing both of his arms down along his body and behind him in a straight motion and then return them to the normal conducting position, all in time with the music.

He was a picturesque conductor in many respects, and most critics thought him dramatic and imaginative. A very small percentage thought him overdramatic, but even these acknowledged his effectiveness. One fine description of the impression he gave an audience was reported in an 1896 Chicago newspaper:

> It is not the usual monotonous devotion of a conductor to the performance of his band, but the charm entering into the spirit, the intricacies, the elucidation of the music played. When Sousa plays a march his arms swing in direct, soldierly, undeviating lines back and forth like military pendulums; when he has a circus galop on hand he throws back his head, snaps his baton and in every move indicates the whip, the spur, the dainty balance of a rider or the pompous entrance of a hippodrome. He throws himself into a soulful quietness for a nocturne and rises in a smiling suggestion of evolutions in the rendition of a dance or rondo caprice, and the beauty of

> it all is that nobody listening is aware that Sousa does anything more than the ordinary plug brass band leader.
>
> His methods are artistic and too delicately adroit and skillful to carry any sort of a notion of posing, and his simplicity in responding to applause is perfectly beautiful. If the average actor could achieve a Sousa pretense of extreme modesty, not to say bashfulness, at honors thrust upon genius, his fortune would lie in responding to curtain calls.[15]

It was Sousa who brought ragtime to Europe, and this caused no small stir in music circles. The French composer Claude Debussy caustically acknowledged this and then offered some choice words on Sousa's conducting: "At last! The King of American music is here. Monsieur Sousa will reveal to us its beauties and how it is to be used in the best society. One must have a special gift to conduct this music [ragtime]. Thus M. Sousa beats time in circular motions, mixes an imaginary salad, sweeps away invisible dust, and snatches a butterfly from the bell of a contrabass tuba."[16] Sousa had the last laugh, however, for his influence was soon to be seen in Debussy's "Golliwog's Cake Walk."

What endeared Sousa most to the world was his obsession with pleasing the public. His sense of duty to an audience bordered on the fanatical. Many times he appeared when his physical condition made conducting burdensome, but he would have had it no other way. He was as reliable and faithful a performer as any audience could ever hope for. Nothing associated with his entire organization was misrepresented, including everything from the advertised selections to the actual starting time. And since he appeared backstage long before concert time, the same was expected of every musician. If, by some incredible happenstance, the auditorium was not filled to capacity, Sousa would insist that his musicians still give their very best efforts. He believed that the faithful should be rewarded, not punished.

A Sousa Band program was literally all music, as will be discussed in the next section. It was a rare occasion when Sousa permitted a pause or took the time to address the audience, and his unique style of compact programming has seldom been duplicated. As Sousa himself said: "I take it that people come to a concert for music and not to watch a conductor's face or back or gloves. It seems to me they're entitled to their money's worth!"[17]

ON PROGRAMMING

If Sousa's philosophy of programming could be summarized briefly, it would be: "What do you like? I'll play it if it kills me!" The Sousa

[15] Amy Leslie, *Chicago News*, February 3, 1896.
[16] Unidentified clipping from Paris newspaper in the 1903 Sousa Band press book. Probably April or May, 1903.
[17] *Boston Post*, October 1, 1922.

Cover of *Ally Sloper's Half Holiday*, March 4, 1905. As a conductor, Sousa was not without his critics, but they were a very small minority. Even those who disliked his style acknowledged his individuality and effectiveness.

concept of programming combined skill, variety, and showmanship. His unprecedented success as a bandmaster is testimony to the wisdom of this simple but effective philosophy. After most other touring bands were forced out of business by movies, radio, and the general mobility of the people of the 1920s, Sousa's Band was still playing to "standing room only" crowds.

To say that Sousa was a master showman would be an understatement. He learned the value of showmanship to stage performers as a youth while playing violin in Washington and Philadelphia theater orchestras. There he made keen observations about the music which the general public enjoyed. From that time on, he made it his business to play music to which the masses would respond, and he was eminently successful. He discovered that bands, which were relatively unhampered by tradition, had the potential for reaching more people than orchestras.

Showmanship was essential to every Sousa program, and the Sousa Band was an aggregation of showmen. "The man who does not exercise showmanship is dead," he said many times.[18] Many excellent musicians were never accepted by the Sousa Band because they did not fit into this mold. This talent was necessary not only for solo work but also for the presentation of Sousa's unique humoresques.

It was Sousa's observation that life was more hurried in the United States than in most other countries. Being restless, audiences expected more in the way of showmanship. He often changed a program at the last minute by playing an appropriately titled song, to capitalize on something of current interest, and he kept up to date by scanning several newspapers every day. His awareness was vividly illustrated at a concert in Columbus, Ohio, shortly after the death of President William McKinley.

> One of the most graceful and beautiful acts John Philip Sousa has ever performed in Columbus was done Friday night at the concert at the Great Southern. The last number before the intermission had just been played and the magnificent finale of Giordano's grand scene and ensemble, "Andrea Chenier," had barely died away when the world's greatest bandmaster again raised his baton. Instantly a profound hush fell upon the audience, for something not on the program was coming. No one knew what. Then softly in strains sweeter than Apollo's lute, in harmony that seemed to have its source in realms celestial, there stole upon the ear that wondrous creation of the Christian hymnology, "Nearer My God to Thee." The audience hardly breathed for with one wave of the master-hand they were suddenly lifted from the midst of the grandest band concert ever given in the Ohio capital and set down beside the catafalque of the dead president. Tears welled in nearly every eye as that divine hymn was played. It seemed as if its matchless beauty had never been realized before. And midst the solemn, breathing sound, faint as the distant echo from some sacred shrine, there came the

[18] "Keeping Time" (part 5). *Saturday Evening Post*, December 5, 1925.

tolling of the funeral bell. No words can picture the effect. The eyes of strong men blurred as the tide of an irrepressible emotion welled within, and heads were bowed in grief. If Sousa had never done anything else to make him the idol of the public, that simple, soulful, unheralded tribute to the fallen chieftain should lift him to the pinnacle. It was a song without words, but words were never so eloquent as the heavenly music of that incomparable band.[19]

Capturing the spirit of the American audience, a Sousa Band concert was an ideal of variety. Sousa felt that variety was typically American, contrasting with practices in Europe, where it was his observation that music was often prescribed by national barriers. People who attended Sousa Band concerts left the hall knowing that they had been entertained, intellectually stimulated, and thrilled by the sight of an internationally famous composer leading one of the world's finest musical organizations in the performance of his own music. As a Seattle reviewer aptly put it: "A concert by Sousa's Band is more than a mere concert—it is a dramatic performance, a stirring lesson in patriotism, and a popular musical event, all on the same program."[20]

Those attending a fast-moving Sousa Band performance would most likely never forget it. Each program was originally conceived, with something of interest to everyone. The curtain went up; out came Sousa, who took one short bow, and quickly stepped up on to the podium; and immediately the band began. Sousa would permit no pauses of over twenty or thirty seconds, and he never left the conductor's stand except for intermissions. This was the supreme test of the musicians' endurance, but they gave "the Governor" all they had without complaint. The practice of omitting long pauses was almost universally praised, most notably in Europe. One common comment, which pleased Sousa, was that this was characteristically American, showing vitality and enthusiasm.

Sousa's most radical departure from traditional programming was his distinctive use of encores. He did not believe in milking applause from an audience. Instead of taking repeated bows, he would commence an encore within five to ten seconds after the completion of a number, before the applause had stopped. He alleged that he could gauge the appreciation of an audience instantly and felt obliged not to keep them waiting.

It was a tradition with the Sousa Band to play two or more encores after each programmed selection except for the one just before intermission. Thus a concert with nine pieces listed on the printed program actually ended up with twenty-five to thirty-five numbers. Encores contrasted with the preceding number and could be anything from currently popular

[19] "Our Observation Car," *Columbus* (Ohio) *Dispatch*, September 21, 1901.
[20] *Seattle* (Washington) *Post-Intelligencer*, October 1, 1927.

songs to short classics. Quite often, however, they were Sousa marches. This was another tradition with the Sousa Band and was expected. Upon sensing the need of an encore, Sousa would indicate his choice to the bandsmen closest to him. The word was rapidly passed through the band, because he was quickly upon the podium again and ready to begin. There was insufficient time to locate the selection in the "encore books" in such a short time, so the bandsmen had to memorize what they could. This wasn't always possible, but there were enough musicians who knew the introductory measures to get the piece started while their side partners found it in the books. They developed a sort of verbal shorthand in order to carry out this procedure. "Cap" meant the Sousa march "El Capitan," "Post" meant "The Washington Post," "Stars" meant "The Stars and Stripes Forever," and so forth. Sousa deliberately mixed up the encores to keep the musicians alert.

The encores were an outgrowth of Sousa's preoccupation with the notion that he should do everything in his power to please an audience. "The inspiration that comes from the . . . audience is the greatest compliment that a musician can have. It is his reward and deserves a turn. . . . If I can please my audiences with more, I am willing to please them. It is the work that I was put in the world to do."[21] As the encore was being played, it was announced to the audience by means of a large show card at stage right which was held aloft or placed on an easel by the librarian, a percussionist, or Sousa's valet.

Sousa's disregard for tradition and precedent was well founded. When objections came from a very small minority of musicians or critics, he countered with the very valid argument that his public did not mind at all. Rather, they loved it. His programming was unorthodox in that he sometimes chose to follow a serious selection with a light or humorous one. This brought an occasional ripple of censure, and he usually cited a parallel in the theatre:

> I learned very early in life that if musicians depended upon musicians for their support there would be no musicians. The support of all art depends entirely upon those who love art for art's sake, and as music is universal, it becomes necessary to heed the wishes of the masses if one hopes to succeed. It is not incongruous to me to see a comedy scene immediately following a tragic scene in Shakespeare or any other of the master dramatists, or laughter following tears in the romantic drama. Therefore, as I have nature and the best examples of men as my champions, I have no hesitation in combining in my program clever comedy with symphonic tragedy, rhythmic march or waltz with sentimental tone pictures.[22]

[21] *Washington* (D.C.) *Star*, January 20, 1900.
[22] "Why Is Sousa?" *Adelaide* (Australia) *Advertiser* (n.d., but probably July, 1911), quoted in *Musical Courier*, August 10, 1911.

To support his theory that by nature people prefer entertainment to education, he noted that fifty comedy companies would prosper while one troupe presenting tragedy would earn a precarious livelihood. He entertained, but he educated his audiences in such a pleasant way that few could find fault. In doing so he brought great music to many who had a limited musical background. He not only played the standard clas-

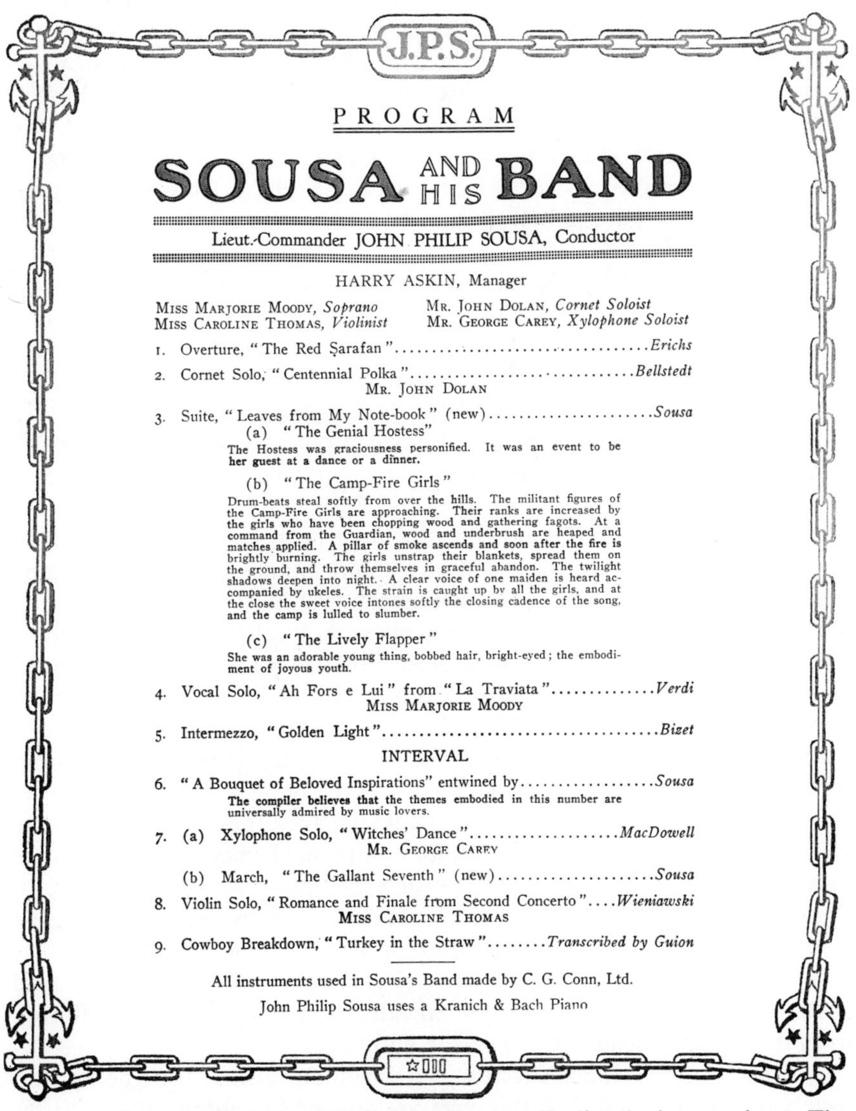
J.P.S.

PROGRAM

SOUSA AND HIS BAND

Lieut.-Commander JOHN PHILIP SOUSA, Conductor

HARRY ASKIN, Manager

MISS MARJORIE MOODY, *Soprano* — MR. JOHN DOLAN, *Cornet Soloist*
MISS CAROLINE THOMAS, *Violinist* — MR. GEORGE CAREY, *Xylophone Soloist*

1. Overture, "The Red Şarafan" .... *Erichs*
2. Cornet Solo, "Centennial Polka" .... *Bellstedt*
   MR. JOHN DOLAN
3. Suite, "Leaves from My Note-book" (new) .... *Sousa*
   (a) "The Genial Hostess"
   The Hostess was graciousness personified. It was an event to be her guest at a dance or a dinner.
   (b) "The Camp-Fire Girls"
   Drum-beats steal softly from over the hills. The militant figures of the Camp-Fire Girls are approaching. Their ranks are increased by the girls who have been chopping wood and gathering fagots. At a command from the Guardian, wood and underbrush are heaped and matches applied. A pillar of smoke ascends and soon after the fire is brightly burning. The girls unstrap their blankets, spread them on the ground, and throw themselves in graceful abandon. The twilight shadows deepen into night. A clear voice of one maiden is heard accompanied by ukeles. The strain is caught up by all the girls, and at the close the sweet voice intones softly the closing cadence of the song, and the camp is lulled to slumber.
   (c) "The Lively Flapper"
   She was an adorable young thing, bobbed hair, bright-eyed; the embodiment of joyous youth.
4. Vocal Solo, "Ah Fors e Lui" from "La Traviata" .... *Verdi*
   MISS MARJORIE MOODY
5. Intermezzo, "Golden Light" .... *Bizet*

INTERVAL

6. "A Bouquet of Beloved Inspirations" entwined by .... *Sousa*
   The compiler believes that the themes embodied in this number are universally admired by music lovers.
7. (a) Xylophone Solo, "Witches' Dance" .... *MacDowell*
   MR. GEORGE CAREY
   (b) March, "The Gallant Seventh" (new) .... *Sousa*
8. Violin Solo, "Romance and Finale from Second Concerto" .... *Wieniawski*
   MISS CAROLINE THOMAS
9. Cowboy Breakdown, "Turkey in the Straw" .... *Transcribed by Guion*

All instruments used in Sousa's Band made by C. G. Conn, Ltd.

John Philip Sousa uses a Kranich & Bach Piano

On tour, the printed Sousa Band programs usually listed nine numbers. The band consistently played from twenty-five to thirty-five numbers, however, because of Sousa's generous and unique presentation of encores.

sics, but he pioneered new works. For example, he was playing music from Wagner's *Parsifal* ten years before that opera was performed at the Metropolitan Opera House. An examination of his programs shows that he played a considerable amount of contemporary music. He was perhaps more progressive in his programming than any other bandmaster of his day.

An indispensable service was rendered by the Sousa Band in its performance of classics in remote areas. On the extensive tours, the band played in many cities in which a symphony orchestra had never been seen. Sousa recognized the embryonic state of art in the United States and accepted the responsibility of doing something about it. He once stated bluntly, in comparing his accomplishments with those of American symphony orchestra conductors: "I think I have done more missionary work for the better class of music than all the rest of them put together."[23]

The Sousa Band programs were eclectic in nature, and Sousa was a shrewd programmer. The tour programs usually consisted of nine selections, not counting encores, and were continually updated with new trends in music. He was quick to program ragtime, and although he was not fond of it, he acknowledged the appeal of strongly rhythmic music. He noted that ragtime was distinctly American but that it had counterparts in many other countries which had music with marked rhythms, some of it syncopated.

He capitalized on the increased popularity of jazz. His public liked it, so he played it. He was cautious about endorsing it, however; he said that what was good was good, what was bad was very bad, and most of it "made you want to bite your grandmother."[24] He perceived a public preference for lively music after World War I, so the programming of a small amount of jazz was in order. Usually jazz was dealt with in his humoresques, in which small ensembles featured those bandsmen who had experience in this type of music. But very little of any program was allotted to music which he considered to be of a transitory nature.

He slighted no musical form, believing that the secret of success of nearly any type of music lay in its treatment. Everything was played to perfection without regard to its musical importance. According to Sousa: "We play a common street melody with just as much care as if it were the best thing ever put on a program. It becomes respectable. I have washed its face, put a clean dress on it, put a frill around its neck, pretty stockings. It is now an attractive thing, entirely different from the frowzly-headed thing of the gutter."[25]

He was often criticized for playing too much music of local composers wherever he traveled, but this was another of his contributions to the

[23] "Sousa and His Mission," *Music*, July, 1899.

[24] *New York Hearld Tribune*, December 20, 1926.

[25] "Sousa and His Mission," *Music*, July, 1899.

art. It is probable that the Sousa Band played more unpublished music than any other American musical organization of the time. Sousa was always eager to help a struggling young composer—unless the new composition was uninspired. He asked composers, "How did you happen to write this?" If he ascertained that the work was not the product of inspiration, he would refuse to play it.

One composition which was on every Sousa Band concert after 1897, whether on the printed program or not, was "The Stars and Stripes Forever." It was expected, and if Sousa ever entertained any thoughts of not including it, his public demanded it. As the number was begun, audiences would rise to their feet as if it were the national anthem. Many of his bandsmen stated that they could not remember ever playing a concert under Sousa in which that march was not played. On many occasions they were obliged to repeat it several times.

Because so many of the encores were marches of Sousa's, his compositions were scarce on the printed programs. There was either a Sousa suite, humoresque, or fantasy, plus his latest march. The new march was a regular feature each season after 1893, when "The Liberty Bell" was introduced. For the new presentation, as for "The Stars and Stripes Forever," the cornets, trumpets, and trombones would come to the front of the stage and face the audience for a striking finale.

Of the utmost importance to any concert were the soloists, who gave Sousa the opportunity to show off the depth of talent in the band. The featured instrumental solo was usually the second programmed number—after the encores of the first number, of course. Additional solos, duets, trios, or ensembles were played after intermission. This format became a tradition not only with the Sousa Band but with other bands as well. If Sousa did not originate it, at least he standardized the practice.

Glamour was also a part of every Sousa presentation, for he had a succession of lovely sopranos and violinists. One of the prerequisites was indisputable artistry, as evidenced by the number of famous sopranos who furthered their careers with Sousa. A second prerequisite was beauty and grace. These qualities were never lacking, and Sousa insisted upon tasteful costuming which contrasted with the dark uniforms of the men. A third prerequisite, which was equal in importance to the other two, was personality. Sousa has been quoted as saying: "When personality is missing, the ear is bound to tire."[26]

ON INSTRUMENTATION

The title "father of the concert band in the United States" rightly belongs to Patrick S. Gilmore, but it has sometimes been applied to Sousa. Gilmore, whose band represented the better class of bands in America, made a lasting impression on Sousa. Sousa crossed the path of Gilmore

[26] From an unidentified clipping in the 1925 Sousa Band press book.

many times and came to appreciate the seemingly limitless potential in tonal production made possible by a wide variety of band instruments. The Sousa Band was formed at the time of Gilmore's death, and it can be said that Sousa began where Gilmore left off. After a period of experimentation with several instruments used in Gilmore's band and others, Sousa stabilized the instrumentation of his own band around 1898. Few changes were made after that time except for increases in the sizes of individual sections.

He longed for the standardization of band instrumentation in general, not just in the United States. Each country had its own preferences in the use of instruments, as reflected by wide differences in printed music. Inasmuch as Sousa's tastes were cosmopolitan, the use of music printed abroad was an impediment to him. In developing his own concept of band tone, he was obliged to study the instrumentation of overseas bands in order to utilize foreign editions. He was unhappy with most of it, especially the German variety, which he considered too brassy. This forced him to make his own arrangements and transcriptions. Many foreign scores are found among his arrangements and transcriptions of the 1890s, giving evidence of the struggle to cultivate an original concept of band tonal quality. Once this concept was established, it was adopted by others. It is interesting to note that the instrumental makeup of present-day American concert bands, most notably university organizations, varies little from that of the Sousa Band of the late 1890s except in the numbers of instruments used.

What Sousa called "oneness of tone" meant, for the most part, a pleasing balance between woodwinds and brass. To achieve this balance he was eventually using a woodwind-to-brass ratio of nearly two to one. He enlarged the clarinet section, included alto and bass clarinets, revised the saxophone complement, and added a contrabassoon and all the woodwind instruments used in orchestras.

Although the use of the string bass in concert bands came about in Sousa's time, he did not favor it. He believed that the string bass was basically not a marching instrument and that it should therefore not be used in bands. Scholars pointed to his use of the harp, however, which is anything but a marching instrument. His answer to that was that there was not, by any stretch of the imagination, a suitable replacement for the harp among band instruments and that it was also needed for delicate accompaniments of many of the vocal or violin solos he programmed.

When Sousa was converted from an orchestral conductor to a band conductor, he made the conversion wholeheartedly. Although he had harbored a love for bands all his life, it is difficult to understand how a competent violinist could have changed his outlook so radically. But perhaps, as an orchestral musician, he had not fully understood the potential of the wind band until he found himself fully involved in his work as leader of the U.S. Marine Band. He never completely abandoned orchestral writing, however, and the skillful scores of his operettas are evidence of a thorough knowledge of orchestration.

Up until the end of his career, he was making statements to the effect that the violin was the queen of instruments and that nothing was so beautiful, for a limited time, as a large body of strings. But there his fascination with the orchestra ended. He believed that the band was more versatile than the orchestra and that it permitted the playing of a wider variety of music. He also pointed out that bands had a greater influence on the development of music as an art form for the simple reason that they were more available.

He was of the opinion that the rich complexities of sound inherent in the band's instrumentation permitted a wider diversity of effects, making the band superior to the orchestra. He often referred to a band's "multiplicity of quartets." He was critical of the orchestra's imbalance of brass, making the comparison that the brass of the well-balanced band could not overpower the woodwinds as easily as the brass tended to overpower the strings in the orchestra. It was his belief that the band was better equipped to deliver dramatic effects and could be described as masculine, whereas the orchestra was feminine. He was also critical of the orchestra (in contrast to the band) for its reluctance to accept new instruments. Specifically, he did not believe that the orchestra had yet explored all the possibilities of stringed instruments.

Although he scored for a rich reed sound in his band, he clearly had no preference for any given instrument and spoke out strongly against favoring certain instruments: "Some jack-assical conductors claim a preference for some musical instruments, but a real conductor has no preference."[27]

In general he was not outspoken about the tonal production of individual instruments, but he did make subtle changes in his band to obtain the desired blend. He was insistent on a soft, mellow clarinet sound and went to great lengths to prevent an individual clarinetist from producing a sound which did not contribute to the homogeneity of the section. He eventually replaced the E-flat clarinet, which is known for its slightly shrill quality, with additional flutes.

If an individual stood out in the Sousa Band he was quickly corrected. This was a problem each year at the first rehearsal, when new players were admitted, but they soon learned from the example of others that Sousa demanded a "smooth" sound. This was carried to entire sections of the band as well. The tuba, for instance, produces a somewhat directional sound, and he felt this undesirable for nonmelody instruments. For this reason he replaced the tuba with an instrument built to his own

[27] *Sioux City* (Iowa) *Tribune*, November 9, 1920.

specifications—the sousaphone. The sousaphone "projected the sound upward and mushroomed it over the entire band and audience."

It was of the utmost importance to Sousa not to have a dominating bass drum. He insisted that the bass drum must be felt rather than heard. On this subject he repeatedly declared that the layman had no idea whatever of the importance of the bass drum in a band but that no band could possibly be greater than its bass drummer. He considered his bass drummers artists in their own right. They were greatly responsible for the distinct "lift" evident in the Sousa Band's performance of marches, and Sousa made as great an effort to recruit outstanding bass drummers as he did soloists.

There were few outstanding original works for band in Sousa's time, and he borrowed heavily from orchestral literature. He used extreme caution in his choice, selecting compositions which made the transition gracefully. He was careful not to use many works of Bach, Mozart, Haydn, and other composers of the baroque and classical eras, feeling that most of their works did not lend themselves to his scheme of instrumentation and that this would have been too great a departure from the composer's intentions. Instead, he relied on transcriptions of works by such composers as Wagner, Tchaikovsky, Richard Strauss, Dvořák, and others whose dynamic contrasts and tone coloring were consistent with the character of his band. On several occasions he hinted that certain masterpieces were better suited to band than to orchestra.

Sousa was among the most imaginative and artistic of all arrangers for band. He knew the band's resources, and his effective use of contrast and climax was readily seen in his arrangements and transcriptions. His concepts of scoring were advanced beyond those in general use in his early career, so he stood alone in this field for many years. He built upon the practices of his predecessors, particularly Gilmore, whose pioneering efforts he graciously acknowledged on many occasions; in turn, his varieties in tone coloring set examples which were to be followed by others. It has been said that Richard Strauss was deeply impressed by Sousa's instrumentation, most notably his muted brass effects, and that he used them in certain of his later works. Sousa claimed to be the first to use mutes for cornets and trombones in a band, and this practice is widely used today in both bands and orchestras.[28]

His idea of an ideal arranger was one who knew the capabilities of each instrument and whose imagination was not bounded by tradition. He thought that Wagner was the paragon of creative orchestrators, that he was unsuccessfully imitated, and that many master composers had

[28] "The Muted Brass" (an interview with Sousa), *Philadelphia Record*. Undated clipping in the 1919 Sousa Band press book. Another Sousa quote on this subject is found in an unidentified newspaper clipping (evidently a Boston paper from late 1929) in the Sousa scrapbook at the Boston Public Library.

groped for ideas in orchestral coloring. He thought the ill-informed orchestrator tended to obscure the central ideas of a composition with excessive coloration. Believing that the potential of wind groups was far greater than usually realized by most composers, Sousa urged arrangers not to restrict wind instruments to current practices. He deplored the inference that wind instruments should be associated only with marching or jazz groups and said that an arranger or transcriber was limited only by his own creative faculties and command of tonal effects.

Some of Sousa's finest examples of band scoring were the transcriptions used as accompaniments for vocal or violin solos. These were delicately scored, and he relied heavily on unobtrusive combinations of woodwinds. He especially loved the lush sound of the clarinet voices, but he would gladly have traded the clarinet for an instrument which would have given the combined qualities of the flute and violin.

One thing which distinguished Sousa as a transcriber of orchestral works for band was his use of the original orchestral keys. Generally speaking, orchestral music is set in sharp keys rather than flat keys for the convenience of string players, whose instruments have strings tuned to sharp keys. Similarly, band music is generally set in flat keys for the convenience of brass and woodwind players because most band instruments are pitched in flat keys. Sousa seldom simplified his transcriptions, that is, changed them from sharp to flat keys, preferring to be faithful to the composers' intentions by retaining the original keys. This placed an additional responsibility on his musicians, and for this reason he preferred to enlist players who had experience in both orchestral and band work.

Sousa's use of one particular brand of instruments was justified to a certain extent in the production of his "oneness of tone." For many years he endorsed Conn instruments and permitted only a few exceptions in cases of a musician's personal preference. This was also a business proposition, but it did help unify the overall tonal quality of the band. The Conn Corporation furnished instruments to the bandsmen, plus monetary incentives to Sousa and a few of the soloists, in exchange for endorsements and advertising space in the printed programs. The programs, incidentally, also declared Sousa's endorsement of Steinert pianos, but he had another make in his own home much of the time.

The number of various instruments used in the Sousa Band, as well as the total number in the band, has been a subject of debate among bandsmen for many years. The point of confusion is that Sousa changed numbers of instruments each season and sometimes even during a season. To clarify this point, Table 2 is presented. As discussed earlier in this chapter, the instrumentation stabilized about 1898 after a period of experimentation. In 1892 the Sousa Band started with a total membership of forty-six players, approximately the same number as in the Marine

TABLE 2.
INSTRUMENTATION OF THE SOUSA BAND IN SEVERAL YEARS

	1892	1898	1900 First European tour	1910-1911 World tour	1915	1919	1922	1928
Flute/piccolo	2	2	4	4	4	2	4	6
Oboe/English horn	2	2	2	2	2	2	3	2
B-flat clarinet	12	14	16	14	20	14	22	23
E-flat clarinet	2	2	2	1	2	1	0	0
Alto clarinet	1	1	2	1	1	0	1	0
Bass clarinet	1	1	2	1	0	1	2	1
Bassoon/contrabassoon	2	2	3	3	2	2	3	2
Saxophone	3	3	5	3	5	6	8	7
Total woodwinds	25	27	36	29	36	28	43	41
Cornet	4	4	4	4	6	5	5	6
Trumpet	2	2	2	2	2	2	2	2
Fluegelhorn	0	1	2	0	0	0	0	0
French horn	4	4	4	4	4	4	4	4
Trombone	3	3	4	4	6	4	5	4
Euphonium/baritone	2	2	2	2	2	2	3	2
Tuba/sousaphone	3	4	4	4	6	4	5	6
Total brass	18	20	22	20	26	21	24	24
Percussion	3	3	3	3	3	3	3	3
Harp	0	0	0	1	1	1	1	1
Total	46	50	61	53	66	53	71	69

Band he left. He maintained this number until 1896. The band was then gradually expanded until there was an average of seventy. This average was maintained all through the 1920s, but the band was augmented or reduced for specific events. See Table 2 for the number of players used for the tours.

ON THE FUTURE OF MUSIC IN AMERICA

Sousa was optimistic—and outspoken—about the future of music in America, but he was cautious about predicting trends in specific types of composition. However, he did make noteworthy predictions about the course of serious composition. Several times he stated that American composers would depart from classical standards and that the form of music known as the symphony would become outdated.

If for no other reason than the growing numbers of Americans, he believed that America would eventually produce many great composers. While America was strong in technological fields and in business matters, he recognized a lack of self-confidence in many art forms. He believed in the inevitable maturing and flowering of American music, however, citing as evidence the rapidly growing number of excellent American musicians available for his own band.

In retrospect, it can truly be said that as music in America has taken on new perspectives, a dedicated musician named John Philip Sousa played a prominent part in its development.

5
The Incredible Sousa Band

THE BEGINNING OF AN AMERICAN INSTITUTION

David Blakely, Sousa's first manager, was a man with a keen business sense and an awareness of public tastes. Before entering the field of concert management, he was a man of many distinctions. At one time he was Minnesota's Secretary of State. He had been founder and editor of the *Chicago Evening Post*, had a controlling interest in Minneapolis and St. Paul newspapers, and was president of the Blakely Printing Company of Chicago. After leaving the field of journalism, he managed the Theodore Thomas orchestra and then the band of Patrick S. Gilmore. He also managed the American tour of the Austrian composer Eduard Strauss.

The successful tours of the U.S. Marine Band under Sousa in 1891 and 1892 were ably managed by Blakely, and Sousa had learned to respect his judgment. Thus, when a Marine Corps surgeon ordered Sousa to Europe to recuperate after the strain of the 1891 tour, Sousa heeded Blakely's advice to visit Paris and hear the Garde Républicaine Band. Blakely had a good reason for suggesting this; the Garde Républicaine was then regarded as the finest band in the world. When he persuaded Sousa to resign from the Marine Corps and form his own civilian band, the standard for comparison was to be the Garde Républicaine. In fact, one of the most important clauses of the Sousa-Blakely contract of June 27, 1892, read as follows: "It shall be the aim and duty of the said Sousa by individual effort, and band rehearsals and practice, and by the preparation and furnishing of music, to make this band equal in executive ability to the band of the Garde Républicaine in Paris."

No expense was spared in engaging the finest musicians for the new band. At least ten distinguished European musicians and many of America's finest orchestral and operatic musicians joined the ranks.

Courtesy Marjorie Moody Glines

The founder of the Sousa Band was the distinguished David Blakely, a clever and ambitious promoter. It was he who persuaded Sousa to resign from the U.S. Marine Corps and to organize his own concert band.

Among them were Arthur Smith, cornetist of the Coldstream Guards Band of England; Henry D. Koch, one of the famous European family of French horn players; John S. Cox, flutist, from Scotland; Arthur Pryor and Frank Holton, trombonists; Joseph Michele Raffayola, euphonium soloist; Richard Messenger, oboist; Walter Smith, cornetist; and two others from Sousa's own U.S. Marine Band. Patrick Gilmore had died just prior to the time the Sousa Band was organized, and within a year, nineteen of Gilmore's finest players had joined Sousa. Among them were such outstanding artists as Herbert L. Clarke, Gustave Stengler, Herman Conrad, and William Wadsworth.

With such a group of celebrated artists, it might be expected that a leader would experience difficulty in establishing complete command. But after only a few moments of the first rehearsal, it was obvious that the martinet Sousa was running the band in his own way and that the men were actually enjoying this arrangement. He gained their confidence immediately.

Blakely and Sousa did not decide upon a permanent name for the band during the first year, but "Sousa" was almost always in the billing, as specified in the contract. The first name was "Sousa's New Marine Band," but this was soon dropped because of objections from Washington. Upon reaching Chicago it was billed as the "World's Fair Band." After a few years as "Sousa's Unrivaled Band," "Sousa and His Peerless Band," and "Sousa's Grand Concert Band," the name "Sousa's Band" and "Sousa and His Band" were used exclusively.

As discussed in chapter 2, Blakely attempted to end the first tour of the band because a poorly arranged schedule resulted in financial difficulties, but Sousa would not permit this. The wisdom of his stand was soon borne out, much to Blakely's embarrassment. The band subsequently proved to be so astonishingly successful that Blakely did not believe the success could be lasting. To gain assurance he put the band to a supreme test in July, 1893. During an engagement at New York's fashionable Manhattan Beach, he invited many critics and prominent musicians to come hear the band and offer their criticism, good or bad. To his amazement he received an avalanche of flattering testimony, both personally and through the press. Sousa had passed the test. Convinced that he had a star in his palm, Blakely never again doubted Sousa's drawing power.

A UNIQUE MUSICAL ORGANIZATION

If, in its day, the band of John Philip Sousa was the finest organization of its kind, why was this so? Some insight was offered by Sousa himself:

> I candidly believe that there is not a better band in the world. There are many reasons for it. It plays under the very best auspices in the world,

better than any other, because it is always before a public that pays a large sum of money, and it is together all the time. We have so much money at our back that we can get the very best players there are, and the reputation of the band draws the players to it. Besides, I have some ability as a drill master, and with all this combination there was never such an effect. . . . Now, take a symphony orchestra; they have a season of twenty weeks, and then scatter. . . . We give one great big performance, sustain our reputation—or think how they are going to roast us. Everything must go as fine as possible. We play here two nights, and we go somewhere else—a new public and a new set of critics. It is bridal night with us all the time.[1]

The Sousa Band was totally dependent upon public approval for its survival, and it was something of a miracle in show business for a musical organization of its size to have played to capacity houses for thirty-nine years. In a single season it presented formal concerts to approximately two million people. And no other musical organization of its time—or perhaps any other time—under a single conductor, traveled so extensively. One of Sousa's ambitions was to travel a million miles with his band, an ambition realized in 1927.[2]

Because Sousa was known as the "March King," the Sousa Band is often thought of as a marching band. Actually, it was a concert band that marched only seven times in its nearly four decades of existence. The first occasion was the parade held at the dedication of the World's Fair in Chicago in 1893. On the second occasion, the band happened to be in Cleveland on the morning of May 5, 1898, when Troop A of the Ohio National Guard departed for the Spanish-American War, and the band escorted them in the parade to the depot.[3] Later that year, on the evening of September 11, the band was appearing in Pittsburgh and marched in a parade celebrating the return of the Eighteenth Regiment, Pennsylvania Volunteers. Then on September 30, 1899, the band was in New York City for the victory parade of Admiral Dewey. The fifth marching appearance of the band was on July 4, 1900, when it marched through the streets of Paris at the Paris Exposition after the unveiling of the Lafayette statue. The sixth and seventh marching appearances were on April 12, 1916, and April 12, 1917, when the band marched in parades sponsored by the New York Hippodrome.

The goal of nearly every serious band musician in the United States was to play with the Sousa Band. One reason was that membership in

[1] "Sousa and His Mission," *Music*, July, 1899.
[2] According to a press release of the Sousa Band office, the millionth mile was reached as the train carrying the Sousa Band crossed the interstate bridge traveling from the state of Washington into Portland, Oregon, on October 8, 1927. This estimate might have been in error, because a 1929 release stated that the band had traveled over 1,272,000 miles.
[3] Sousa's march "The Black Horse Troop" (1924) was dedicated to this military unit twenty-six years later.

Courtesy Ralph Corey, Jr.

The Sousa Band marched only seven times in thirty-nine years. In this rare photograph it is seen escorting Troop A of the Ohio National Guard to the Cleveland train depot and off to the Spanish-American War on May 5, 1898.

August 1913

Sun. 10	Allentown	Pa.	M & E	Central Park
Mon. 11	Ocean Grove	N.J.	M & E	Auditorium
Tue. 12	Dover	N.J.	Matinee	Baker Theatre
	Del. Water Gap	Pa.	Evening	Castle Inn Music Hall
Wed. 13	Pottsville	Pa.	M & E	Academy of Music
Thu. 14	Shamokin	Pa.	M & E	G. A. R. Opera House
Fri. 15	Harrisburg	Pa.	M & E	Paxtang Park
Sat. 16	Harrisburg	Pa.	M & E	Paxtang Park
Sun. 17	Willow Grove	Pa.	M & E	Willow Grove Park
(Daily for 22 days)				

September 1913

Mon. 8	Pittsburgh	Pa.	M & E	Exposition
(Daily for 12 days, Sunday excepted)				
Sun. 21	Columbus	Ohio	M & E	Southern Theatre
Mon. 22	Delaware	Ohio	Matinee	City Opera House
	Marion	Ohio	Evening	Chautauqua Pavillion
Tue. 23	Findlay	Ohio	Matinee	Majestic Theatre
	Lima	Ohio	Evening	Faurot Opera House
Wed. 24	Indianapolis	Ind.	M & E	Murat Theatre
Thu. 25	Huntington	Ind.	Matinee	New Huntington Theatre
	Fort Wayne	Ind.	Evening	Majestic Theatre
Fri. 26	Goshen	Ind.	Matinee	Jefferson Theatre
	Elkhart	Ind.	Evening	New Bucklen Theatre
Sat. 27	Kalamazoo	Mich.	M & E	Fuller Theatre
Sun. 28	Detroit	Mich.	M & E	Detroit Opera House
Mon. 29	Port Huron	Mich.	Matinee	Majestic Theatre
	Mt. Clemens	Mich.	Evening	Bijou Theatre
Tue. 30	Pontiac	Mich.	Matinee	Howland Theatre
	Flint	Mich.	Evening	Stone Theatre

October 1913

Wed. 1	Bay City	Mich.	Matinee	Washington Theatre
	Saginaw	Mich.	Evening	Academy of Music
Thu. 2	Owosso	Mich.	Matinee	Owosso Opera House
	Lansing	Mich.	Evening	Gladmer Theatre
Fri. 3	Adrian	Mich.	Matinee	Croswell Opera House
	Ann Arbor	Mich.	Evening	Whitney Theatre
Sat. 4	Toledo	Ohio	M & E	Valentine Theatre
Sun. 5	Cleveland	Ohio	M & E	Hippodrome
Mon. 6	Akron	Ohio	M & E	Grand Opera House
Tue. 7	Sharon	Pa.	Matinee	Morgan Grand
	Youngstown	Ohio	Evening	Grand Opera House
Wed. 8	Corry	Pa.	Matinee	Library Theatre
	Jamestown	N.Y.	Evening	Samuels' Opera House
Thu. 9	Buffalo	N.Y.	M & E	Elmwood Music Hall
Fri. 10	Lockport	N.Y.	Matinee	Temple Theatre
	Niagara Falls	N.Y.	Evening	International Theatre
Sat. 11	Rochester	N.Y.	M & E	Shubert Theatre
Sun. 12	Syracuse	N.Y.	M & E	Wieting Opera House
Mon. 13	Oneida	N.Y.	Matinee	Madison Theatre
	Utica	N.Y.	Evening	Majestic Theatre
Tue. 14	Amsterdam	N.Y.	Matinee	Opera House
	Schenectady	N.Y.	Evening	Van Curler Opera House
Wed. 15	Albany	N.Y.	M & E	Harmanus Bleecker Hall
Thu. 16	Hudson	N.Y.	Matinee	The Playhouse
	Poughkeepsie	N.Y.	Evening	Collingwood Opera House
Fri. 17	Great Barrington	Mass.	Matinee	Mahaiwe Theatre
	Pittsfield	Mass.	Evening	Colonial Theatre
Sat. 18	Worcester	Mass.	M & E	Mechanics Hall
Sun. 19	Malden	Mass.	Matinee	Auditorium
	Boston	Mass.	Evening	Colonial Theatre
Mon. 20	Portland	Me.	M & E	Jefferson Theatre
Tue. 21	Augusta	Me.	Matinee	Opera House
	Waterville	Me.	Evening	City Opera House
Wed. 22	Bangor	Me.	M & E	Opera House
Thu. 23	Brunswick	Me.	Matinee	Cumberland Theatre
	Lewistown	Me.	Evening	Empire Theatre
Fri. 24	Portsmouth	N.H.	Matinee	Music Hall
	Dover	N.H.	Evening	Opera House
Sat. 25	Manchester	N.H.	M & E	Franklin Street Church
Sun. 26	Malden	Mass.	Matinee	Auditorium
	Boston	Mass.	Evening	Colonial Theatre
Mon. 27	Fall River	Mass.	M & E	Savoy Theatre
Tue. 28	Milford	Mass.	Evening	Opera House
Wed. 29	Providence	R.I.	M & E	Infantry Hall
Thu. 30	Springfield	Mass.	M & E	Court Square Theatre
Fri. 31	Derby	Conn.	Matinee	Sterling Theatre
	South Norwalk	Conn.	Evening	Armory; or Music Hall

The Sousa Band tours were strenuous, as this route sheet illustrates. There were two concerts per day, seven days per week, for months at a time.

November 1913

Sat. 1	New Haven	Conn.	M & E	Woolsey Hall
Sun. 2	Troy	N.Y.	M & E	Rand Opera House
Mon. 3	Saratoga Springs	N.Y.	Matinee	Broadway Theatre
	Glens Falls	N.Y.	Evening	Empire Theatre
Tue. 4	Oneonta	N.Y.	Matinee	Oneonta Theatre
	Binghamton	N.Y.	Evening	Stone Opera House
Wed. 5	Waverly	N.Y.	Matinee	Loomis Opera House
	Elmira	N.Y.	Evening	Lyceum Theatre
Thu. 6	Lock Haven	Pa.	Matinee	Martin Theatre
	Williamsport	Pa.	Evening	Lycoming Theatre
Fri. 7	Wilkesbarre	Pa.	M & E	Grand Opera House
Sat. 8	Scranton	Pa.	M & E	Lyceum Theatre
Sun. 9	New York City	N.Y.	Evening	Hippodrome

the Sousa Band established a man's reputation once and for all. No finer recommendation could be found; a man who had played with Sousa seldom experienced difficulty in finding employment elsewhere. Positions in the Sousa Band were not always open, however, because of the surprisingly small turnover. A total of less than 500 different men played regularly in the band during its life-span. The auditioning policy changed over the years. At first Sousa himself auditioned each man. Later, auditions were held by section leaders. Then, in the 1920s, musicians were sometimes admitted on the recommendations of other band members.

The personality of the band changed gradually. In the beginning it was an organization of older men led by a younger man. In the band's final years, an old man was leading young men. The number of European musicians also diminished with time. There were several reasons for this. Sousa had become outspoken on the subject of Americanism, and he realized that his band was constantly being referred to as an "American institution." Then, too, there were growing numbers of versatile, proficient American musicians.

The changing character of the band posed a question which was debated among former members for many years and was never resolved: was the band of seasoned artists in pre-World War I days superior to the band of younger musicians in the 1920s? With changing times Sousa had considerable difficulty obtaining polished musicians for the long, arduous tours, and he often complained privately that increasing numbers of them were finding steady jobs in big cities. On the other hand, the younger musicians were quicker to adapt to the music of the 1920s, and Sousa was thus enabled to include such music as jazz on his concerts.

Musicianship was, of course, the most important prerequisite for the Sousa musician, but other things were equally important. One had to be a "regular fellow," that is, able to get along with others under trying circumstances. And he had to be a showman. Showmanship was essential for the humoresques which invariably found their way into the tour programs. Endurance was also extremely important because of the length and frequency of the concerts. Even the soloists were expected to play every note of every concert, which often lasted three hours. Some thought Sousa unreasonable in this respect, but he disregarded

Courtesy Col. Osmund Varela

For the first two seasons the Sousa Band uniform was medium blue with red and gold trim. (Because of the orthochromatic film used at that time, the blue appears as a lighter color.) Thereafter, the uniforms were black or navy blue. This is Henry Koch, French horn player of the 1890s, also one of Sousa's copyists and arrangers.

Defense Department (Marine Corps)

Emblems such as these provided the only color seen on the black Sousa Band uniforms.

his own welfare and likewise expected his men to put forth every effort to please audiences. Rookie musicians usually had difficulty adjusting to this pace. Cornetist Frank Simon used to tell the story of how his lips became black and blue after his first few days with the Sousa Band.

The tours, which usually lasted from six to ten months, were almost unbelievably strenuous. Quite often the band played in two towns in a single day. They performed seven days a week, and it was not unusual

Courtesy Louis Morris

Sousa might not have known of this picture because he frowned upon diversions during rehearsals. It was taken in the New York Hippodrome at a rehearsal for the 1919 season.

for them to play in a dozen different towns a week. There were no air-conditioned trains and diners. Meals came irregularly, and each night was spent in a different hotel. The men became highly efficient in arranging for their meals and sleeping accommodations, because the trains left on time and the concerts were begun promptly at the scheduled times. Extremities of weather brought additional hardships, but this was all part of the job. The Sousa Band man was a hardy man, one with stamina and fortitude. Present-day musicians would not tolerate this grueling work, but there is no Sousa to inspire them.

Each man furnished his own uniform and was expected to keep himself presentable. Few had more than one uniform, so keeping them cleaned and pressed was difficult. One of the tricks they used for keeping their trousers pressed was to sprinkle them with water and place them under-

neath their mattresses at night. The uniforms were semimilitary in appearance and were worn constantly, regardless of the weather. No summertime concerts were ever given in shirt sleeves.

The uniforms traditionally were black or near-black, with black braid and black velvet trim on the coats. For the first two years of its existence, however, the band's uniforms were medium blue with red and gold trim. Caps with gold trim were used until 1901, after which they were plain. Between 1894 and 1919 the standard uniform was dark (navy) blue, and thereafter it was black. The only ornamentations were small emblems. Sousa's uniforms were similar to those of the bandsmen except for his white uniforms, which he used on Sundays (and sometimes Saturdays) and special occasions. During the 1920s he wore his navy uniform most of the time.

Rehearsals of the band were pleasant but orderly and demanding. They were not begun until every man was in his place or satisfactorily accounted for. First, scales were played very slowly so that undesirable qualities of tone production and intonation were revealed. They would then proceed to rehearse the regular program, with Sousa quietly and patiently explaining what he wanted. He was strict in his "oneness of sound" concept and expected a suitable blend of each section with no individual players predominating. At the first rehearsal of the 1893 season, he rehearsed the clarinet section in the first few measures of an overture for approximately three hours to get the tonal quality he desired. The amount of time spent in rehearsals decreased over the years; in 1892 the rehearsals lasted twelve days, and in the 1920s only two days were allotted. It should be noted that rehearsals were very seldom held for the extended outdoor concert series at such places as Willow Grove or Manhattan Beach; rehearsals were for tour programs only.

ONE BIG HAPPY FAMILY

The Sousa Band was such a closely knit organization that in many respects it was a traveling fraternity. The men had much in common, not the least of which was a conspicuous respect for each other. This relationship was fostered by Sousa, whom they all addressed as "Mr. Sousa" and referred to as "the Governor" or "the boss." In the 1920s they affectionately referred to him as "the old man." Each of the men was, by Sousa's proclamation, "young man." Sousa was genuinely loved and respected, and it was a rare band member who would not have done anything in his power to please him or promote the good of the band.

Sousa permitted absolutely no vanity among the bandsmen, even from the soloists who came to him from Gilmore's Band, where vanity was not only allowed but actually encouraged. Sousa showed amazing impartiality, and this resulted in an almost complete absence of jealousies. There was also an almost unbelievable religious tolerance among the bandsmen, and it was an unwritten law of the band that one band member was never to ridicule another because of his religion.

There were many fathers and sons as well as brothers in the band. For example, Morris Reines and his three sons, Abraham, Philip, and Leo, all played bassoon at one time or another. Edmund A. Wall and his two sons, Edmund C. and Charles, played clarinet. August Helleberg, Sr., and his two sons, August, Jr., and John, played tuba. There were also the three Heney brothers, Edward, William, and John, and the three Schueler brothers, Henry, John, and William. Sousa was as proud of this family participation as were the men themselves.

Wives seldom traveled with the band; those who did found it burdensome, and few ever stuck it out for an entire season. Sousa was extremely polite to them but did not encourage them to follow the band. He even showed signs of discomfort on the rare occasions when his own wife accompanied him for a series of engagements. Visits by wives were acceptable while the band was playing lengthy engagements in one location,

Courtesy Donald C. Gardner

''Sir Knight John Philip Sousa and the Masonic Members of His Band, Season 1921-1922.''
Depending on the year, from one third to one half the Sousa Bandmen were members of some Masonic order.

Courtesy Leon E. Weir

No matter how strenuous the tours of the band, its members managed to find time for a little nonsense (above and following pages).

Courtesy Ralph Corey, Jr.

Courtesy Roy M. Miller

Courtesy Leon E. Weir

Courtesy Robert V. Rose

Courtesy Leon E. Weir

Courtesy Robert V. Rose

but Sousa realized that traveling wives meant that band members' minds were not 100 percent on their work.

The exhausting tours would have grown boring were it not for a little horseplay now and then. Former Sousa bandsmen love to recall the pranks they played on one another to brighten dreary moments. Sousa, being a wit himself, was amused and looked the other way. Practically the only thing of this nature that he disapproved of was the men's subtle flirting with girls in the audience during a performance. When it became noticeable, he uttered a few sharp words and put an end to it—at least temporarily.

Sports were diversions which delighted the men. While the band was playing long summer stands in some cities, the men formed their own baseball team. Games were played with local teams, some of considerable repute. The Sousa team usually fared quite well. The games with teams of rival bands, such as Pryor's Band, were the most interesting. Sousa himself participated in the games as long as he was able. For reasons not fully understood, the band baseball players eventually shied away from outside competition and began intramural games between the woodwinds and the brasses.

During a few seasons in the early 1920s, the band also sported a basketball team, but the team's record was not enviable. They were flashy early in a game but lacked endurance and would usually take a licking in a game of regulation length. Newsmen could not pass up the opportunity to poke fun at the rotundity of the players, with such humorous comments as "the high rise and low fall of their bosoms."[4]

Stylish Willow Grove Park at Philadelphia was the spot best loved by both Sousa and the band. Sousa was revered in Philadelphia, and to him, Willow Grove was a sentimental journey. Music was foremost with the management there, and the park was a shrine for art lovers. For several years it was considered the summer musical capital of America. The Sousa Band was booked for periods of up to eleven weeks from 1901 through 1926 (except for 1911, when the band was on the world tour) for a very good reason: Sousa could keep the park out of the red. Although many other famous orchestras and bands played there, it was Sousa who drew the crowds. The orchestra of Victor Herbert and the band of Arthur Pryor were also perennial favorites, but Sousa broke all attendance records and conducted more concerts than anyone else. As an added attraction, he engaged more vocal soloists and insisted on many solos and ensembles from within the band. Starting in 1913, one day of each week was reserved for Sousa compositions exclusively.

The bandsmen looked forward to Willow Grove as a relief from the monotony of constant travel, even though the engagement posed extreme demands on their musicianship. Many of their families joined

[4] *Yakima* (Washington) *Herald*, December 26, 1923.

Courtesy Col. Osmund Varela

The black-bearded pitcher (seated, center) of the 1904-1905 Sousa Band baseball team was Sousa himself. The young man wearing the "Nassau" jersey is John Philip Sousa II, not a member of the band. On July 4, 1900, the Sousa Band team played the first game of baseball ever played in Paris.

Courtesy Joan Ambrose

Willow Grove Park just outside Philadelphia was, for many years, the most important summer music-center of America. Sousa's Band played twenty-five lengthy engagements there, starting in 1901.

Courtesy Harold B. Stephens

The genial Herbert L. Clarke became the most highly regarded cornetist of all time during his years with Sousa. His compositions for the cornet are still popular. After retiring from the Sousa Band he became one of America's leading bandmasters.

Courtesy Robert Hoe, Jr.

Alessandro Liberati

Courtesy Oliver R. Graham

Bohumir Kryl

Courtesy Glenn D. Bridges

Walter Rogers

Courtesy Oliver R. Graham

Herman Bellstedt

Courtesy Frank Simon

Frank Simon

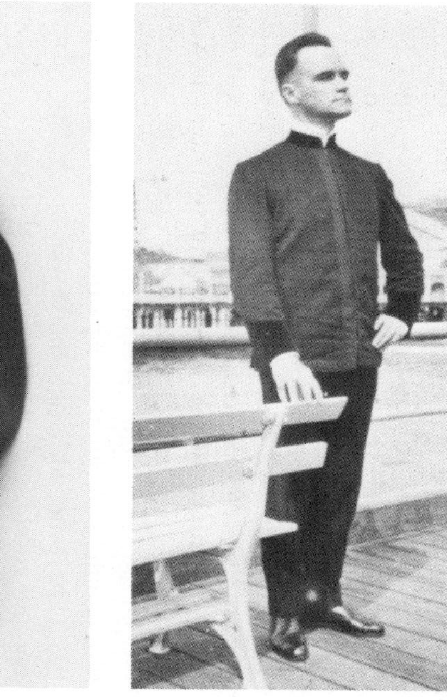

Courtesy Norman E. Hinkel

John Dolan

Sousa traditionally featured a top cornetist with his band. Some of the important ones are pictured on these two pages.

them there for vacations. A large percentage of the men roomed in private homes, another pleasant change from the routine of hopping from one hotel to another.

The park itself was beautiful. It had been built by and was operated by the Philadelphia Rapid Transit Company, whose trolley lines terminated there.[5] No liquor was permitted, and policemen were on duty at all times.

The long and tedious train rides are well remembered by former Sousa men. There were usually two passenger cars used by the Sousa Band. These were sometimes referred to as the "gentlemen's" car and the "roughneck's" car or simply as the smoker and the non-smoker. Sousa, the soloists, and those wishing to converse or enjoy the scenery were usually in the "gentlemen's" car. Several card games, including a poker game or two, could be found in the other. The men usually kept the same seats all the time, although there was never any formal assignment. Courtesy and good conduct prevailed at all times.

EMINENT SOLOISTS

One thing that distinguished Sousa's organization from most others of its kind was that it was truly a virtuoso group. Each season several top-name soloists were featured. Many of the instrumental soloists added to the overall program interest by composing their own solos. Among the more outstanding solos were the cornet pieces by Herbert L. Clarke, Walter Rogers, Herman Bellstedt, Frank Simon, and Eugene LaBarre; the trombone solos of Arthur Pryor and Leo Zimmerman; and the saxophone solos of H. Benne Henton and Jeane Moeremans. Sousa had many reasons for programming soloists. He knew from his own experience that solos contributed to the individual musician's confidence and poise by affording him a direct appeal to the audience. Also, the depth of the band's talent was revealed. But the main reason was that solos added variety and showmanship to the programs.

Soloists on practically all instruments were featured, but the brass soloists were the most popular with the public. Each tour concert included at least one brass soloist and sometimes two. Most of the finest brass players in the United States eventually gravitated to the Sousa Band, usually early in their careers. Three whose names rank with the finest of all time on their respective instruments were cornetist Herbert L. Clarke, trombonist Arthur Pryor, and euphonium player Simone Mantia. In the opinion of most Sousa bandsmen (including Sousa) and other veteran

[5] Two Sousa compositions were written in honor of Willow Grove Park and its management. The first was a concert piece, "Willow Blossoms" (1916). The second was "March of the Mitten Men" (1923), named for Thomas Mitten, head of the Philadelphia Rapid Transit Company, which owned the park.

Courtesy Col. Osmund Varela

The title "Paganini of the Trombone" described Arthur W. Pryor, Sousa's peerless trombonist. He played ten thousand solos with Sousa before resigning to organize his own band. Pryor's Band became one of the finest in America, perhaps second only to Sousa's.

bandsmen as well, these three men were without equals. Such claims were, of course, influenced by personal association. The claims were not groundless, however, because Sousa afforded his soloists opportunities not offered by any other organization. Another distinguishing factor was the fantastic endurance they all developed as members of Sousa's troupe.

Courtesy Col. Osmund Varela

The feats of Simone Mantia, Italian-born euphonium player, are legendary in the band world. He also had great facility on the trombone. He resigned from Sousa's Band in 1903 to be Pryor's assistant conductor.

Herbert L. Clarke (1867-1945) had nearly every faculty a cornetist could hope for: a brilliant technique, a delicate lyric style, and extremes of range and dynamics. He joined Sousa in 1893, left after one season, and then returned to play almost continuously from 1899 until 1917. He was assistant conductor for several seasons. As the premier soloist with the Sousa Band for so many years, he became a legendary figure among cornet and trumpet players. Among the other outstanding Sousa cornet soloists were Walter Rogers, Herman Bellstedt, Bohumir Kryl, Allesandro Liberati, Frank Simon, and John Dolan. Simon was the first to use the post horn for encore numbers. But perhaps the man most often compared with Clarke was John Dolan. It is unfortunate that Dolan did not mix well with the other bandsmen and did not meet the public well, for he was a superb artist.

Arthur Pryor (1870-1942) was called the "Paganini of the trombone," and judging from comments handed down by his contemporaries, the title was appropriate. He was with Sousa from 1892 until 1903. Appointed assistant conductor, he directed many recordings of the Sousa Band even after he was no longer a member. His specialties were an extraordinary technique, a unique rapid vibrato, three-note chords, and resounding pedal notes. No one was ever quite able to fill his shoes, although he was succeeded by such noteworthy trombonists as Leo Zimmerman, Gardell Simons, and Ralph Corey. Corey, the "village cutup," added much extramusical lore to the band; he was very popular with the ladies and was the checkers champion of the band.

The claim to fame of Italian-born euphonium soloist Simone Mantia (1873-1951) was his dazzling technique. He played even the most difficult solos with amazing speed and accuracy. He also had a high degree of proficiency on the trombone and even substituted for Pryor on occasion. Strangely, most of Sousa's euphonium soloists were of Italian extraction: Joseph Raffayolo, John Perfetto, Joseph DeLuca, and Mantia. The notable exception was Noble Howard, an American who was with the band in the late 1920s.

Among the woodwind soloists were several peerless performers. In the 1890s, E. A. Lefebre was recognized as the greatest saxophone player in the world and was known as the "Saxophone King." A later performer, H. Benne Henton, was referred to as the "Saxophone Prince." Two other outstanding saxophone artists were Jeane H. B. Moeremans, for whom Sousa wrote "Belle Mahone," and Harold B. Stephens. More popular than any individual saxophonist was the saxophone octet of the late 1920s, which added variety and humor to programs. They had been preceded by a saxophone sextet. The following was typical of the octet's press reviews:

> The saxophones ranged in size from the little tenor down to the monster bass "Dutch pipe" blown by Fred Monroe, whose . . . introductions of the various numbers brought waves of laughter. "Our next number," said Fred, "will be a little ditty entitled 'The Light That Lies in a Lady's Eyes Just Lies and Lies and Lies!' " Then he announced that they would play "It's Better to Have Loved and Lost—Yes, Much Better," which turned out to be the Democratic battle hymn, "Happy Days Are Here Again."[6]

[6] *Raleigh* (North Carolina) *News and Observer*, November 15, 1930.

Courtesy Leon E. Weir

One of the highlights of a Sousa Band concert during the 1920s was the saxophone octet. It presented a brief but highly entertaining show.

Few piccolo soloists were ever featured, but the artistry of Marshall P. Lufsky and his predecessor, Eugene C. Rose, cannot be forgotten; both were recording artists as well as soloists with the Sousa Band. The only clarinetist featured regularly was Joseph Norrito, who was with the band for over thirty years. Percussionists did not get into the spotlight regularly until later years, when George J. Carey and Howard Goulden were featured on the xylophone.

The ladies appearing with the Sousa Band were either vocalists, violinists, or harpists. The renowned violinist Maud Powell began her brilliant career with Sousa. Her stay was short, however, and the violinist most familiar to Sousa audiences over the years was Florence Hardeman. Another popular favorite was Nicoline Zedeler.

A large number of women vocalists sang with Sousa at one time or another, many of them making brief appearances at such places as Willow Grove. Those making the tours were all sopranos, either coloratura or lyric. Sousa had three requirements: talent, beauty, and stage presence. One of cornetist Frank Simon's favorite stories was about Sousa's reaction when he excitedly told Sousa that he had discovered a great talent in a young soprano named Marjorie Moody. Sousa listened to Simon's description of her vocal attributes, hesitated a moment, and then asked, "Is she pretty?" Indeed Miss Moody was, and she charmed Sousa Band patrons almost continuously from 1917 on. In all, she sang over 2,500 concerts with Sousa.[7]

Virginia Root was another of the sopranos whose longevity with the Sousa Band was noteworthy. It was she whom Sousa chose for the world tour of 1910-1911, and she was with the band for several other seasons. Miss Root was the granddaughter of George Frederick Root, composer of such popular songs as "Tramp, Tramp, Tramp the Boys Are Marching," "The Battle Cry of Freedom," and "Just Before the Battle, Mother."

The most renowned Sousa vocalist was the coloratura soprano Estelle Liebling, who came from a long line of distinguished musicians. It was her brother Leonard who wrote the libretto for Sousa's operetta *The American Maid* (1909). Her range was extensive and her production of high notes brought many fine reviews. She sang over 1,600 concerts with the Sousa Band.[8] One thing Miss Liebling had in common with all the Sousa sopranos was a voice with great carrying power. They all performed without the aid of microphones.

The "royal suite," or "imperial suite," was a term used by the bandsmen when referring to the party of Sousa and the women of the band. For the sake of propriety, Sousa insisted that the women room together and avoid unnecessary association with the bandsmen. It was his policy for the women to have their meals with him in public. One

[7] Author's estimate.
[8] Mme. Liebling's estimate.

Maud Powell, one of the most distinguished women violinists, began her career with the Sousa Band.

of their fringe benefits was that Sousa usually paid for their meals, and he often humorously complained that they "ate up one side of the menu and down the other."

BUSINESS ASPECTS

In Sousa's writings one finds that he consistently voiced opposition to governmental subsidy for musical organizations and for art in general.

It was his observation that, almost without exception, the successful composer depended upon his art for a living, not for a handout. According to his theory, governmental aid was a good thing for the perpetuation of the art, but in the end it was a drawback. Musical organizations subsidized by the state, he asserted, were like hardy plants brought up in a hothouse. Under those conditions, he noted, conductors tended to play only what they preferred, resulting in a musical fare of limited scope.

Courtesy Edna Jellinek

The young Marcella Lindh (née Rosalind Marcella Jacobson) was the first soprano to sing with the Sousa Band. She later became a popular operatic figure in Europe.

Courtesy Marjorie Moody Glines

The talented and lovely Marjorie Moody was with Sousa longer than any other vocalist. She sang more than twenty-five hundred concerts over a period of fourteen years. Sousa held her in high esteem and dedicated two songs to her: "There's a Merry Brown Thrush" (1926) and "Love's Radiant Hour" (1928).

In his travels abroad he observed that music seemed to have national boundaries. In this regard he was particularly critical of France.

He thought that all musical organizations should sustain themselves just as his own organization did. However, not all musicians and artists were as richly blessed with natural gifts as he. Not all composers and

Courtesy Nora Fauchald Morgan

The beautiful Nora Fauchald, Sousa's "Norwegian Nightingale," presents ample evidence that Sousa was successful in selecting sopranos who were talented, personable, and attractive.

conductors had the inclination to cater to the masses by directing their art toward the field of entertainment, and his views were largely unheeded. Then too it must be remembered that his own reputation as an extremely popular composer was partly responsible for the drawing power of the Sousa Band. This matter could be debated endlessly. But for what it

The Library of Congress

The versatile Estelle Liebling sang with Sousa on two continents and later distinguished herself in many fields. She was the most renowned of all Sousa sopranos.

is worth, the fact remains that the Sousa Band was the most successful band in musical history without receiving the slightest bit of governmental patronage. Sousa maintained that neither he nor the band would have worked as hard had they been furnished with comfortable salaries. As it was, their business success depended upon their musical reputation, and with this at stake they could not lower their standards for a single concert.

If Sousa had had a better mind for business, the Sousa Band might have been organized years earlier. But he was naive in business matters until he met David Blakely. Shortly afterward he stopped selling his marches to Harry Coleman for thirty-five dollars each and began a much more profitable association with the John Church Company. He did his own personal negotiating with publishers, but band business matters were left to his managers. Sousa became a millionaire in spite of being a poor businessman.

The general managers of the Sousa Band were David Blakely, Frank Christianer, Everett Reynolds, George Frederick Hinton, James S. Barnes, George N. Loomis, Edwin Clarke, and Harry Askin, in that order. Not all were equally effective. The three who handled the job most capably were Blakely, Hinton, and Askin. Blakely founded the band and, except for the first short tour, handled matters admirably. Like Blakely, Hinton was at his best as a press agent. Sousa had high regard for Hinton's handling of the European tours, and it was he who created the "S.O., U.S.A." farce which got out of hand. The band management apparently was slipping from the time of the 1910-1911 world tour until 1918, when Harry Askin took over.

Askin was a genius at promotion, and previous experience as manager of the New York Hippodrome served him well. Publicity stunts and bold press releases were his specialties. According to some of the releases from his publicity mill, George Carey's $5,000 xylophone, twelve feet long, was the largest ever built and accommodated eight players; Gus Helmecke's bass drum heads cost $500 each and were made from zebra skin, the only known material able to withstand the temperature and humidity extremes encountered in the travels of the Sousa Band; the band's huge Chinese gong formerly belonged to a Manchurian executioner who used it to announce the hours of fate; and so forth. These were merely sidelights, for Askin's best publicity centered around Sousa himself. With Sousa's varied interests—horses, trapshooting, hunting, writing, baseball, or his fancy of the moment—he was sure to appeal to some segment of the public.

There were actually several managers of the Sousa Band at any given time, but their functions were entirely different. The ones discussed above were the general managers, or those in charge of all business operations at the home office. The others were the traveling managers and the personnel managers. The duties of the traveling manager were first to book engagements in advance and then to accompany the band, collect receipts, and act as paymaster. The personnel manager was a member of the band and was its union representative. His duties were to engage the musicians and to arbitrate in personnel and salary matters.

The Harry Askin organization of the 1920s consisted of four full-time employees. Askin was the general manager and had his office at 1451 Broadway in New York City. Miss Lillian Finegan was the one and only secretary who handled all correspondence and clerical work and who was held in high esteem by Sousa. William (''Willie'') Schneider was the amiable and intelligent young traveling manager who had endeared himself to Sousa by virtue of his efficiency. Jay Sims was the personnel manager who had good working business relations with musicians all over the United States. The remaining people in Askin's employ were part-time publicity writers, the most notable being Elbert Severance.

The logistics of transporting the personnel and equipment of the Sousa Band from city to city on its transcontinental tours was the management's number one concern. The concert schedules were closely coordinated with existing railroad schedules. ''Specials,'' or nonscheduled trains, were set up only as a last resort because of the expense involved. Nevertheless, there were more ''Sousa Band specials'' than they wished for. The next most expensive mode of travel was the ''extras,'' or independent sections run behind the scheduled train. There were many of these, and they were also loosely referred to as ''specials.'' But almost always the Sousa Band was transported from place to place in two, or sometimes three, cars hooked onto an existing train. The ''specials'' were usually scheduled at critical times in a tour and had to make good time. The management noted that these trains actually broke many existing speed records between towns, but the railroads were conspicuously quiet on the subject.

For a while in the early 1920s there was talk of a Sousa Band caravan of busses and trucks instead of trains, but the matter was dropped after the management made a feasibility study. The proven dependability of railroads in all kinds of weather was the determining factor. Seldom did the trains fall appreciably behind schedule, but to be on the safe side arrangements were made to leave one town as soon as possible after a concert in order to be at the next town in plenty of time. The management knew that Sousa was a punctual man and did its best to maintain his peace of mind. The bandsmen also cooperated, and when one of them missed a train there were always extenuating circumstances.

One of the management's proudest moments in making efficient railroad connections was in 1923 when Sousa was sent on a detour between regularly scheduled engagements to receive an honorary degree. After giving matinee and evening performances in Akron, Ohio, Sousa and the band headed west. Matinee and evening concerts were scheduled in Hammond, Indiana, for the following day. On the morning of the

Hammond concerts, however, Sousa was to be in Milwaukee to receive an honorary Doctor of Music degree from Marquette University. He and the band proceeded on separate trains. With the aid of a police escort from the Milwaukee train depot to the university's gymnasium, he barely made it. Immediately after the ceremony he was again escorted to the train depot. At Hammond he was given another police escort from the train depot to the concert hall. This time he didn't quite make it, but this had already been allowed for by the management. The band began the concert with Sousa's humoresque "Showing Off Before Company." In this composition the bandsmen appeared singly or in groups and played various compositions to demonstrate their individual abilities, and Sousa entered last. The bandsmen were instructed to "stretch it out." They did, and Sousa arrived just in time for his entry. The audience had no knowledge that he was just pulling into town when the concert began.

For the bandsmen the most exciting tour concerts were the opening concert, often played in a small town to test the program, and the final concert, usually played in New York City. But in between the routine was the same—concerts intermixed with train rides. This routine was taxing, especially for those spending their first season with the band. For this reason the management made every effort to obtain the best passenger cars available. A comfortable car meant satisfied musicians, and satisfied musicians meant relaxed performances. The cars were almost always day coaches, but occasionally there would be a car with drawing rooms for members of the "royal suite." Sleepers were seldom used, but when they were it was usually only in the western states where the distances between populated areas were greater. Seldom did the trains have diners, but when they were available Sousa would sometimes foot the bill for the entire band.

It is a testimony to the safety of railroads that the Sousa Band was involved in only a few train accidents. Mishaps in 1906, 1907, and 1925 were minor, but seven band members were injured in a wreck in Colorado in 1929. In this incident a "special" traveling over little-used tracks between Pueblo and Trinidad derailed thirteen miles west of Walsenberg on the way to Trinidad. None of the injuries was serious, and the railroad promptly settled with the individual bandsmen.

Not only did the band management try to obtain the best train cars, but it also attempted to secure superior hotel accommodations. For the sake of the band's reputation, Sousa insisted that the men stay in better-grade hotels. The men paid for the rooms themselves,[9] and a satisfactory amount was included in their salaries with the understanding that this was to be used for rooms in better hotels.

A change in management structure resulted in failure to secure adequate reservations in early January, 1920, and this led to what has

[9] After 1920 a member of the band was given the responsibility of making accommodations.

been referred to as the "strike" of the band. Accommodations had not been reserved sufficiently in advance for a stretch of the tour through Tennessee and North Carolina. Consequently, for a period of approximately two weeks, several of the men had been unable to find rooms and had ended up sleeping on chairs in hotel lobbies, pool tables, or anywhere else they could find a spot to relax. In one North Carolina town there were few rooms available because of the presence of many tobacco salesmen.[10] Realizing that there would be insufficient rooming, the men held a "gripe" meeting. It was decided that those who could not find accommodations would express their disapproval by not performing the matinee concert the following day.

When Sousa faced the audience for that matinee concert, less than two dozen men were onstage. He was shocked. But he was determined to present a concert and announced that dissatisfied patrons could have their money refunded. The bandsmen did the best they possibly could, switching back and forth between their own parts and the parts of the missing musicians, and the concert went on. Not one listener asked for a refund, but Sousa was furious. As cornetist Frank Simon put it: "If ever I saw fire in a pair of black Spanish eyes, it was then!"[11] Sousa was a man slow to anger, but he was also slow to forgive. Failure to perform for a paying audience was, in his mind, unforgivable, except in a case of extreme emergency. The season was just ending, and he told the personnel manager that those who had failed to perform that day were never to be hired again. It is a matter of record that, with the exception of bass drummer August Helmecke and possibly one other, none of these men ever again played with the Sousa Band. The "strike" was thus a turning point in the band's history.

Former members of the Sousa Band—particularly those who were involved and lost their jobs—have avoided detailed discussions of the "strike." The affair marked the only time of wholesale dissatisfaction with conditions. Sousa gave considerable thought to the causes and resolved to improve conditions so that such an incident would not recur. Many of the new members the following year did not know of the incident.

The pay of the lower chair members rose from thirty-five dollars per week in 1892 to seventy-four dollars per week in the late 1920s. This was consistently above existing rates except during the last years of the band when the management decided to go along with rates set by the musicians' union. The high pay enabled Sousa to select the musicians he wanted. The finest artists flocked to Sousa because he offered security, challenging work, and the satisfaction of playing before highly

[10] Several Sousa band men have stated that the "strike" took place in Winston-Salem, North Carolina, but newspaper reviews of the concerts there and elsewhere in the area make no mention of it.

[11] Interview with the author, November 29, 1963.

appreciative audiences. Some made enough money to sustain themselves between seasons without additional work, but the majority kept active with other organizations. In Sousa's case, high pay led to high standards. As he once explained: "I have refused to cut down the number of players or the rates of pay. I can lay the flattering unction to my soul that I have raised the status of bandsmen in the United States, in Canada, and in England. How could I lower the standard which I have set up by sacrificing artistic excellence to mere commercialism?"[12] The first chair musicians were given premium pay and the soloists considerably more. Inasmuch as the concert receipts were in cash, the bandsmen were paid in cash.[13] Payday was once a week. There were no agents in the Sousa Band; that is, no percentages were paid to intermediate parties who influenced employment; the musicians were paid directly.

In the Sousa Band's thirty-nine-year lifespan there were only a few times when Sousa was temporarily incapacitated and unable to perform. Assistant conductors then took over. But no matter how attractive the programs, attendance would drop off. In show business terminology, Sousa was the "whole show." This was dramatically demonstrated two years after his death when cornetist Eugene LaBarre attempted to revive the Sousa Band as the "Sousa Men's Band" in New York City. He assembled a group of fifty-five former Sousa Band musicians who donated their services for a concert at Rockefeller Center on Easter Sunday, April 1, 1934. They had hoped to stimulate public interest and attract a sponsor. The public loved it, but those were depression days, and no sponsor came forth. Furthermore, another bandsman tried to elevate himself to leadership of the group, and the project collapsed after only one concert. With it went the hopes of those who had cherished the name of Sousa. Without Sousa there could be no Sousa Band.

THE IMPACT OF SOUSA BAND ALUMNI

For several decades the list of former members of Sousa's Band read like a veritable "Who's Who in American Music." They carried the name of Sousa to all corners of America, and even abroad, with one proud spirit. Many of them rose to fame far greater than they had achieved while members of Sousa's troupe. Nearly all continued performing on their chosen instruments and took up teaching. Some laid down their instruments to take up the baton, keeping alive the Sousa tradition for still another generation. A few became notable composers, and others became prominent educators. Only a minority abandoned music to pursue

[12] "What Sousa Pays His Men," *Musical America*, September 3, 1903.

[13] The bank structure of America was not as solid in Sousa's day as it is today. The band management therefore insisted on cash payments. Rarely did they accept bank drafts, and almost never did they accept checks.

other professions, but even then many years passed before they chose other fields of endeavor. Of these, several became doctors, dentists, attorneys, or noteworthy businessmen.

Of those who became conductors, most chose band work rather than orchestral work. When the elite organization known as the American Bandmasters Association was founded in 1929, three Sousa alumni were among the nine charter members: Herbert L. Clarke, Frank Simon, and Arthur Pryor.[14] A fourth, Victor J. Grabel, had played under Lt. Sousa at the Great Lakes Naval Training Station during World War I. As the ABA grew in stature to become the most prestigious band organization on this side of the Atlantic, four former Sousa men were subsequently elected to its presidency: Clarke, Simon, Howard Bronson, and Peter Buys.

Bohumir Kryl was one of the first alumni to make a name for himself as a conductor. He had come to the United States in 1889 with a diversified background—cornetist, sculptor, and acrobat. His skill as a sculptor is seen in the war memorial in Indianapolis. After leaving Sousa in 1894, he soloed with several other bands. He then organized his own touring band, which existed for thirty-five years. Later he formed a popular all-girl symphony orchestra which was also a touring organization. He was known in the musical world as an extremely frugal man and left an estate of over one million dollars.

After having performed over ten thousand solos with Sousa, Arthur Pryor resigned in the summer of 1903 and became one of America's greatest bandmasters. Although one of Sousa's more worthy competitors, he remained on the best of terms with him. It is generally acknowledged that Pryor's Band rivaled Sousa's Band in technical excellence. While retaining his fame as a trombone soloist, he became a studio director for the Victor Talking Machine Company, a position he held for over thirty years. With Victor he participated in approximately one thousand recordings, directing not only his own band but Sousa's and several others as well. Pryor's Band made six transcontinental tours between 1903 and 1909 and was active for many summers at such places as Asbury Park (New Jersey) and Willow Grove. In later years it was heard over the NBC radio network. Pryor was also a prolific composer of band works; he had over three hundred pieces to his credit.

When Herbert L. Clarke retired from the Sousa Band at the age of fifty in 1917, he no longer played cornet in public. He established himself as a conductor, first with the Anglo-Canadian Band of Huntsville, Ontario, and then, for twenty years, with the Long Beach (California) Municipal Band. The latter was a full-time professional band and was staffed by several former Sousa musicians. Several of his cornet solos became classics among brass players, and he also had several fine band

[14] Sousa was named first Honorary Life President of the ABA at the time it was founded.

transcriptions to his credit. Clarke's name will always be associated with Sousa's because the Clarke Library at the University of Illinois is adjacent to the Sousa Library and because his grave is but a few feet from Sousa's at Congressional Cemetery in Washington.

Frank Simon, accused of being one of the ringleaders in the "strike" of 1920, was one of those not called back the following season. Several years later he and Sousa were reconciled. From that time on, Sousa had no greater devotee. Simon founded the famed ARMCO Band in Middletown, Ohio, in 1921 and developed it into a splendid professional band; for years it was featured on the NBC radio network. He then became bandmaster at the Cincinnati Conservatory of Music, was later a member of the faculty of music at the University of Arizona, and was active in other radio work. He was twice awarded honorary Doctor of Music degrees. For many years he worked tirelessly and unselfishly as a conductor of Sousa memorial concerts and as a consultant at Sousa clinics held at various educational institutions. It is largely through his efforts that Sousa's interpretations of the marches have been kept alive. Just prior to his death in 1967, Simon supervised the recording of thirty-six Sousa marches for the American School Band Directors Association.

Eugene LaBarre, organizer of the ill-fated "Sousa Men's Band" in 1934, also established himself as a bandmaster of note. In Detroit he led the Elk's Band, the Detroit Fire Department Band, the Dodge Brothers Motor Band, and finally the Detroit University Band. In New York he led the New York Police Department Band and then the famed 1939 World's Fair Band. This was one of the finest bands ever assembled in America, and among its members were thirty-eight Sousa alumni. LaBarre ended his career with a six-year tenure as conductor of Herbert L. Clarke's former band, the Long Beach Municipal Band.

Among those who laid aside their instruments to make their marks in other areas of music, flutist Meredith Willson rose to a pinnacle of success through creative composition after a career as a professional musician. His spectacular Broadway musical *The Music Man* is rich in band lore and is among the most popular Broadway productions of all time. Another of his popular musical scores was *The Unsinkable Molly Brown*. At various times in his illustrious career he has also been a radio and television star, a conductor, a lecturer, and an author.

Another Sousa man who gave up performing to make a notable contribution in another area of music was trombonist Frank Holton. Holton established an instrument manufacturing company, and this company is still in existence. Many former Sousa Band men endorsed the Holton line of instruments, not the least of whom were Arthur Pryor and Frank Simon. Assisting Holton at one time was former Sousa clarinetist Eugene Slick, a master instrument craftsman, who designed one of the company's finest saxophones.

Courtesy Meredith Willson

The dynamic show-business personality Meredith Willson is today the most celebrated Sousa Band alumnus. An outstanding flutist, he trouped with Sousa during the 1921, 1922, and 1923 seasons.

The women of the Sousa Band also fared well. Virtually all of the violinists continued their careers as concert artists or as members of leading orchestras. Maud Powell, for example, became one of the world's greatest women violinists. The vocalists also made their marks. Marcella Lindh returned to Europe, settling in Budapest, and was soon an established operatic figure. Her husband was a noted industrialist and was knighted by King Franz Joseph of Hungary. Of all the sopranos, the most illustrious career belonged to Estelle Liebling. She was highly successful as an operatic singer, choral conductor, author, lecturer, composer, and arranger, but she is best remembered as an educator. Many notable sopranos benefited from her tutelage and publications.

Of the Sousa alumni entering the field of education, a number taught on the university level. Anton Horner, regarded as America's top French horn player during the forty years he was with the Philadelphia Orchestra, was also on the faculty of the Curtis Institute of Music; euphonium player A. J. Garing, after conducting the New York Hippodrome orchestra, was band director at the Georgia Institute of Technology. Trombonist Jaroslav Cimera, composer and author of several musical instruction books, was a member of Northwestern University's faculty; William J. Bell, tuba player, taught at Indiana University; and percussionist John J. Heney became director of the Stetson University Band. Cornetist Ernest Williams founded his own school, the Ernest Williams School of Music in New York City. He had previously been the director of several bands and orchestras as well as a faculty member at Ithaca College. He was also an author, composer, and arranger and was awarded an honorary Doctor of Music degree.

Arthur Pryor was not the only Sousa alumnus to enter the recording business. Cornetists Henry Higgins and Walter B. Rogers also became studio directors. Higgins was associated with Victor. Rogers was studio director for Paroquette, Emerson, Brunswick, and Victor, and he made a number of fine recordings with his own studio band. Jaraslov Cimera also started his own small recording company, and one of his releases was a recording of Sousa's voice which had been dubbed from a radio program.

Because of their age, only a few former Sousa men entered military service. Of those, clarinetist Howard C. Bronson had the distinction of holding the highest rank of any American military musician. As chief of the U.S. Army's music branch during World War II, he was a full colonel. Francis W. Sutherland also distinguished himself, rising to the rank of major as leader of the famed 7th Regiment (107th Infantry) Band of the New York National Guard. He was the first of the Sousa men to enlist in the U.S. Army during World War I and was leader of the 27th Division (104th Field Artillery) Band. Sousa composed "The Gallant Seventh" march in honor of Sutherland. Oscar B. Short, another Sousa cornetist, first with the U.S. Navy Band and then the U.S. Marine Band, blew taps at several ceremonies held at Sousa's grave. He shared this honor with Dana Garrett, another former Sousa cornetist.

Many Sousa men became conductors of civic or fraternal bands, but cornetist Birley Gardner's occupation was unique. After many years as soloist with the Long Beach Municipal Band, he became director of

Courtesy Norman E. Hinkel

Gus Helmecke, legendary bass drum specialist, was with Sousa for twenty-two years. Sousa often remarked that Helmecke had the heart of a great artist. He could produce a wide variety of sounds with his drum and even in his eighties he practiced for half an hour each day.

the Navaho Indian Band at Window Rock, Arizona. Among the directors of civic bands, cornetist Albertus Meyers led the Allentown (Pennsylvania) Band for over forty years; cornetist Russell D. Henegar led the Sioux Falls (South Dakota) Municipal Band, also for over forty years; clarinetist William P. Schueler became conductor of the Daytona Beach (Florida) Municipal Band; his brother, trombonist John P. Schueler, directed the Utica (New York) Civic Band; the genial and popular Donald Bassett, former clarinetist under Sousa, Pryor, and Simon, became conductor of the Dayton Municipal Band; saxophonist Arthur A. Rosander led the John Wanamaker Band of Philadelphia to the Paris International Exhibition Prize in 1927; Peter Buys, arranger and clarinetist, led the famed Hagerstown (Maryland) Municipal Band; flutist William Kunkel conducted the Albuquerque Municipal Band, Shrine Band, and Civic Symphony; flutist Joseph Lefter directed the Sunshine City Band at St. Petersburg; saxophonist Paul Christiansen directed the Huron (South Dakota) Municipal Band. And the list goes on and on.

Many former Sousa instrumentalists continued to grace the American scene by sticking with their respective instruments. Bass drum specialist August ("Gus") Helmecke retired at the age of eighty-two after literally pounding the life out of thirteen drums. He was percussionist with the Metropolitan Opera Orchestra for several seasons and was the mainstay of the famed Goldman Band in New York City until his retirement. William J. Bell, truly a virtuoso of the tuba and known as the "dean of American tuba players," not only played with many top symphony orchestras and bands but also became a noted composer and clinician. Euphonium player Simone Mantia had left Sousa to become assistant conductor of Pryor's Band but continued to be America's top euphonium player. He also maintained his proficiency on the trombone and was personnel manager of the Metropolitan Opera Orchestra for approximately twenty-five years. Also a personnel manager, French hornist Maurice van Praag was with the New York Philharmonic for thirty-six years. Cornetist Ernest Pechin was soloist with several top bands and orchestras before becoming a studio conductor for radio station WGN in New York City.

The above list of Sousa Band alumni is by no means complete. However, a full accounting for the careers of all former Sousa musicians is beyond the scope of this book. Even without a complete list, it is obvious that former Sousa musicians had a considerable impact on the music of America.

THE SOUSA BAND LIBRARY

The Sousa Band music library is believed to have been the largest privately owned collection of its kind. It was valued at $500,000, and what was not taken on tour was stored in New York City warehouses. The music

Courtesy William J. Bell

William J. Bell was such a sensation on the tuba that he held first chair with Sousa at the age of twenty-one. He left the Sousa Band in 1924 and eventually became America's most celebrated tuba player. He had an army of devoted students.

taken on tour was insured for values of up to $25,000. Sousa gave considerable thought to the disposition of the library during his final years. As early as 1924 he told newsmen that the bulk of it would be bequeathed to the Library of Congress and that the remainder would go to other public libraries, but he later changed his mind.[15]

The 1931 season was less than two weeks long, and it was probably then that Sousa made definite plans for the band library. He gave two portions to individuals, but the remainder was not disposed of until after his death. Today it may be considered as being divided into five distinct segments.

One segment, given away in 1931, had an interesting history. This was given to his associate and close friend Victor J. Grabel, who had been one of his bandmasters at the Great Lakes Naval Training Station during World War I. Sousa was especially pleased with the ambitious young Grabel's work, and the two became warm friends. The segment of the library given to him was that of the original Sousa Band, dating from 1892 to 1897. It had been forfeited to the heirs of manager David Blakely in the lawsuit following his death. In 1924 the Blakely heirs found themselves in financial straits and offered to sell it back to Sousa. He explained that he had since replaced it with newer music and that it was therefore obsolete and of little value to him. Nevertheless he bought it back for $500. This was then picked over; what little was of interest to him was added to the current band library, and the rest was put in storage. He took this out of storage and gave it to Grabel in 1931.

Grabel made good use of the music as conductor of the Chicago Concert Band. But a few years later he felt the effects of the depression and sold approximately two trunk loads of it to an associate, Louis Blaha, a school band director. When Blaha died the music was left to his school, the J. Sterling Morton High School in Cicero, Illinois, where it remains today. When this was catalogued in 1969, several missing Sousa manuscripts were discovered.

Grabel apparently kept the remainder of his Sousa library intact and donated it to Stetson University at Deland, Florida, early in 1945, when he became director of bands there. There was a total of thirty trunk loads—6,000 pounds—of music in this collection of over 1,400 selections. Grabel had evidently never catalogued the collection, so it was completely catalogued in 1966 at Stetson. As might be expected, many Sousa manuscripts turned up. In 1969 the Grabel library at Stetson was transferred to the U.S. Marine Corps Museum at Quantico, Virginia.

Another portion of the band library was given to A. Austin Harding at the University of Illinois at approximately the same time Grabel received his. This was a small collection of several dozen published selections, mostly Russian. Today Harding's music is in the custody of the Band Department of the University of Illinois at Champaign, Illinois.

[15] *Philadelphia Public Ledger*, July 25, 1924.

The most significant section of the band library was presented to the University of Illinois by Sousa's widow shortly after his death. Sousa had great admiration for the work of Harding and was of the opinion that the University of Illinois Band was the best college band in the world. Sousa and Harding had become good friends, and Sousa had promised to bequeath most of the band library to the university. In 1929 Sousa had dedicated his march "University of Illinois" to Harding and the university. There were forty trunk loads, or 18,000 pounds, of music in this segment of the library, most of which has been catalogued and filed in a special room at the University of Illinois Band Department building. There are approximately 4,000 selections.

The fifth and final segment of the Sousa Band library was the subject of much searching, and its whereabouts was not made public until 1967 when it was donated to the U.S. Marine Band in Washington, D.C. This portion consisted of slightly over 100 compositions plus the encore books of the band. Former members of the Sousa Band had fond memories of these books, and they were much discussed over the years. No one knew what had happened to them, and the speculation was often quite wild. There is, however, a logical explanation for their mysterious disappearance for over thirty-five years.

The complete Sousa Band library had not been stored in one place, but in three different New York City warehouses, presumably as a precautionary measure. At the first location was the section given to Grabel and, presumably, that given to Harding. At the second location was the greater part of the library, that which was bequeathed to the University of Illinois. The encore books were not at this location, and the band's librarian, Clarence ("Buss") Russell, could not account for their whereabouts. For years several of the former Sousa men had intimated that Russell had kept them for himself. This was far from the truth, however. Actually, the encore books and the other music with them had been stored in two trunks in a third location, unknown even to Sousa's immediate family. These trunks went unclaimed at the warehouse until 1940, at which time they were purchased with other unclaimed articles by Reginald Walker, a neighbor of the Sousas, for the price of storage costs. Several years later they became the possession of Walker's son, Charles Hyde Walker. While the son was playing in the high school band at Port Washington, New York, the music was used occasionally by his band. Then in 1967 Walker donated the music to the U.S. Marine Band. A public announcement was made on the anniversary of Sousa's birth on November 6. The only Sousa manuscript found in this collection was the band score of "The Liberty Bell" march.

THE SOUSA BAND FRATERNAL SOCIETY

When Patrick S. Gilmore died in 1892, his bandsmen so cherished his memory that they engaged a succession of conductors and kept the

Courtesy Leonard B. Smith

Twelve years after Sousa's death his former musicians organized the Sousa Band Fraternal Society. They meet each year in New York City on the Saturday nearest his birthday. Shown here is the 1954 meeting, marking the hundredth anniversary of Sousa's birth.

band alive periodically for several years. John Philip Sousa was held in even greater esteem by his bandsmen, but when he died in 1932 there was little opportunity for a revival of his band because of the depression of that era. But there was much consideration given to the possibility of forming a fraternal association, particularly by bandsmen in the New York area. The idea germinated for twelve years.

In the spring of 1944, seven former members of the Sousa Band gathered in Forest Hills, New York. The occasion was a dinner given in honor of Howard Bronson by Fred Gretsch, an instrument manufacturer. They talked seriously of formally organizing the much-discussed fraternal association. The Sousa men at this meeting were cornetists Eugene LaBarre and Francis W. Sutherland, percussionists August Helmecke and William T. Paulson, clarinetist Howard C. Bronson, bassoonist Sherley C. Thompson, and tuba player William J. Bell. Four other meetings were later held, two in Thompson's home in Forest Hills, and two at Steinway Hall in New York City. The last meeting at Steinway Hall, on September 13, 1944, was an organizational meeting, and the Sousa Band Fraternal Society was founded.

Courtesy Louis Morris

Many prominent musicians were members of the Philadelphia chapter of the Society. Clarinetist Louis Morris (far left), was Sousa's copyist. Saxophonist Rudolph Becker (seated, center), was a member of the original Sousa Band in 1892.

The new organization had as its purpose to reunite the former members of the band and to perpetuate the name of John Philip Sousa. It was agreed that they would hold annual dinner meetings in New York City on the anniversaries of Sousa's birth.[16] Membership was to be limited to those who had made at least one transcontinental tour with the band, but this requirement was relaxed to admit some who had not completed an entire tour. Although former bandsmen were widely scattered, a concerted effort was made to contact all Sousa alumni. By the time of the first annual dinner meeting, held at the Blue Ribbon Restaurant on November 6, 1944, there were seventy-seven members. By 1959 the membership had swelled to an all-time high of 235.

A Washington, D.C., chapter was also formed, and instead of dinner meetings, brief ceremonies were held at Sousa's grave. Another group held annual meetings in St. Petersburg, Florida. A Philadelphia chapter was also formed and was active until the early 1950s. In Los Angeles it was customary to arrange for a Sousa memorial concert to be played by the Long Beach Municipal Band just before its annual dinner.

The dinner meetings are pleasant and memorable, and several have been covered by the press. After the dinner and a business meeting, there is an afterglow. Each member present tells anecdotes based on his personal experiences in the band, and this can go on for hours. Fellowship is foremost, with bandsmen of different years comparing notes. Humorous stories involving Sousa are always the most popular.

Since the organization is comprised of men in their advanced years, it has little interest in sponsoring major projects. But it is always willing to assist in the promotion of Sousa memorial concerts, and in 1952 it lent its support to a bill in Congress which would have made "The Stars and Stripes Forever" the national march of the United States. To celebrate the one hundredth anniversary of Sousa's birth in 1954, the organization commissioned four composers to write marches for the occasion. The most ambitious project of the society has been their own cheerful newspaper, the *Sousa Band Fraternal Society News*, published "every now and then." Its three editors have given unselfishly of their time to make it a success: Sherley C. Thompson (1944-1949),[17] Eugene Slick (1949-1967), and Edmund C. Wall (1967-).

The Society consists exclusively of former Sousa Band members. The only exceptions have been Sousa's two daughters, who were made honorary members. In 1947 some of the Philadelphia members proposed that the membership be extended to descendants of Sousa Band alumni, but this was voted down. The issue has been brought up several other times but has been consistently rejected. It has also been proposed several times that former members of Sousa's navy band at Great Lakes be

[16] This has since been changed to the Saturday nearest Sousa's birthday.

[17] Thompson was co-editor of *The Official Encyclopedia of Baseball*.

Courtesy Harold B. Stephens and Leon E. Weir

Many Sousa alumni drifted to sunny California, as can be seen by the number attending this 1946 dinner meeting of the Sousa Band Fraternal Society's Los Angeles chapter.

admitted, but this too has been consistently voted down. The members have decided that the organization should go down in history as a "last man's" organization.

Some day a solitary Sousa Band alumnus will travel to New York City and have a dinner in honor of his beloved former bandmaster. This will mark the expiration of the Sousa Band Fraternal Society, an organization unique in the annals of American music.

6
Marching On

Considering that John Philip Sousa was not only the most popular musician of an era but a dedicated patriot as well, it is only proper that his countrymen have honored his memory in many different ways. Almost immediately after his death efforts were begun to erect memorials of one type or another. Appropriately, musicians themselves were responsible for the most impressive of these—the Sousa Stage in the John F. Kennedy Center for the Performing Arts in Washington—but it took thirty-six years to overcome obstacles.

The first attempt to erect a Sousa memorial in Washington, D.C., came in 1933. It was ill-timed, however, because of the country's depression, and the memorial never progressed beyond the planning stage.

Five years later, in 1938, a grandiose memorial was planned. The American Federation of Musicians and ASCAP were among the more powerful organizations behind this effort.[1] At first they planned to build a home for retired musicians, but being optimistic, they set their goal at $750,000 for an elaborate auditorium in Washington to be known as Sousa Memorial Auditorium. To stimulate interest, a series of radio broadcasts was planned, and the Mutual Broadcasting Company made good their promise of carrying the initial broadcast. The country's financial status had again been miscalculated, however, and the directors of the memorial were forced to capitulate. All that remains of this memorial is a bronze model statue of Sousa and a marble decorative seat. The

[1] Benjamin A. Rolfe of the ABA spearheaded this movement, assisted by bandmasters Arthur Pryor, Edwin Franko Goldman, Francis Sutherland, and Joseph Maddy; Gene Buck, President of ASCAP; and Joseph N. Weber, President of the American Federation of Musicians. Among other sponsors were Alfred E. Smith, Governor of New York; Fiorello LaGuardia, Mayor of New York City; news commentator Lowell Thomas; cartoonist Robert L. Ripley; Eugene Mayer, publisher of the *Washington Post*; and the Conn Instrument Corporation.

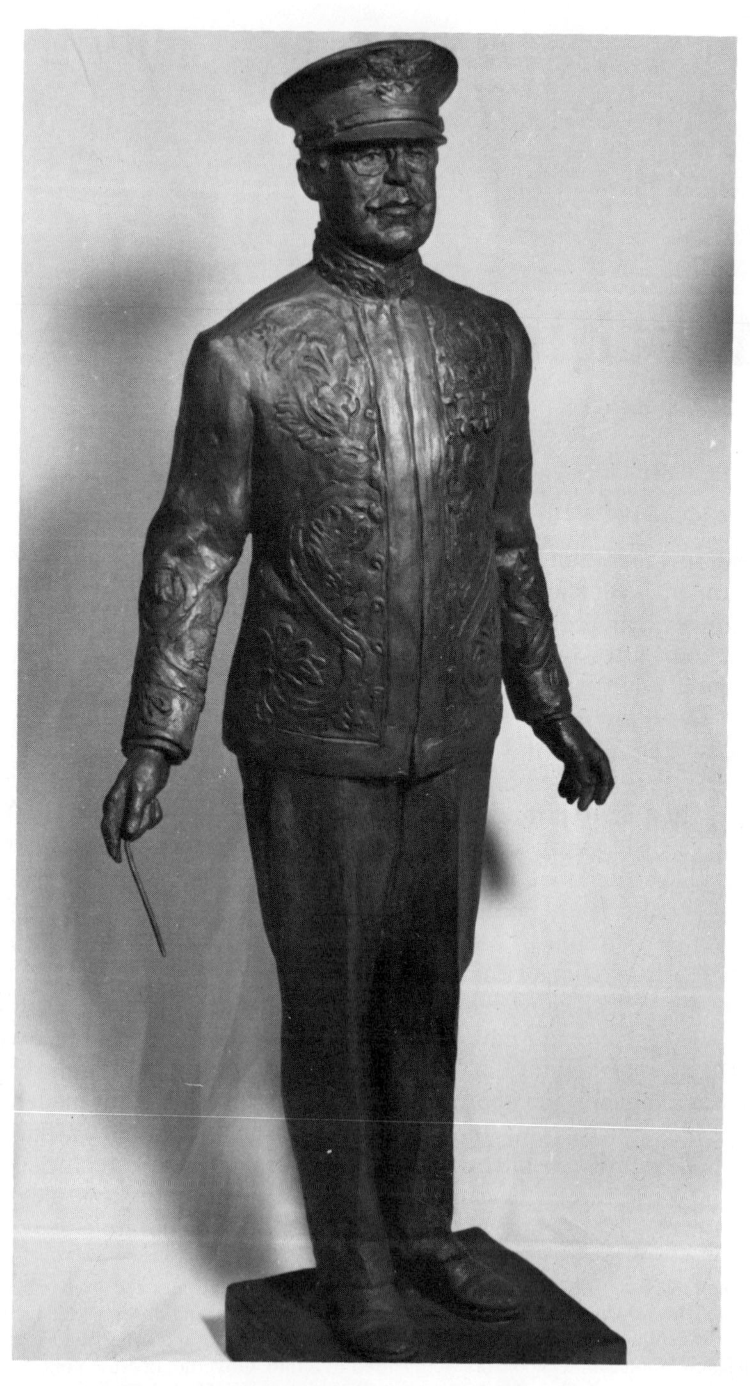

Walter Russell's miniature bronze statue was the model for a statue in the proposed Sousa Memorial Auditorium of 1938.

statue became a family treasure, and the marble seat was used as a monument for Sousa's grave in Congressional Cemetery. Both were the work of the noted sculptor Walter Russell.

In 1955 the American Federation of Musicians renewed interest in a Sousa memorial. Little was accomplished until the American Bandmasters Association entered the scene, headed by Lt. Col. William F. Santelmann, retired director of the U.S. Marine Band. They proposed that Sousa's former home at 318 Independence Avenue, SE (now B Street), be made into a museum.[2] This met with the approval of Sousa's two daughters, who offered the property and agreed to donate manuscripts and other memorabilia. Two bills were introduced in the House of Representatives to provide for the preservation and maintenance of the building.[3] But after the building was vandalized and later condemned, the Sousa family had it restored and then sold it.

Lt. Col. George S. Howard, retired director of the U.S. Air Force Band, and Mr. James L. Dixon, a Washington realtor, became cochairmen of the Sousa Memorial Committee, and in 1963 it was decided that the Sousa memorial should be a part of the proposed John F. Kennedy Center for the Performing Arts. The first plans called for a band shell with an all-weather rooftop. But as the design of the center developed, it was deemed more appropriate to use the stage of the concert hall as a memorial, with plaques indicating the names of donors.

Contributions for the Sousa Stage came from all over the world, but mostly they came from United States school bands, which held hundreds of Sousa memorial concerts in a nationwide fund-raising campaign. Their goal of $100,000 was met in 1969, and this was matched by government funds. The American musician's dream of a memorial to Sousa, begun in 1933, was finally realized.[4]

While the musicians' early efforts were in progress, many other Sousa memorials sprang up. The first was the John Philip Sousa Memorial Fountain in Philadelphia's Willow Grove Park, near the pavilion where Sousa's Band had played for so many seasons. The huge fountain was illuminated by colored floodlights and was dedicated in the summer of 1934. It has since been razed.

Another fitting memorial, this one at the University of Illinois, progressed slowly but came to be recognized as an important Sousa shrine.

[2] This was the first home Sousa owned. He resided there from 1890 until 1892 while conductor of the U.S. Marine Band.

[3] H.R. 6983, May 8, 1961, and H.R. 8364, July 25, 1961. Another bill, H.R. 9027, September 1, 1961, would have named a new wing of the Library of Congress after Sousa. It was not built.

[4] Among other organizations joining in this final effort were the American School Band Directors Association, the College Band Directors National Association, the National Band Association, the National Catholic Bandmasters Association, ASCAP, the National Association of Band Instrument Manufacturers, various music publishers, Kappa Kappa Psi (music honorary), and the Sousa Band Fraternal Society.

Courtesy Col. George S. Howard

Bands all over the United States held Sousa memorial concerts to raise money for the Sousa Stage in the John F. Kennedy Center for the Performing Arts.

The beautiful illuminated John Philip Sousa Memorial Fountain in Willow Lake, at Willow Grove Park, was dedicated in 1934.

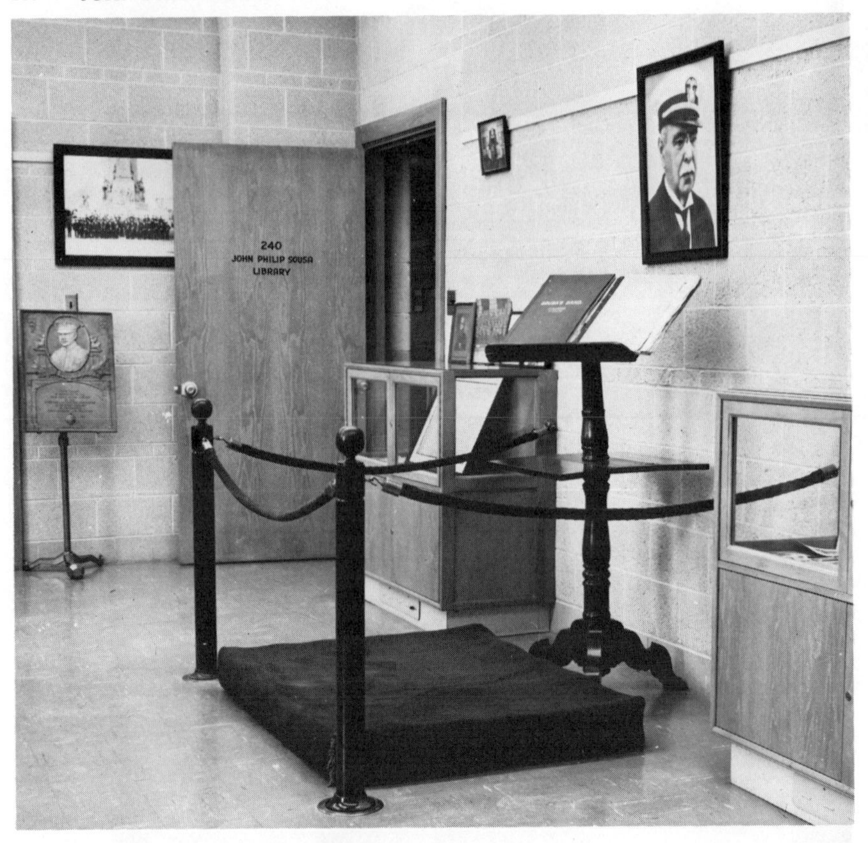

No one is permitted to stand on Sousa's podium at the University of Illinois, signifying that Sousa will never have a successor.

After a large part of the Sousa Band music library was donated to the university by Sousa's widow in 1932, manuscripts and other items were put on display in a room at the main library. When the Band Department acquired its own building in 1958, the present John Philip Sousa Library was established there. Sousa's podium and music stand are on display, as are many other items of interest. The Sousa Band library is stored in file cabinets along the walls.

The next Sousa memorial appeared in 1939 in the form of a bridge in Washington, D.C. The name "John Philip Sousa Bridge" was suggested by the Southeastern Citizens Association, and this was approved by Congress. The bridge crosses the eastern branch of the Potomac River, where Sousa hunted and fished as a boy.

Four public schools have been named for Sousa. The first, a junior high school in Washington, D.C., was built in 1950. The second was also a junior high school, built in 1957 in Port Washington, Long Island,

Courtesy Maj. Edward D. Connin

The John Philip Sousa Bridge in Washington crosses the Anacostia, or eastern branch of the Potomac River, on Pennsylvania Avenue. Sousa is buried nearby in Congressional Cemetery.

Irvin Simon

The John Philip Sousa Junior High School in Port Washington, New York, is one of four schools named for Sousa.

New York. Still another junior high school, in the Bronx, New York, and an elementary school, in Chicago, were built in 1959.

Another memorial was dedicated on Sousa's birthday in 1961 by the publishers of the newspaper he helped make famous by his march "The Washington Post." This memorial took the form of a meeting room and is called the John Philip Sousa Community Room.

A memorial of a different nature was dedicated in 1967: the John Philip Sousa Memorial Shrine located within a museum atop the Foshay Building in Minneapolis. Sousa composed a march on the occasion of the dedication of the building in 1929 ("Foshay Tower Washington Memorial"), and the story of Sousa's association with William B. Foshay is told in the form of a display in the museum.

It was inevitable that an outdoor band shell would bear Sousa's name, and such a band shell was constructed in 1967. It is the John Philip Sousa Memorial Band Shell in Port Washington, near Sousa's

Val Gelo

The John Philip Sousa Memorial Band Shell in Port Washington's Sunset Park is a reality largely because of the inspired efforts of Mrs. William V. Pearsall.

Long Island home. The idea originated in World War II, when it was proposed to honor Port Washington High School members serving in the armed forces, but the project did not gather momentum until 1963, when Mrs. William V. Pearsall started a concentrated drive. She gained the support of American Legion Post 509 and its auxiliary and worked tirelessly until the band shell became a reality.

Port Washington remembers Sousa in many ways. There is not only the Sousa band shell and the Sousa school, but there is also a street called Sousa Drive. And among commemorative trees in the community, an oak tree and a linden tree were planted in his honor. The Cow Neck Historical Society (Port Washington Historical Society) has a Sousa room with a display of memorabilia donated by the Sousa family and other individuals.

By far the largest collection of Sousa memorabilia is found in a section of the U.S. Marine Corps Museum—the Band Americana Collection. This collection, the creation of MGySgt. Joan Ambrose, is located in Washington, D.C., at the Navy Yard. It includes the former Grabel library of music from the original Sousa Band library, the Sousa Band encore books, copies of Sousa's published works, and the bulk of his personal library of rare books. It also includes many of his medals, trophies, and other career mementos, as well as an assortment of photographs, batons, and personal effects. Of much interest to scholars are the eighty-five Sousa Band press books and a few of the band's financial records.

In addition to the various memorials, Sousa has been honored in many other ways—for example, by countless memorial concerts and "tribute to Sousa" half-time shows at football games. Many special Sousa concerts have been held by those of his former bandsmen who became conductors of their own bands. The Ringgold Band of Reading, Pennsylvania, the band conducted by Sousa the evening before he died, presents a Sousa memorial concert each year on the anniversary of his death. Another annual Sousa memorial concert is held in New York by members of the John Philip Sousa American Legion Post No. 1112. This post is an all-musician post, and all its members belong to Local 802, American Federation of Musicians, the local to which Sousa belonged. The New York City post was chartered in 1933 and was the first of two American Legion posts to be named after Sousa. A second one, Post 770 in Chester, Pennsylvania, was named for Sousa in 1945 but was renamed the Glenn Miller Post in 1946.[5]

Another annual event honoring Sousa is the ceremony held at his grave on the anniversary of his birth. Surprisingly, these ceremonies are not planned by any one individual or organization. Each year at least

[5] Research done by C. W. Geile, Director of Internal Affairs, The American Legion National Headquarters.

Without fail, some organization or individual places a wreath on Sousa's grave on the anniversary of his birth.

one wreath is placed on his grave. Among those holding the ceremonies have been the U.S. Marine Band, the Boy Scouts of America, the Sousa Band Fraternal Society, Almas Temple Shrine of Washington, and members of Sousa's family.

An annual affair of another nature, which honors many young musicians as well as Sousa, is the presentation of the John Philip Sousa Band Awards. Begun in 1954, this event is sponsored by the publishers of *Instrumentalist* magazine. Approximately four thousand awards each year are bestowed on high school bandsmen who have displayed superior musicianship and outstanding character and cooperation. The winners are usually selected by their fellow bandsmen by secret ballot. They are awarded medals and their names are inscribed on plaques bearing the names of previous recipients.

Several activities marked the hundredth anniversary of Sousa's birth in 1954. Memorial concerts were performed throughout America and music journals carried much Sousa lore. By coincidence, the copyright of "The Stars and Stripes Forever" had just expired, and dozens of new arrangements and transcriptions of the piece were published. Sousa's

Courtesy the *Instrumentalist*

Each year hundreds of outstanding high-school musicians receive the John Philip Sousa Band Award.

daughters deemed this the proper time to donate many of their father's manuscripts to the Library of Congress, and an impressive program was held there when the manuscripts and other articles were displayed. The Sousa Band Fraternal Society held its most memorable meeting that year and commissioned four composers to write new marches, as mentioned in the preceding chapter.[6] A significant honor also came from abroad. Sculptor Arnold Hartig created a medal of Sousa at the request of the

[6] These were "John Philip Sousa Centennial" (William Letcher), "The March King" (Leonard B. Smith), "March Nonpareil" (Charles O'Neill), and "Sousa Band Fraternal March" (Peter Buys).

Courtesy Kenneth Berger and Edward M. Petrushka

A centennial medallion was struck by the Austrian Mint in 1954.

Austrian Mint, and a commemorative medallion was struck. Frank Simon, former Sousa Band cornetist, personally awarded many of these to bands which presented Sousa memorial concerts.

Over the years many individuals have felt that "The Stars and Stripes Forever" merited official government recognition. Ten bills proposing that the march be named the national march of the Unites States were introduced in Congress.[7] All failed, however, because of disjointed efforts and lack of effective planning. The sponsors did not solicit adequate nationwide support, and Congressmen interpreted this to mean that the general public was not wholeheartedly demanding such action. Also, they

[7] H.R. 10369, 1932; H.J. Res. 278, 1932; H.J. Res. 117, 1933; H.J. Res. 246, 1935; H. Res. 118, 1935; H.J. Res. 368, 1937; S.J. Res. 160, 1954; S.J. Res. 47, 1955; H.J. Res. 270, 1955; and H.J. Res. 81, 1957.

Twentieth-Century-Fox

The Twentieth-Century-Fox movie of 1952, *Stars and Stripes Forever*, was based on Sousa's career and featured Clifton Webb as Sousa. Co-stars were Debra Paget, Robert Wagner, and Ruth Hussey.

did not see a need for both a national anthem and a national march. Another factor in the bills' failure was that some of the march's copyrights were still active.

Sousa's life has been documented several times in the form of movies. The most significant was the Twentieth-Century-Fox movie of 1952, *Stars and Stripes Forever*, in which Clifton Webb played the role of Sousa. After running for several years in movie houses, its life was extended by television showings. Although it was popular with the public, a handful of informed persons were critical of the lack of historical accuracy. The movie covered seven years of Sousa's life, commencing with his discharge from the Marine Corps in 1892, and focused on the first years of the Sousa Band. Sousa's daughter Helen felt that her father was cast as an ineffective man,[8] and a few former members of the Sousa Band were highly critical of Webb's portrayal of Sousa as a conductor.[9] The public was unaware of these inaccuracies, however, and the movie was a noteworthy success.

Among other films of Sousa's life was *Sound of a Giant*, written and produced in 1966 by Thomas E. Simonton for television station WRC in Washington, D.C. Another was *Marching Along with Sousa*, produced in 1956 by the famed bandmaster Raymond F. Dvorak of the University of Wisconsin. The most impressive of the documentary films was *The March King: John Philip Sousa*, produced in 1969 by Kenneth Corden of the British Broadcasting Corporation for the series known as "Workshop." This was an hour-long film for which the Detroit Concert Band, under the direction of Dr. Leonard B. Smith, was selected to make the sound track and pose as the Sousa Band for some of the scenes.[10]

[8] Letter from Mrs. Helen Sousa Abert to the Sousa Band Fraternal Society dated December 14, 1952, printed in the *Sousa Band Fraternal Society News*, January, 1953. In this letter she revealed that the movie's producers had negotiated with her mother as early as 1943 but had been discouraged by Mrs. Sousa's restrictions. After Mrs. Sousa died, Mrs. Abert lifted many of the restrictions. In her criticism she said, ". . . It is as if they had been handed a blueprint of a jet plane, and had come up with a mousetrap, and not even a better mousetrap.

[9] In the preparation of this book, the author had several interviews with Dr. Frank Simon, former Sousa Band cornet soloist and assistant conductor. In an interview on November 13, 1964, Dr. Simon said that approximately forty Sousa Bandmen had been invited to a preview and that several of them walked out in disgust. He stated that some of them actually wept because they felt Sousa had been improperly portrayed.

[10] This selection was based on Dr. Smith's reputation of keeping the Sousa march style alive. Another factor in the selection was the opinion of several knowledgeable persons who felt that Smith's band was the finest civilian band in the world and therefore the most logical choice. Broadcasts of the Detroit Concert Band have for many years featured seldom-heard Sousa marches as well as the perennial favorites. For this documentary program the band was augmented to sixty-six men to simulate the size and appearance of the Sousa Band. The tuba section included America's foremost tuba player, William J. Bell, former first tuba player of Sousa's Band and one of the few remaining Sousa musicians still performing. The author was privileged to play in this same section.

New York City Ballet

Hershy Kay's *Stars and Stripes Ballet* is based on ten Sousa marches. The work was conceived by its choreographer, George Balanchine.

The "Famous American" series of postage stamps was issued in 1940. The composers represented were Sousa, MacDowell, Herbert, Foster, and Nevin.

Of many radio programs devoted to Sousa's life and career, one of the finest was "In Search of Sousa." This program included several interviews with former Sousa Band musicians and was produced for the Canadian Broadcasting Corporation in 1966 by Tony Thomas.

It would be difficult—if not impossible—to list all the musical compositions dedicated to Sousa. Most of those written after his death were medleys or paraphrases of his marches, but many of those written during his lifetime were original compositions. The best known of the paraphrases is "Tribute to Sousa," by Maurice C. Whitney. The most notable original composition based on Sousa's marches is Hershy Kay's *Stars and Stripes Ballet*. This was commissioned by the New York City Ballet for its 1957-1958 season. Its lively and gay strains are in keeping with the character of Sousa's music, and it has been well received.

There have been in the past or are today many other memorials to Sousa, such as the American postage stamp bearing his likeness, a World War II Liberty ship bearing his name, and the ever-present sousaphone. Sousa's first and last homes—his birthplace in Washington,

Official Coast Guard photograph, Courtesy
Mariners Museum, Newport News, Virginia

The S.S. *John Philip Sousa* was a World War II Liberty ship.

D.C., and his Sands Point home—have plaques denoting their historical importance.[11]

Of all the memorials erected to musicians, Sousa's living memorial—the Sousa Band Fraternal Society—is unique. When a conductor's musicians honor him by annual meetings decades after his death, his profound influence on their lives may be appreciated. Perhaps their humble memorial meetings are the greatest tribute of all.

It is somewhat ironic that the Sousa Band Fraternal Society has excluded from its membership those navy musicians who served under Sousa during World War I, for many of them were better men for having passed through his sphere of influence. Victor J. Grabel, for instance, who became one of America's foremost bandmasters, wrote this moving tribute shortly after Sousa's death:

> After John Philip Sousa—there is no other. Bandmaster pre-eminent; composer of unrivaled popularity; sterling patriot; ardent sportsman; accomplished writer; charming storyteller; gentleman supreme—tho honored by presidents and kings, and decorated by many foreign governments, he remained the simplest and most kindly of men. . . .
>
> Sousa's Band—a name of magical import! . . . Without the genius and personality of John Philip Sousa it could never have become a reality—without his guiding hand it passes into that eternal silence where are stored our most treasured memories.
>
> Affectionately known as the "March King," his real kingdom was in the hearts of all music lovers—his crown jewelled with kindly deeds.
>
> Now he is gone—and there is no other.[12]

[11] The plaque on the birthplace was donated by the Capitol Hill Restoration Society. The Sands Point home bears a plaque of the U.S. Department of the Interior.
[12] *American Bandmasters Annual*, 1932.

APPENDIX 1
The Works of John Philip Sousa

Operettas (15)

The American Maid (The Glass Blowers) (1909)
The Bride Elect (1897)
El Capitan (1895)
The Charlatan (The Mystical Miss) (1898)
Chris and the Wonderful Lamp (1899)
Desiree (1883)
The Devil's Deputy (unfinished) (1893)
Florine (unfinished) (1881)
The Free Lance (1905)
The Irish Dragoon (1915)
Katherine (1879)
The Queen of Hearts (1885)
The Smugglers (1882)
The Victory (unfinished) (1915)
The Wolf (1888)

Marches (136)

"Across the Danube" (Opus 36) (1877)
"America First" (1916)
"Anchor and Star" (1918)
"Ancient and Honorable Artillery Company" (1924)
"The Atlantic City Pageant" (1927)
"The Aviators" (1931)
"The Beau Ideal" (1893)
"The Belle of Chicago" (1892)
"Ben Bolt" (1888)
"The Black Horse Troop" (1924)
"Bonnie Annie Laurie" (1883)
"Boy Scouts of America" (1916)
"The Bride Elect" (1897)
"Bullets and Bayonets" (1919)
"El Capitan" (1896)
"A Century of Progress" (1931)
"The Chantyman's March" (1918)
"The Charlatan" (1898)
"The Circumnavigators Club" (1931)
"Columbia's Pride" (1914)
"Comrades of the Legion" (1920)
"Congress Hall" (1882)
"Corcoran Cadets" (1890)
"The Crusader" (1888)
"Daughters of Texas" (1929)
"The Dauntless Battalion" (1922)
"The Diplomat" (1904)
"The Directorate" (1894)
"Esprit de Corps" (Opus 45) (1878)
"The Fairest of the Fair" (1908)
"The Federal" (1910)
"Flags of Freedom" (1918)
"La Flor de Sevilla" (1929)
"Foshay Tower Washington Memorial" (1929)
"The Free Lance" (1906)
"From Maine to Oregon" (1913)
"The Gallant Seventh" (1922)
"George Washington Bicentennial" (1930)
"The Gladiator" (1886)
"Globe and Eagle" (1879)
"The Glory of the Yankee Navy" (1909)
"Golden Jubilee" (1928)
"The Golden Star" (1919)
"The Gridiron Club" (1926)
"Guide Right" (1881)
"Hail to the Spirit of Liberty" (1900)

"Hands Across the Sea" (1899)
"Harmonica Wizard" (1930)
"The High School Cadets" (1890)
"Homeward Bound" (probably 1891 or 1892)
"The Honored Dead" (1876)
"Imperial Edward" (1902)
"In Memoriam" (1881)
"The Invincible Eagle" (1901)
"Jack Tar" (1903)
"Kansas Wildcats" (1931)
"Keeping Step with the Union" (1921)
"King Cotton" (1895)
"The Lambs' March" (1914)
"The Legionaires" (1930)
"The Liberty Bell" (1893)
"Liberty Loan" (1917)
"The Loyal Legion" (1890)
"Magna Charta" (1927)
"The Man Behind the Gun" (1899)
"Manhattan Beach" (1893)
"March of the Mitten Men" ("Power and Glory") (1923)
"March of the Pan Americans" (1916)
"March of the Royal Trumpets" (1892)
"Marquette University March" (1924)
"Mikado March" (1885)
"The Minnesota March" (1927)
"Mother Goose" (1883)
"Mother Hubbard March" (1885)
"National Fencibles" (1888)
"The National Game" (1925)
"The Naval Reserve" (1917)
"New Mexico" (1928)
"The New York Hippodrome" (1915)
"Nobles of the Mystic Shrine" (1923)
"The Northern Pines" (1931)
"The Occidental" (1887)
"Old Ironsides" (1926)
"On Parade" ("The Lion Tamer") (1892)
"On the Campus" (1920)
"On the Tramp" (1879)
"Our Flirtation" (1880)
"The Pathfinder of Panama" (1915)
"Pet of the Petticoats" (1883)
"The Phoenix March" (1875)
"The Picador" (1889)
"Powhattan's Daughter" (1907)
"President Garfield's Inauguration March" (Opus 131) (1881)
"The Pride of Pittsburgh" ("Homage to Pittsburgh") (1901)
"The Pride of the Wolverines" (1926)
"Prince Charming" (1928)
"The Quilting Party March" (1889)
"Recognition March" (1880 or before)
"Resumption March" (1879)
"Review" (Opus 5) (1873)
"Revival March" (1876)
"Riders for the Flag" (1927)
"The Rifle Regiment" (1886)
"Right Forward" (1881)
"Right-Left" (1883)
"The Royal Welch Fusiliers" (No. 1) (1929)
"The Royal Welch Fusiliers" (No. 2) (1930)
"Sabre and Spurs" (1918)
"Salutation" (1873)
"The Salvation Army" (1930)
"Semper Fidelis" (1888)
"Sesqui-Centennial Exposition March" (1926)
"Solid Men to the Front" (1918)
"Sound Off" (1885)
"The Stars and Stripes Forever" (1896)
"The Thunderer" (1889)
"Transit of Venus" (1883)
"The Triton" (1892)
"Triumph of Time" (1885)
"Universal Peace" (probably 1925 or 1926)
"University of Illinois" (1929)
"University of Nebraska" (1928)
"USAAC March" (1918)
"U.S. Field Artillery" (1917)
"The Victory Chest" (1918)
"The Volunteers" (1918)
"The Washington Post" (1889)
"Wedding March" (1918)
"The White Plume" (1884)
"The White Rose" (1917)
"Who's Who in Navy Blue" (1920)
"The Wildcats" (1930 or 1931)
"Wisconsin Forward Forever" (1917)

"The Wolverine March" (1881)
"Yorktown Centennial" (1881)
Untitled march (1930)

Suites (11)

At the King's Court (1904)
Camera Studies (1920)
Cubaland (1925)
Dwellers of the Western World (1910)
Impressions at the Movies (1922)
The Last Days of Pompeii (1893)
Leaves from My Notebook (1922)
Looking Upward (1902)
People Who Live in Glass Houses (1909)
Tales of a Traveler (1911)
Three Quotations (1895)

Descriptive Pieces (2)

"The Chariot Race" (1890)
"Sheridan's Ride" (1891)

Songs (70)

"Ah Me!" (poem by Emma M. Swallow) (Opus 29) (1876)
"Annabel Lee" (poem by Edgar Allan Poe) (1931)
"The Belle of Bayou Teche" (poem by O. E. Lynne) (1911)
"Blue Ridge, I'm Coming Back to You" (words by John Philip Sousa) (1917)
"Boots" (poem by Rudyard Kipling) (1916)
"Come Laugh and Be Merry" (words by ?) (1916)
"Crossing the Bar" (poem by Alfred Lord Tennyson) (1926)
"Day and Night" (words by Emma M. Swallow) (1873)
" 'Deed I Has to Laugh" (words by John Philip Sousa) (1877)
"Do We? We Do" (words by John Philip Sousa) (1889)
"Fall Tenderly, Roses" (words by John Philip Sousa) (probably late 1860s)
"The Fighting Race" (poem by J. I. C. Clarke) (1919)
"Forever and a Day" (words by Irving Bibo and John Philip Sousa) (1927)
"The Free Lunch Cadets" (words by John Philip Sousa) (1877)
"Hoping" (poem by Jefferson H. Nones) (Opus 39) (1877)
"I Love Jim" (words by Helen Sousa Abert) (circa 1916)
"I Wonder" (words by Edward M. Taber) (1888)
"In Flanders Fields the Poppies Grow" (poem by John D. McCrae) (1918)
"It Was Really Very Fortunate for Me" (words by Charles Brown) (1913)
"It's a Thing We Are Apt to Forget" (words by John Philip Sousa) (1900 or after)
"I've Made My Plans for the Summer" (words by John Philip Sousa) (1907)
"The Journal" (words by John Philip Sousa) (1924)
"Lonely" (poem by Jefferson H. Nones) (Opus 32) (1877)
"Love Me Little, Love Me Long" (words by John Philip Sousa) (Opus 37) (1877)
"Love That Comes When May-Roses Blow" (words by John Philip Sousa) (1889)
"The Love That Lives Forever" (words by George P. Wallihan) (1917)
"Lovely Mary Donnelly" (poem by William Allingham) (1918)
"Love's Radiant Hour" (words by Helen Boardman Knox) (1928)
"The Magic Glass" (poem by Charles Swain) (Opus 31) (1877)
"Maid of the Meadow" (words by John Philip Sousa) (1897)
"Mallie" (words by J. W. Heysinger) (n.d.)
"Mavourneen Asthore" (words by Albert S. Nones) (1878)
"The Milkmaid" (poem by Austin Dobson) (1914)
"My Own, My Geraldine" (poem by Francis C. Long) (1887)

"My Sweet Sweetheart" (words by Jack Nilpon) (n.d.)
"Nail the Flag to the Mast" (poem by William Russell Frisbie) (1890)
"O My Country" (words by B. Lowlaws) (1874)
"O Ye Lillies White" (poem by Francis C. Long) (1887)
"Only a Dream" (words by Mary A. Denison) (Opus 25) (1876)
"Only Thee (poem by Charles Swain) (Opus 24) (1876)
"O'Reilly's Kettledrum" (words by Edward M. Taber) (1889)
"Pretty Patty Honeywood" (poem by Cuthbert Bede) (1881)
"Pushing On" (words by Guy F. Lee) (1918)
"A Rare Old Fellow" (poem by Barry Cornwall) (1881)
"Reveille" (poem by Robert J. Burdette) (1890)
"Sea Nymph" (words by B. P. Wilmot) (n.d.)
"A Serenade in Seville" (words by James Francis Cooke) (1924)
"Smick, Smack, Smuck" (words by John Philip Sousa) (1878)
"The Song of the Dagger" (words by John Philip Sousa) (1916)
"The Song of the Sea" (words by Emma M. Swallow) (Opus 27) (1876)
"Star of Light" (poem by Bessie Beach) (1882)
"Stuffed Stork" (words by John Philip Sousa) (1894)
"Sweet Miss Industry" (poem by S. Conant Foster) (1887)
"Tally-Ho!" (poem by Joaquin Miller) (1885)
"There's a Merry Brown Thrush" (poem by Lucy Larcom) (1926)
"There's Something Mysterious" (words by Hunter MacCulloch) (1889)
"Though Dolly Is Married" (words by M. E. W.) (n.d.)
"The Toast" (words by R. H. Burnside) (1918)
"We Are Coming" (poem by Edith Willis Linn) (1918)
"We'll Follow Where the White Plume Waves" (words by Edward M. Taber) (1884)
"When He Is Near" (words by Mary A. Denison) (1880)
"When the Boys Come Sailing Home!" (words by Helen Sousa Abert) (1918)
"While Navy Ships Are Coaling" (poem by Wells Hawks) (1923)
"Wilt Thou Be True" (poem by E. Cook) (1873)
"The Window Blind" (words by Edward M. Taber) (1887)
"Yale Marching Song" (words by Joseph Grant Ewing) (1920)
"You'll Miss Lots of Fun When You're Married" (words by Edward M. Taber) (1890)
"2:15" (words by Edward M. Taber) (1889)
Untitled song (words by James Adams) (n.d.)
Untitled song (words by Emma M. Swallow) (1874)

Other Vocal Works (7)

"The Last Crusade" (ballad) (poem by Anne Higginson Spicer) (1920)
"The Messiah of Nations" (hymn) (poem by James Whitcomb Riley) (1902)
"Non-Committal Declarations" (vocal trio) (words by John Philip Sousa) (1920)
"Oh, Why Should the Spirit of Mortal Be Proud?" (hymn) (poem by William Knox) (1899)
"Te Deum in B-Flat" (words by John Philip Sousa) (Opus 12) (1874)
"The Trooping of the Colors" (pageant) (1898)
"We March, We March to Victory" (processional hymn) (words by Gerard Moultrie) (1914)

Waltzes (11)

"The Coeds of Michigan" (1925)
"The Colonial Dames Waltzes" (1896)
"Intaglio Waltzes" (1884)
"The Lady of the White House" (1897)
"Moonlight on the Potomac Waltzes" (Opus 3) (1872)
"Paroles d'Amour Valses" (1880)
"La Reine d'Amour Valses" (Opus 9) (1874)
"La Reine de la Mer Valses" (1886)
"Sandalphon Waltzes" (1886)
"Sardanapolis" (1877)
"Wissahickon Waltz" (1885)

Various Dance Forms (13)

"Alexander" (gavotte) (1876 or 1877)
"The Coquette" (caprice) (1887)
"Cuckoo" (galop) (1873)
"The Gliding Girl" (tango) (1912)
"Love's But a Dance, Where Time Plays the Fiddle" (fox trot) (1923)
"Myrrha Gavotte" (Opus 30) (1876)
"On Wings of Lightning" (galop) (Opus 26) (1876)
"Peaches and Cream" (fox trot) (1924)
"Presidential Polonaise" (1886)
"Queen of the Harvest" (quadrille) (1889)
"Silver Spray Schottische" (1878)
"With Peasure" ("dance hilarious") (1912)

Humoresques (14)

"Among My Souvenirs" (1928)
"The Band Came Back" (1895)
"Follow the Swallow" (1926)
"Gallagher and Shean" (1923)
"Good-bye" (1892)
"A Little Peach in an Orchard Grew" (1885)
"Look for the Silver Lining" (1922)
"The Mingling of the Wets and Drys" (1926)
"Oh, How I've Waited for You" (1926)
"Showing Off Before Company" (1919)
"Smiles" (1919)
"The Stag Party" (circa 1885)
"Swanee" (1920)
"What Do You Do Sunday, Mary?" (1924)

Fantasies for Band (20)

"Assembly of the Artisans" (1925)
"The Blending of the Blue and the Gray" (1877)
"The Fancy of the Town" (1921)
"In Parlor and Street" (1880)
"In Pulpit and Pew" (1917)
"In the Realm of the Dance" ("In the Realm of the Waltz") (1902)
"Jazz America" (1925)
"The Merry-Merry Chorus" (1923)
"Music of the Minute" (1922)
G8r" (1922)
(1916)
with the Dance" (1923)
"Rose, Thistle and Shamrock" ("Patrol of the United Kingdom") (1901)
"The Salute of the Nations" (1893)
"Songs of Grace and Songs of Glory" (1892)
"Sounds from the Revivals" (1876)
"A Study in Rhythms" (1920)
"Tipperary" (1915)
"Tyrolienne" (between 1880 and 1892)
"When My Dreams Come True" (1929)

Fantasies for Orchestra (3)

"In the Sweet Bye and Bye" (1876)
"The International Congress" (1876)
"Medley" (1877)

Fantasies for Individual Instruments (4)

"Adamsonia" (violin, flute, or cornet) (1879)
"Home, Sweet Home" (violin, flute, or cornet) (1879)
"Out of Work" (violin or flute) (1880)
"Under the Eaves" (violin or flute) (1880)

Incidental Music (6)

Cheer Up (1916)
Everything (1918)

Hip Hip Hooray (1915)
Matt Morgan's Living Pictures (1876)
Our Flirtations (1880)
The Phoenix (1875)

Overtures (4)

"The Lambs' Gambol" (1914)
"Rivals" (1877)
"Tally-Ho!" (1886)
"Vautour" (Sans Souci) (1886)

Concert Pieces (2)

"The Summer Girl" (1901)
"Willow Blossoms" (1916)

Instrumental Solos (4)

"An Album Leaf" (violin) (circa 1863)
"Belle Mahone" (saxophone) (1885)
"Nymphalin" (violin) (1880)
"La Reine d'Amour" (cornet) (1879)

Trumpet and Drum Pieces (12)

"Four Marches for Regimental Drums and Trumpets" (1884)
"Funeral March" (1886)
"Gallant and Gay We'll March Away" (1886)
"Good Bye, Sweet Nannie Magee" (1886)
"Hannah, My True Love" (1886)
"Here's Your Health, Sir!" (1886)
"Hurrah! We Are Almost There" (1886)
"Waltz" (1886)
"With Steady Step" (1886)

Arrangements and Transcriptions (322)

Classical works	69
Operetta orchestrations	6
Opera and operetta arrangements for piano	15
Various dance forms	16
Songs	54
Instrumental solos or ensembles	119
Marches	11
Miscellaneous compositions	32

Books (7)

The Fifth String (novel) (1902)
Marching Along (autobiography) (1928)
National, Patriotic and Typical Airs of All Lands (compilation) (1890)
Pipetown Sandy (novel) (1905)
Through the Year with Sousa (almanac) (1910)
The Transit of Venus (novel) (1919)
The Trumpet and Drum (a handbook of instruction for the field-trumpet and drum) (1886)

Articles (132)

"According to Sousa," *Daily Express* (London), January 11, 1905.
"All's Well with the Musical World," *Wurlitzer Magazine* (Cincinnati), December 10, 1920.
"American Music in Paris," wire service article, May 12, 1900.
"American Musical Taste," in *Modern Music and Musicians*, part 2, vol. 3, 1912.
"Appreciations of Rachmaninoff from Famous Musicians in America," *Etude*, October, 1919.
"As to Military Bands," *Independent*, September 2, 1897.
"The Band," *American Bandsman*, November 15, 1908.
"Being a Musician," *Circle*, September, 1909.
"The Business of the Bandmaster," *Criterion*, August, 1905.
"A Century of Music," *New York World*, December 31, 1899.

"Commander John Philip Sousa Tells of His Tour with the Offenbach Orchestra," *Etude*, July, 1930.
"Development of Military Band," *Focus* (New York), February 7, 1903.
"Differences of Opinion as to Correct Metronomic Tempo Indications," *Metronome*, April, 1917.
"The Experiences of a Bandmaster," *Youth's Companion*, September 27, 1900.
"A Fable with a Moral," *M.A.P.* (London), January or February, 1911.
"Facetiae in Music," *Town Topics* (New York), December 12, 1907.
"Following the Band," *Country Gentleman*, September, 1928.
"The Force of Music," *American Legion Weekly*, September 1, 1922.
"From the Gardens of Paradise to the Great Industrial Plants," *Etude*, June, 1923.
"The Future of Grand Opera in America," *Sun* (New York), August 10, 1913.
"The Future of Music in America," *Pacific Monthly*, May, 1899.
"The Greatest Game in the World," *Baseball Magazine*, February, 1909.
"Here's Sousa's First Self-Written Interview," *Los Angeles Times*, October 16, 1911.
"His Experiences as a Bandmaster," *Pearson's Weekly* (London), April, 1903.
"A Horse, a Dog, a Gun, and a Girl," *American Shooter*, August 15, 1916.
"How I Built the Sousa Band," *Life* (Australia), January 9, 1911.
"How I Earned My Musical Education," *Etude*, November, 1908.
"How to Make Programs," *Musical Record*, December, 1893.
"The Ideal Band," *Independent*, January 25, 1900.
"If I Had to Begin All Over Again," *Etude*, December, 1916.
"I'm Not Saying Good-Bye," *Pearson's Weekly* (London), September 1, 1911.
"In the Days of My Youth," *M.A.P.* (London), October 19, 1901.
"Jazz Will Never Replace Great American Marches," wire service article, April 27-28, 1928.
"John Philip Sousa on Trap Shooting in America," *Sketch* (London), January 18, 1911.
"Keeping Time" (six-part autobiography), *Saturday Evening Post*, November 7, 14, 21, 28, 1924; December 5, 12, 1925.
"King David First Bandmaster," *Spokane Chronicle*, August 6, 1915.
"The King of Instruments?" *Etude*, April, 1932.
"Leave German Music to Germans," *Musical Leader*, October 10, 1918.
"Let's Go Down the Highroad of Music—Together," *Music Magazine*, September, 1929.
"Making America More Musical," *Woman's Home Companion*, July, 1925.
"The March King Answers Questions from Beginners" (26 articles), *Chicago Daily News*, *Cleveland News*, and *Detroit News*, 1927-1928.
"The Menace of Mechanical Music," *Appleton's Magazine*, September, 1906.
"Misplaced Men Drag Way Through Life," wire service article, October, 1922.
"The Most Familiar Melody in the World," *Great Lakes Recruit*, March, 1918.
"Music, an Ideal Christmas Present," *Etude*, December, 1921.
"Music Becomes a Profession," 1926 Sousa Band souvenir program.
"Music We Must Have," *Chicago Tribune*, November 23, 1890.
"Musical Instruments Like Men in Disposition," *Northward-Ho!*, September (?), 1912.

"My Contention," *Music Trades*, Christmas Issue, 1906.
"My Dreadful Past," *Pearson's Weekly* (London), September 3, 1911.
"My Hobby—Trapshooting," *Country Life in America*, June, 1914.
"Oh, Listen to the Band!" Sousa Band souvenir program, 1920.
"Parents of Patriotism Are Mother and Music," *Chicago Examiner*, March 7, 1918.
"Playing 'The Star Spangled Banner' 'Round the World," *Ladies' Home Journal*, December, 1917.
"Queer Instruments in the Modern Military Band," wire service article, November, 1902.
"Ready! Pull! Dead!" *New York Sun*, June 14, 1914.
"Sidelights on Music," *Pittsburgh Dispatch*, September 18, 1907.
"Songs of a Century That Never Grow Old" (22 articles), wire service articles, 1924.
"Songs of the Sea," *Great Lakes Recruit*, December, 1917.
"Sousa on the Influence of the Band in Musical Education," *Metropolitan Magazine*, July, 1900.
"Sousa—Who Has Made $1,000,000 with His Brass Band," *Farm and Fireside*, January, 1924.
"The Star Spangled Banner in Petrograd," *New York Telegram*, circa 1916.
"Start with a Tune," *Evening Mail* (New York), October 14, 1921.
"Success in Music and How to Win It," in advertising booklet of C. G. Conn Ltd., 1926.
"The Symphony Orchestra and the Concert Band," *Etude*, May, 1917.
"Then and Now," *Etude*, May, 1921.
"The Ultimate Musical Choice," *Etude*, July, 1930.
"The Victrola and I," *Victor Talking Machine Magazine*, December, 1920.
"The Wave of Musical Creation Will Next Reach America," wire service article, October, 1913.
"We Must Have Standard Instrumentation," *Musical Observer*, July, 1930.
"What the Band Means to Your Home Community," *Etude*, September, 1931.
"What Constitutes True Beauty in a Woman," *Great Lakes Recruit*, January, 1918.
"What Every Music Lover Should Know About the Band," *Etude*, February, 1927.
"What Our National Anthem Should Be," *New York Times*, August 26, 1928.
"What 'Rag Time' Means," *New York World*, April 7, 1901.
"When the Band Begins to Play," *American Legion Monthy*, July, 1931.
"Where Is Jazz Leading America?" *Etude*, August, 1924.
"Why Not Give Music This Christmas?" *Better Homes and Gardens*, December, 1930.
"Why the World Needs Bands," *Etude*, September, 1930.
"A Word as to Orchestration," *Music*, March, 1897.
"The Year in Music," *Town Topics* (New York), December 6, 1906.

Letters-to-the-Editor (20)

Augusta (Georgia) *Chronicle*, March 17, 1916.
Boston News, April 13, 1904.
Daily Mail (London), April 22, 1905.

Daily Telegraph (London), April 27, 1905.
Etude, April, 1908.
Etude, May, 1921.
Etude, January, 1926.
Literary Digest, October 14, 1916.
New York Herald, June 25, 1922.
New York Herald, August 19, 1922.
New York Herald Tribune, July 16, 1925.
New York Telegram, March 8, 1920.
New York Times, November 7, 1915.
Paris Herald (2 letters), July, 1900.
Presto, September 27, 1917.
Times (London), January 16, 1903.
Times (London), February 27, 1905.
Washington Post, circa 1890.
Westminster (England) *Gazette*, September 2, 1911.

APPENDIX 2

The Family of John Philip Sousa

John Antonio Sousa (Father)

In various documents the name Sousa appears as Soussa, Sioussa, Sioucca, Soucca, Souca, Souza, Sausa, and Saucca. Actually, the name is Sousa and is of Portuguese origin. Among the distinguished Portuguese ancestors of John Antonio Sousa are Thomas de Sousa, the first Captain General of Brazil; Alfonse de Sousa, Viceroy of India; Goncalo de Sousa, Chief Justice of Portugal; and Louis de Sousa, a writer. John Philip pronounced his name Sōṓ-sa. The public, however, has always pronounced it Sōṓ-za.

John Antonio Sousa was named after his father, and his mother's name was Josephine de Blanco. During the Peninsular War, probably in 1822, John Antonio's parents fled Portugal for political reasons and settled in Seville, Spain. There John Antonio was born on September 22, 1824. He evidently received an excellent education and could speak several languages by his early teens, at which time he left home.[1] He went to Italy and then became an interpreter aboard a British warship. It is possible that he spent some time in Britain. Little is known of his activities during the next few years, but he received a bullet wound in the arm, presumably during his service with the British Navy in the Amazon. After his duty with the British Navy he joined the United States Navy. He is believed to have served during the latter part of the Mexican War in 1847 or 1848. During this period he acquired the classification of musician, but it is not known what instrument or instruments he played.

He was stationed in Brooklyn, New York, as a musician at the Navy Yard about 1848. While there he met his future wife, Marie Elisabeth Trinkaus. The Sousas moved to Washington, D.C., early in 1854, and John Antonio enlisted in the U.S. Marine Band on March 23, 1854.

Antonio was of the Catholic faith until late 1854 or early 1855, at which time he turned Protestant. At first he attended the Concordia German Evangelical Church (Lutheran) and later Christ Episcopal Church.[2] As a Catholic he had

[1] According to a family story, he was interested in the stage and would slip out at night to attend performances. One night the home was burglarized when he left it unguarded, and he fled home to escape punishment.

attended St. Peter's Church in Washington and had sung bass in the choir there.

During the Civil War period he served with the Marine Band, playing trombone and fife, and he probably saw actual combat too. He continued his service with the Marine Band as a trombonist and served almost twenty-five years. He retired on March 1, 1879, and spent the rest of his life in Washington working as a cabinetmaker and upholsterer. He was a Mason, being a member of Naval Lodge No. 4 in Washington, and he also belonged to the George Meade Post, Grand Army of the Republic. He died on April 27, 1892, and is buried in Congressional Cemetery.[3]

Marie Elisabeth Sousa (Mother)

Marie Elisabeth Trinkaus was born in Hesse Darmstadt (Frankish Prumbach), Bavaria, on May 20, 1826. Her father, Peter Trinkaus, was the mayor (burgomeister) of a small town, and her mother was Catherine Schafers. Marie Elisabeth came to the United States about 1846 and resided with relatives in Brooklyn. There she met and married John Antonio Sousa. After moving to Washington in 1854, she remained there until her death in 1908.

She was a deeply religious person, and in her early life she was known as "Cloister Elise" because of her saintly disposition. She was originally Lutheran, but after changing her membership from the Concordia German Evangelical Church to Christ Episcopal Church, she was active in that church's work for approximately fifty years. She had a remarkable influence on John Philip, and he was guided by her principles throughout his life. When she died on August 25, 1908, he sent the following telegram to his brother Antonio: HEAVEN HAS ADDED ONE MORE ANGEL TO ITS LEGION. LET US BOW TO THE WILL OF GOD.[4]

She is buried in the Antonio Sousa plot in Congressional Cemetery.

Catherine Margaret Sousa (Sister)

Catherine Margaret was the first of John Antonio and Marie Elisabeth Sousa's ten children and was born on December 6, 1890, in Brooklyn, New York. "Teeny," or "Tiny," as she was called, is the only one of Sousa's brothers or sisters mentioned in his autobiography, *Marching Along*. This tends to strengthen the belief that she was his favorite. As the eldest child, she had to help bring up the younger children. One of her familiar sayings was "Mother had the babies, and I raised them." She was married to Alexander C. Varela,

[2] There are two family stories about how Antonio came to change his religion. According to one, he was upset about a priest's unwillingness to come to his home in the rain when his child, Josephine, died. Another story holds that he was attended by friendly Masons once when he was ill, later joined the order, and then met with the disfavor of his church.

[3] The Antonio Sousa plot consists of three adjoining burial lots. Three people would normally be buried in this space, but the graves are deep and the caskets are stacked. The bodies of eleven people are buried in this plot. They are: John Antonio and Marie Elisabeth Sousa; their children Josephine, Ferdinand, Rosina, Annie Frances, and Antonio A.; and four others not identified. Some time after Antonio's death, John Philip had the present monument erected.

[4] *Washington Post*, August 25, 1908.

a chemist and photographer, in 1869. Except for six years in California, she spent most of her life in Washington, D.C. She died on December 28, 1939, and is buried in Congressional Cemetery.

Josephine Sousa (Sister)

The second of the ten Sousa children, Josephine, was born in Brooklyn sometime between late 1851 and early 1854. She died in Washington about the time of John Philip's birth. Therefore, she could have been no more than three years old when she died. She is buried in the Antonio Sousa plot in Congressional Cemetery.[5]

John Philip Sousa

John Philip was the third of the family of ten and was the oldest boy.

Ferdinand M. Sousa (Brother)

Ferdinand, the fourth child, was born in Washington on February 6, 1857.[6] He lived only two months and died on April 16, 1857. He is buried in the Antonio Sousa plot in Congressional Cemetery.[7]

Rosina Sousa (Sister)

Rosina was the fifth child and was born in Washington in March, 1858.[8] She lived two years and died on March 2, 1860. She is buried in the Antonio Sousa plot in Congressional Cemetery.

George Williams Sousa (Brother)

George Williams was the sixth child and was born in Washington on February 7, 1859.[9] He served thirty years in the U.S. Marine Band and was a member during his brother's tenure as leader. He was a percussionist, and during the last decade of his enlistments he was band librarian.[10] After retirement he entered the poultry business in Hampton, Virginia. He died in Elizabeth City, Virginia, on January 20, 1913, and is buried in Greenlawn Cemetery in Hampton.

[5] Cemetery records show that her body was moved from another grave to the Antonio Sousa family plot in March, 1860.

[6] This birthdate was computed from the record of death in the District of Columbia Public Health Department.

[7] His body was transferred to the Antonio Sousa family plot in March, 1860, with Josephine's.

[8] This birthdate was computed from the record of death in the District of Columbia Public Health Department.

[9] This birthdate was computed from information on his death certificate. Concerning the name Williams, it should be noted that a Mrs. Elizabeth Williams was a witness at the baptism of his younger sister, Mary Elisabeth. It is possible that Mrs. Williams was a close friend of the Sousa family and that George was named for her. Sometime later the letter *s* was dropped from his middle name.

[10] Obituary in the *Washington Times*, January 20, 1913.

Annie Frances Sousa (Sister)

Annie Frances, the seventh child, was born sometime during the first half of 1863.[11] She died on June 27, 1865, and was the fourth and last of the Sousa children to die in infancy. She is buried in the Antonio Sousa plot in Congressional Cemetery.

Mary Elisabeth (Elise) Sousa (Sister)

Elise, the eighth child and the youngest girl, was born in Washington on December 18, 1865.[12] Her first husband was Robert Camp Bernays, a Washington conductor and Director of the Bernays School of Music. After Bernays died in 1891, she married James McKesson Bower, an officer in the U.S. Navy. She lived her later years in Grand Rapids, Michigan, and died there on March 16, 1940. She is buried in the Orangeville Cemetery in Orangeville, Illinois. Elise was the hub of Sousa family ties, and the family seemed to drift apart after her death.

Antonio Augustus Sousa (Brother)

Tony, the ninth child, was born on March 25, 1868, in Washington, and is also listed in various references as Anthony and Antony.[13] He was active in several fields. At one time he was a letter carrier and post office clerk. A talented writer, he contributed to the sports columns of Washington papers, wrote verse, and collaborated with Edward Lewellyn on an opera. He was an avid sportsman and was particularly fond of wrestling, baseball, and cricket. While working for the U.S. Department of Agriculture, he contracted tuberculosis and was sent to Colorado to recuperate. But on May 8, 1918, he died there, at Rocky Ford. His body was returned to Washington for burial in the Antonio Sousa plot in Congressional Cemetery.

Louis Marion Sousa (Brother)

Louis, the tenth and youngest of the Sousa children, was born in Washington on January 13, 1870, and spent his entire life there.[14] He was employed in the Navy Yard as a machinist for almost thirty years. He also worked as a mechanic and at several other occupations. He died on August 19, 1929, and is buried in Congressional Cemetery.

[11] This birthdate was computed from the death record at Christ Church. There is no record of her death at the District of Columbia Public Health Department because their records for the Civil War years are incomplete. Were it not for the record at Christ Church, there would be no knowledge of the existence of a tenth child in the family, except for John Philip's occasional statements that he came from a family of ten.

[12] Elise's birthdate was believed to have been 1867 until the record of her baptism, on May 6, 1866, was found in Christ Church records.

[13] This birthdate was found on the record of his baptism, on July 5, 1868, at Christ Church.

[14] This birthdate was computed from information on his death certificate.

Jane van Middlesworth Sousa (Wife)

Jane van Middlesworth Bellis was born in Philadelphia on February 22, 1862 or 1863,[15] the daughter of Henry Bellis and Louise Hyle Cornish. Henry Bellis was a carpenter (stair builder) and later the proprietor of a photographic studio on the Boardwalk at Atlantic City, New Jersey. Jane resided in Philadelphia until her marriage on December 30, 1879.

Jane, or Jennie, was an amateur vocalist but apparently did not perform in public after her marriage. She was a member of the Daughters of the American Revolution but few other organizations. She was an excellent horsewoman, and her other athletic interests were tennis, sailing, and trapshooting. Gardening was another of her pastimes, and John Philip often mused that the vegetables she grew received such lavish care that they cost several dollars each. She nearly always declined interviews, remaining in the background, and was content with her life as a housewife. Seldom did she accompany John Philip on his tours except for those overseas.

Another of her interests was writing, and a few of her efforts were published. Among these were "By a Lady," a verse satirizing Sousa's song, "Love Me Little, Love Me Long," published in *Town Topics* (New York), March 15, 1910; "A Chat from Australia," an article in the *Musical Courier*, September 13, 1911; "His Lost Love," a poem in *Harper's Weekly*, August 10, 1912; and "A Plea for Peace," a poem in *Munsey's Magazine*, March, 1913.

[15] The actual birthdate of Jane van Middlesworth Sousa has been a well-kept secret. On p. 63 of Sousa's autobiography, *Marching Along*, he tells of marrying Jennie Bellis while she was yet sixteen. He also mentioned this in many interviews. From performance dates (found in Philadelphia and New York newspapers) of a Philadelphia *H.M.S. Pinafore* company in which they both performed, the author has established the date of their meeting as February 22, 1879.

Subtracting sixteen from 1879 gives 1863 as Jennie's birthdate. But the date on her grave marker in Congressional Cemetery in Washington is 1862, not 1863. Sousa's younger daughter, Mrs. Helen Sousa Abert, intimated to the author in an interview that the marker date was correct, and it has since been learned that it was she who gave written instructions to the monument maker. Mrs. Abert also gave 1862 as the birthdate when she applied for her mother's Social Security death benefit. However, Priscilla Sousa, the older daughter, filled out her mother's death certificate in New York and gave 1863 as her birthdate.

The confusion does not end here by any means. Mrs. Sousa apparently did not want her exact age known (assuming she knew it herself). For example, her age is given as 19, not 16, on her marriage record, which is on file in the Public Archives of Philadelphia. This implies that her birthdate was 1860, not 1862 or 1863. (This could have been an intentional error. It is not the only bit of misinformation on the record; Sousa's birthplace is erroneously listed as Philadelphia.)

Her age is not listed on her application for membership in the Daughters of the American Revolution in 1907, and the author has been unable to locate any birth or baptismal records. But when she applied for a Social Security number in 1938, she gave her birthdate as 1866.

From the evidence at hand, it is obvious that Mrs. Sousa was born between 1860 and 1866; 1862 or 1863 appears to be the most likely date. The date inferred by Sousa is 1863, but the probability that his daughter Helen came across proof of the 1862 birthdate must not be overlooked.

After the death of John Philip, Jane lived the rest of her life at the Sands Point home near Port Washington, Long Island, except for some of the winters, when she resided in New York City apartments. She died in her Manhattan apartment at 30 Sutton Place on March 11, 1944, and is buried in the John Philip Sousa plot in Congressional Cemetery.[16]

John Philip Sousa, Jr. (Son)

John Philip Jr., the first of three children, was born at 420 Eighth Street, SE, Washington, D.C., on April 1, 1881. He was educated in Washington and New York City schools and graduated from Princeton University in 1904. In 1905 he married Eileen Adams of New York. He was active in several businesses, primarily in the manufacturing field. A lover of sports, he played on the Princeton baseball team and was also very much interested in hunting, fishing, and tennis. He died in La Jolla, California, on May 18, 1937, and is buried in the John Philip Sousa plot in Congressional Cemetery.

Jane Priscilla Sousa (Daughter)

Jane Priscilla, the second of John Philip's three children, was born at 420 Eighth Street, SE, Washington, D.C., on August 7, 1882.[17] She was educated in Washington and New York City schools and graduated from Vassar in 1903. She never married and resided with her parents until their deaths. She then spent the rest of her life at the Sands Point home on Long Island. Although not a serious music student, she played the piano and composed at least one song ("Me and Ma' Old Banjo," published by Sol Blom in 1904). She was active in society. In ill health after an auto accident in 1954, she died in New York City on October 28, 1958, and is buried in the John Philip Sousa plot in Congressional Cemetery.

Helen Sousa (Daughter)

Helen, the third and youngest of John Philip Sousa's children, was born at 204 Sixth Street, SE, Washington, D.C., on January 21, 1887. Her family moved to New York in 1892, and she received her education there. She married Hamilton Abert, a New York stockbroker, in 1912, and was active in society. She authored a few magazine articles about her father and also wrote lyrics for two of his songs ("I Love Jim" and "When the Boys Come Sailing Home!") and one of his marches ("On the Campus"). After the death of her mother, she managed the family's business matters (John Philip Sousa, Incorporated). She and Mr. Abert were divorced before his death.

[16] This plot was designed to provide space for John Philip Sousa, his wife, and his three children. There are individual markers plus a large decorative marker.

[17] According to an old family story, her name was changed from Priscilla Jane to Jane Priscilla so that her initials would be the same as her father's.

APPENDIX 3

The Residences of John Philip Sousa

1854 Washington, D.C. Born at 636 G Street, SE (third house east of Christ Episcopal Church) on November 6.

1855 to 1859(?) Washington, D.C. G Street, SE, between Fifth and Sixth Streets, approximately one block west of 636. Family moved here a few months after living at 636.

1859(?) to May(?) 1876 Washington, D.C. 502 Seventh Street, SE (southeast corner of Seventh and E Streets). Father built this house. In various Washington directories the house number is given as 500, 502, 527, or 528.

May(?) 1876 to December, 1879 Philadelphia. Presumably living in boarding houses until married (December 30, 1879).

December, 1879 to October(?) 1880 Philadelphia. Presumably living in one or more rented houses. Was touring with *Our Flirtations* show from August until September 30, 1880, taking his wife with him, but he may have maintained a home in Philadelphia until early October, 1880.

October(?) 1880 to early 1881 Washington, D.C. 502 Seventh Street, SE (the family home), then an unknown address on A Street, SE.

Early 1881 to 1882 or 1883 Washington, D.C. 420 Eighth Street, SE.

1882 or 1883 to early(?) 1891 Washington, D.C. 204 Sixth Street, SE.

Early(?) 1891 to early 1893 Washington, D.C. 318 B Street, SE. (B Street is now Independence Avenue.) First house of his ownership.

Late 1892 or early 1893 to 1895 New York City. Hotel Beresford, 1 West Eighty-first Street.

1895 to 1896 or 1897 New York City. Presumably at Hotel Beresford or Carnegie Hall.

1896 or 1897 to 1898 or 1899 New York City. Carnegie Hall, 883 Seventh Avenue, presumably in one of ten roof-story apartments.

1898 or 1899 to 1900 or 1901 New York City. Hotel Grenoble, 880 Seventh Avenue.

1900 or 1901 New York City. Hotel Netherlands, 783 Fifth Avenue.

1901 or 1902 to January(?) 1905 New York City. Presumably the Hotel Netherlands or the Madison Square Apartments.

January(?) 1905 to February(?) 1911 New York City. Madison Square Apartments, 37 Madison Avenue.

February(?) 1911 to July(?) 1914 New York City. In one or more apartments or hotels, probably the Astor Hotel, 1517 Broadway.

July(?) 1914 to 1932 Port Washington, Long Island, New York. 14 Hicks Lane, in the area known as Sands Point, or Barker's Point. Known as "Wildbank," this home was leased to the Sousas before they purchased it in 1915. It remained in the possession of the Sousa family until 1965.

APPENDIX 4

John Philip Sousa's Military Career

First Enlistment, U.S. Marine Corps

John Philip Sousa enlisted as an apprentice, or "boy," in the U.S. Marine Band in Washington, D.C., on June 9, 1868. His age was thirteen years, seven months, and three days.[1] The term of this enlistment was to have been seven years, five months, and twenty-seven days (at which time he would have reached his twenty-first birthday), "unless sooner discharged." He was honorably discharged (settlement of accounts) on December 31, 1871, after having served three years, six months, and twenty-two days.

Second Enlistment, U.S. Marine Corps

Six months and eight days after his discharge, on July 8, 1872, Sousa enlisted as a third-class musician in the U.S. Marine Band. His age was seventeen years, eight months, and two days, and the term of the enlistment was to have been five years. He received an honorable discharge (special) on May 18, 1875, after having served two years, ten months, and ten days of this enlistment.

Third Enlistment, U.S. Marine Corps

Sousa enlisted for a term of five years as Leader, or Principal Musician, of the U.S. Marine Band on October 1, 1880, at the age of twenty-five years, ten months, and twenty-five days. Although his title was Principal Musician, his initial rank was Private. It is not known how long he held this rank. He received an honorable discharge at the expiration of this enlistment, on September 30, 1885, and re-enlisted two days afterward.

Fourth Enlistment, U.S. Marine Corps

Sousa enlisted for a term of five years on October 2, 1885. His rank during this enlistment is believed to have been Sergeant Major. His title was probably changed from Leader to Director during this enlistment. He received an honorable discharge at the expiration of the enlistment on October 1, 1890, and reenlisted the following day.

[1] On the enlistment paper his age was miscalculated by one month; it states thirteen years, six months, and three days.

Fifth Enlistment, U.S. Marine Corps

Sousa enlisted on October 2, 1890, presumably again for a term of five years. It is believed that he was assigned the rank of Warrant Officer during this enlistment.[2] He received an honorable discharge (settlement of accounts) on July 30, 1892, leaving the Corps at this time to organize his own civilian band. In this enlistment he served one year, nine months, and twenty-eight days.[3]

The total time of Sousa's Marine Corps enlistments was eighteen years, two months, and twenty-seven days.

Navy Enlistment

On May 31, 1917, at the age of sixty-two years, six months, and twenty-five days, Sousa enlisted for a term of four years to organize and train band units of the Naval Training Station at Great Lakes, Illinois. He was assigned the provisional rank of Lieutenant in the Navy Coast Defense Reserve, Class 4, U.S. Naval Reserve Force. The official title of Musical Director of the Great Lakes Naval Training Station was assigned in September, 1918. Assignments carried him to many cities for performances with various groups of Great Lakes musicians, principally with the "Jackie" band. There were several special assignments. In the spring of 1918, for example, he was temporarily assigned to duty "at the port in which the flagship of the Commander-in-Chief, Atlantic Fleet, may be." And in November, 1918, his additional duties were as Musical Director in Toronto, Canada, and New York City.

He was in Toronto with the "Jackie" band when the war ended. Because of an ear infection, he was permitted to return to his home in New York, presumably on November 13, 1918, thereby unofficially ending his term of active duty. At home he was assigned to the Third Naval District and was officially relieved from active duty circa January, 1919.

On February 11, 1920, he was promoted to the provisional rank of Lieutenant Commander in the Naval Coast Defense Reserve, Class 4. On March 15, 1920, he was transferred to Class 6, U.S. Naval Reserve Force. When his original enlistment expired on May 31, 1921, he was re-enrolled. Because of his age he was disenrolled on August 10, 1922.

The total length of Sousa's active navy service, starting with his enlistment date and ending with his departure in Toronto, was one year, five months, and thirteen days.

Total Military Service

The total length of Sousa's active service in the U.S. Marine Corps and the U.S. Navy was nineteen years, eight months, and ten days.

[2] Marine Corps records of Sousa's rank at this time are incomplete. However, Sousa stated on occasion that his rank had been Warrant Officer. One reference to this is his testimony before the House of Representatives Committee on Military Affairs on January 18, 1927, when he appeared on behalf of army bandmasters in their request for advances in pay and rank.

[3] Not subtracted from this figure were the periods he was on leave from the navy to fulfill engagements with the Sousa Band.

Bibliography

Books

Baldwin, Charles E., and Phillips, J. Harry. *History of Columbia Commandery No. 2, Knights Templar 1863-1963*. Washington, D.C.: private publication, 1963.

Berger, Kenneth. *Band Encyclopedia*. Evanston, Ind.: Band Associates, Inc., 1960.

Berger, Kenneth. *The March King and His Band*. New York: Exposition Press, Inc., 1957.

Bridges, Glenn. *Pioneers in Brass*. Detroit: Sherwood Publications, 1965.

Burford, Cary Clive. *We're Loyal to You, Illinois*. Danville, Ill.: The Interstate, 1952.

Gelatt, Roland. *The Fabulous Phonograph*. New York: Appleton-Century, 1954.

Goldman, Edwin Franko. *Band Betterment*. New York: Carl Fischer, Inc., 1934.

Heney, John J. *The Correct Way to Drum*. St. Augustine, Fla.: Heney School of Percussion, 1934.

Jacob, H. E. *Johann Strauss, Father and Son*. New York: Greystone Corp., 1939.

Lingg, Ann M. *John Philip Sousa*. New York: Henry Holt and Co., 1954.

The Lynn Farnol Group, Inc. *The ASCAP Biographical Dictionary, 1966 Edition*. New York: ASCAP, 1966.

Schwartz, Harry W. *Bands of America*. Garden City, N.Y.: Doubleday and Co., Inc., 1957.

Smart, James R. *The Sousa Band: A Discography*. Washington, D.C.: Library of Congress, 1970.

Sousa, John Philip. *The Fifth String*. Indianapolis: Bowen-Merrill Co., 1902.

Sousa, John Philip. *Marching Along*. Boston: Hale, Cushman, and Flint, 1928.

Sousa, John Philip. *National, Patriotic and Typical Airs of All Lands*. Philadelphia: Harry Coleman, 1890.

Sousa, John Philip. *Pipetown Sandy*. Indianapolis: Bobbs-Merrill Co., 1905.

Sousa, John Philip. *Through the Year with Sousa*. New York: Thomas Y. Crowell and Co., 1910.

Sousa, John Philip. *The Transit of Venus*. Boston: Small, Maynard and Co., 1920.

Sousa, John Philip. *The Trumpet and Drum*. Publisher not known. 1886.

Sousa's Band. A promotional book printed and distributed by the management of Sousa's Band in 1897. Contains reprints of several hundred press reviews of concerts by Sousa's Band.

Waters, Edward N. *Victor Herbert*. New York: Macmillan Co., 1955.

Articles

Abert, Helen Sousa. "Happy Memories." *Instrumentalist*, April, 1965.
Abert, Helen Sousa, as told to Al G. Wright. "John Philip Sousa—a Picture Biography." *Instrumentalist*, March, 1967, and May, 1967.
Ambrose, Joan. "John Philip Sousa." Publicity release. U.S. Marine Band, 1962.
Bachman, Harold B. "Victor Grabel: Bandmaster." *Music Journal*, January, 1966.
Bierley, Paul E. "Sousa: America's Greatest Composer?" *Music Journal*, January, 1967.
Bierley, Paul E. "Sousa's Mystery March." *Instrumentalist*, February, 1966.
Cooke, James Francis. Eulogy of Sousa. *Etude*, June, 1932.
Cooke, James Francis. "A Momentous Musical Meeting." *Etude*, October, 1923.
Cooke, James Francis. "The Origin of Sousa's Name." *Etude*, September, 1936.
Downs, Olin. (A biography of Sousa.) *Boston Post*, September 10, 17, 24, October 1, 8, 15, and 22, 1922.
Evenson, Orville. "The March Style of Sousa." *Instrumentalist*, November, 1954.
Glenum, Arthur R. "Sousa, Honorary Director of Almas Military Band." *Almas Life* (Almas Temple, A.A.O.N.M.S., Washington, D.C.), July-August, 1961.
Goldberg, Isaac. "Sousa." *American Mercury*, October, 1932.
Grabel, Victor J. "Tribute." *American Bandmasters Annual*, 1932.
Harris, Milton F. "History and Highlights of the Ringgold Band." Hundredth Anniversary Concert (John Philip Sousa Memorial Concert) program of the Ringgold Band, Reading, Pennsylvania, March 30, 1952.
Harris, Sam. "Sousa As I Knew Him . . ." *Instrumentalist*, March-April, 1951.
Helmecke, August. "Why the Accents Weren't Written In." *Instrumentalist*, March-April, 1951.
Howard, George S. "A New Era for Brass: Sousa's Role." *Music Journal*, January, 1966.
Howard, George S. "That Name Sousa." *Instrumentalist*, April, 1965.
Interavaia, Lawrence J. "Wind-Band Scoring Practices of Gilmore and Sousa." *Instrumentalist*, March, 1965.
"Interview with John Philip Sousa." *Music*, June, 1898.
"John Philip Sousa." *Music*, January, 1894.
"John Philip Sousa—His Spirit Carries On in the Bands He Created." *International Musician*, August, 1953.
Larson, Cedric. "John Philip Sousa as an Author." *Etude*, August, 1941.
Mangrum, Mary Gailey, as told to Harold Geerdes. "Experiences as Violin Soloist with the Sousa Band." *Instrumentalist*, October, 1969.
Mangrum, Mary Gailey, as told to Harold Geerdes. "I Remember Sousa." *Instrumentalist*, December, 1969.
Mayer, Francis N. "John Philip Sousa—His Instrumentation and Scoring." *Music Educators Journal*, January, 1960.
Newcomb, Stanley. "Sousa Down Under." *Instrumentalist,* March, 1967.
Quayle, Nolbert Hunt. "Stars and Stripes Forever—Memories of Sousa and His Men." *Instrumentalist*, September, October, November, and December, 1954; January, February, March, and April, 1955.

Shannon, J. Harry. "Migration from Spain Preceded Establishment of Sousas Here." *Washington Sunday Star*, August 23, 1925.

Shannon, J. Harry. "Early Life of John Philip Sousa, 'The March King,' in Washington." *Washington Sunday Star*, August 7, 1921.

Sousa, John Philip. Articles and letters to the editor. See Appendix 1.

Sousa, [Jane] Priscilla. "My Father . . ." *Instrumentalist*, March-April, 1951.

"Sousa and His Mission." *Music*, July, 1899.

"Sousa as He Is." *Music*, May, 1899.

"Sousa's New Marine Band." *Musical Courier*, November 9, 1892.

Stewart, G. Hollis. "The Royal Welch Fusiliers March." Publicity release. U.S. Marine Corps Historical Section, December 16, 1930.

Stoddard, Hope. "Sousa: Symbol of an Era." *International Musician*, December, 1948.

Thompson, Harry H. "The Marine Band—The Washington Post." *Marine Corps Gazette*, August, 1932.

Yoder, Paul. "The Early History of the American Bandmasters Association." *Journal of Band Research*. Autumn, 1964, and Winter, 1965.

Wells, William Bittle. "John Philip Sousa on Directing." *Pacific Monthly*, May, 1901.

Wilson, J. Ormund. "Eighty Years of the Public Schools of Washington—1805 to 1885." *Records of the Columbia Historical Society*, vol. 1, 1896.

Miscellaneous

Blakely v. Sousa, No. 1, and Blakely v. Sousa, No. 2. State Reports, Vol. 197, The Supreme Court of Pennsylvania at July and October terms, 1900.

Church, Charles Fremont. "The Life and Influence of John Philip Sousa." Ph.D. dissertation, Ohio State University, 1942.

Copyright entry books (unpublished) and the *Catalogue of Copyright Entries* (published), all vols., 1870-1969. The unpublished, handwritten copyright entry books are on file at the Copyright Division, Library of Congress.

"Ex-Lieutenant John Philip Sousa, U.S. Naval Reserve Force (Deceased)." Publicity Release. Department of the Navy, Office of Information, February 13, 1945.

Hearing Before a Subcommittee of the Committee on Military Affairs, Senate, 70th Congress, on S. 750, January 26, 1928.

Hearings Before the Committee on Military Affairs, House of Representatives, 69th Congress, Second Session, on H.R. 444, S. 2337, January 18, 1927.

"Historical Notes on the Participation by the Marine Band in the Ceremonies Attendant to the Funeral and Burial of John Philip Sousa." From *Leader's Ledger*, March 5-10, 1932. U.S. Marine Band, Washington, D.C.

"John Philip Sousa." Publicity Release. U.S. Marine Corps Historical Section, Division of Public Information, 1949.

"John Philip Sousa." Service Records. U.S. Marine Corps Museum, Quantico, Virginia. N.d.

"John Philip Sousa, 1854-1932." List of Sousa's copyrighted works. Library of Congress, Division of Music, July 23, 1935.

"Marine Band Chronology from 1798" (unpublished). U.S. Marine Band, Washington, D.C.

Microfilms of *Public Ledger* and other Philadelphia newspapers, 1876-1881. Free Library of Philadelphia.

Microfilms of *Washington Post* and *Washington Star*, 1867-1892. District of Columbia Public Library, Washington, D.C.

Sousa Band Fraternal Society News, all issues, 1944-. Published in Los Angeles, then Anderson, Indiana, then New York. Complete set at the Library of Congress.

Sousa Band press books. Set of eighty-five hardbound scrapbooks containing approximately 55,000 clippings and programs of the Sousa Band, 1892-1931. In custody of the U.S. Marine Corps Museum.

Sousa scrapbook. Boston Public Library.

Index